THE STRANGER NEXT DOOR

The Stranger Next Door

The Story of a Small Community's Battle
Over Sex, Faith, and Civil Rights

ARLENE STEIN

Beacon Press
BOSTON

Beacon Press
25 Beacon Street
Boston, Massachusetts 02108-2892
www.beacon.org

Beacon Press books
are published under the auspices of
the Unitarian Universalist Association of Congregations.

05 04 03 02 01   7 6 5 4 3 2 1

This book is printed on acid-free paper that meets the uncoated paper
ANSI/NISO specifications for permanence as revised in 1992.

Text design by Elizabeth Elsas
Composition by Wilsted & Taylor Publishing Services

Library of Congress Cataloging-in-Publication Data
Stein, Arlene.
     The stranger next door : the story of a small community's battle over
sex, faith, and civil rights / by Arlene Stein.
        p.   cm.
     Includes bibliographical references and index.
     ISBN 0-8070-7952-9 (cl.:alk. paper)
     1. Gay rights—Oregon.   2. Gays—Oregon.   3. Homosexuality
—Oregon.   4. Homosexuality—Religious aspects.   I. Title.
HQ76.8.U5 S74   2001
305.9'0664'09795—dc21   00-064158

FOR NANCY, LEWIS, AND FRED

Up until now, everything around here has always been, well, *pleasant*. Recently, certain things have become *unpleasant*. It seems to me that the first thing we have to do is to separate out the things that are pleasant from the things that are unpleasant.

Pleasantville, Gary Ross, director

Nothing calms better the dread one cannot eradicate than worrying and "doing something" about the trouble one can fight.

Zygmunt Bauman, In Search of Politics

CONTENTS

THE STRANGER NEXT DOOR

Introduction

Midway between San Francisco and Seattle, in a spectacular verdant valley, is a place I will call Timbertown. Home to eight thousand people, it is in many respects a typical small Oregon community, and a typical small American town, a place that prides itself on the fact that most people know each other, at least by sight, and a place where life goes on and relatively little changes—or so many believe. Yet several years ago, within the space of a few months, the intimate acts of individuals became the subject of a raucous public debate that pitted neighbor against neighbor. Should the community recognize lesbians and gay men as a legitimate minority group, and accord them equal protection under the law?

Since Timbertown possessed little power to create such protections, the question was above all a symbolic one. Nonetheless, it created a storm of controversy few will forget. Families stopped their children from playing with friends whose parents stood on the opposing side of the issue. Husbands and wives quarreled over it, and it sparked fistfights at the high school. The local newspaper, normally preoccupied with news of the timber industry and Little League scores, covered little else for months. Practically overnight, the question of lesbian/gay civil rights became a matter of public debate and acrimony.

Rural Oregon was a rather unlikely site for a battle over homosexuality. In this vast, sparsely populated region of the country, there were few visible signs of queer life outside of the few metropolitan areas: no out homosexuals lobbying for civil rights; no lesbian/gay coffeehouses, newspapers, or running clubs, commonplace in larger towns and cities. Yet suddenly the issue of homosexuality moved to center stage. "Across rural Oregon, where homosexuality used to be the last thing you'd expect anyone to be discussing, much less debating," a newspaper reported, "people are talking about little else."[1]

In 1992, religious conservatives sponsored a highly controversial statewide ballot measure that sought to deny civil rights protections to lesbians and gay men. The initiative, known as Measure 9, lost by a large margin in the state's two most populous metropolitan areas but won across rural Oregon. The following year, in an effort to build upon its successes in rural areas, the Oregon Citizens Alliance, which spearheaded the campaign, targeted eight counties and three dozen small communities where the statewide measure had passed the year before. These measures sought to amend local bylaws to prevent antidiscrimination protections for gays and lesbians and prohibit government spending to promote homosexuality (see Appendix B).

When I moved to Oregon in the fall of 1994, the year after the ballot measures rippled across the state, people were still talking about them. On several occasions, friends warned me to stay out of a particular community when it had passed an ordinance prohibiting lesbian/gay rights the year before; gay rights sympathizers waged unofficial boycotts of these towns. It seemed to me that homosexuality had become a primary way these towns defined themselves, and others defined them. But why, I wondered, did small-town folks find homosexuality, seemingly a nonissue, so confusing and troubling? And why bother organizing against lesbian/gay rights in towns where queer people were barely visible? A second question also emerged: How did small towns defend lesbian and gay rights in the absence of a visible, identifiable gay community?

I became interested in how discussions of homosexuality and lesbian/gay civil rights entered public life in small communities, shaping how "ordinary" people talked about sexuality. Small rural communities have usually been thought of as the repository of traditional American values, conjuring up images of close, face-to-face relationships among like-minded people. In recent decades, a series of sweeping social changes, including the dissemination of new media technologies and the growing movement of urban dwellers into rural areas across the nation, has called this nostalgia-tinged image into question. What happens, I wondered, when small-town people and big-city, indeed *global,* cultures come into contact with one another?

The issue of homosexual civil rights, as it was debated by a small community, provided a lens for looking at this process.

I spent two years talking with community activists on the right and the left, along with city officials, teachers, students, car mechanics, and lumbermen in the small Oregon town. I examined what people said publicly in the debate about homosexuality—in newspapers, radio broadcasts, television interviews, and organizational literature. And I interviewed people who participated in these debates to try to figure out what homosexuality symbolized for them on a deeper level—for those who sought to legislate against gay rights or who defended these rights, as well as for those who had few opinions on the matter.

I had to admit that I was drawn to the project because it offered the chance of entering an alien world: small-town America, and particularly the world of Christian evangelicals. I had read about the Christian Coalition and its efforts to shape American politics, seen films such as *The Apostle,* about a southern Pentecostal preacher, and had followed the Jim and Tammy Faye Bakker scandal in the news. But I had never actually talked with a card-carrying evangelical. Nothing seemed further from my reality as a Jew, an urbanite, and a laborer in the agnostic groves of academia.

As I embarked on this project, friends and colleagues were curious. How would I present myself to my subjects? Would I tell people that I was a Jew? A lesbian? Would I reveal my progressive political sympathies? A colleague of mine, Linda Kintz, had studied the world of Christian conservatism, attending conferences of such organizations as Concerned Women for America. Kintz, a sweet-voiced woman with a smooth Texas drawl, wore a tasteful pantsuit and presented herself as a conservative activist in order to gather what we sociologists call "data." Reporter Donna Minkowitz chose a different strategy: she bound her breasts and donned a goatee makeover to attend rallies of the Promise Keepers, the hugely successful Christian men's organization. But my appearance irrevocably marked me as not-Christian (and not-male). I couldn't pass. Nor did I want to, particularly, as I imagined that interactions with my informants would tell me as much about their world as would their answers to my pointed questions.

Indeed, much of what I learned surprised me. I was struck by how many people expressed opinions about the world that were both honest and forthright yet based upon operating assumptions diametrically opposed to those I took for granted. While I understood diversity and multiculturalism as a positive ideal, for example, others felt threatened by it, and refused to mince words when describing their feelings. The schools "require our children to celebrate cultural diversity," one mother complained. "But what if the families don't want to celebrate?"[2]

Why would individuals come to such different conclusions about something that seemed, to me at least, relatively simple and straightforward? To find out, I would have to enter a particular place, and try to understand its people, and their world. This book, then, is about much more than the gay rights debate. It explores how sexuality became a resonant symbol upon which a group of citizens projected a host of anxieties about the changing world around them, how it divided a small community, and what that tells us about our ability to live with difference. And it documents how a local campaign brought the issue of homosexuality into the public sphere in unprecedented ways, generating discussions of sexuality among those who had never before talked about such matters publicly.

DOES THIS MEAN WAR?

While I spoke with rural Oregonians, ethnic conflicts six thousand miles away transformed Serbs, Croats, and Albanians into bitter, bloody rivals. Though the context was clearly very different, the ethnic conflicts in the former Yugoslavia frequently entered my thoughts. Why do some social differences that are submerged and unremarkable become sources of division? In the United States, few have taken up guns to defend their vision of what is right and true, but Americans have frequently responded violently to such perceived social problems as drug use, abortion, and satanic ritual abuse, to name a few. Stanley Cohen coined the term "moral panic" to describe how some issues—such as pornography, homosexuality, and pedophilia—engage the passion and focus of people in ways that seem to far outweigh their real threat.

But frequently, religious convictions shape political attitudes in ways that go far beyond fleeting panics over disparate issues of concern.[3] Indeed, some would argue that Americans' preoccupation with moral issues, such as homosexuality, is evidence of a "culture war" that is realigning political loyalties along lines of faith. According to sociologist James Davison Hunter, a "culture war" pits traditionalists, who understand the truth in terms of an external, definable, and transcendent authority, usually defined by religious beliefs, against progressives, who see truth as inherent in human beings and the natural order, and constantly in flux. A good number of American Protestants feel themselves to be socially and demographically distant from modern life, a fact that, in Hunter's words, allows them to "avoid sustained confrontation with modernity's most threatening attributes."[4]

As the "culture war" argument goes, religious conservatives use their faith to insulate themselves from the threatening changes around them, looking to traditional values as guides for living. In contrast, liberal secularists are more apt to embrace the changes they see around them, and view the individual as the best arbiter of what is right and wrong. These beliefs about truth—whether it is absolute or relative—shape people's beliefs on a host of issues, such as abortion, gay rights, and welfare reform, cutting across many of the cleavages that organized politics in the past.[5]

If there is in fact a culture war, it isn't all that new, of course. Throughout American history, moral crusades against drinking, campaigns against pedophilia, child abuse, and satanism identified deviant social categories and dramatized and normalized identities and institutions such as the traditional family and Christianity. A wave of religious revivals in 1831 converted large numbers of middle-class Americans to millennial beliefs. The decade that followed saw a massive "protest cycle" in temperance, abolition, and moral-reform movements, each based on a sense that sudden, dramatic change was possible in this world, a view impossible under older Calvinist fatalism.[6]

In the 1920s, cultural clashes about the teaching of evolution in the public schools rippled through the United States, culminating in the Scopes trial, in which a biology teacher was charged with challenging state and biblical law. The clash between Clarence Darrow and William Jennings Bryan was a battle over values—a culture war that pitted modernists against fundamentalists. As liberal critic Horace Kallen put it, "The Great War with tanks and planes and poison gas has been followed by a battle of values, or norms and standards; a struggle of theories of life."[7] Fundamentalists retreated after the Scopes trial, in which creationism was roundly condemned, and for fifty years occupied themselves with building their own culture and institutions, breaking out into public life only occasionally in momentary spurts of activity.

Many members of Timbertown's religious community certainly believed they were engaged in a culture war. As one conservative activist asked: "The question is do you follow God's teachings, or do you defy them? Do you live by the rules that were set down thousands of years ago, or do you live by your own rules?" Many of the evangelical Christians I spoke with viewed the Bible as the word of God, saw salvation as central to religious faith, and attended church at least once a week, if not more. They believed that homosexuality poses a threat because it represents chaotic and morally lax behavior, and that growing tolerance for homosexuality is evidence of the community's declining morals.

But there was much more at stake, a union leader told me. "Christianity has very little do with the appeal of the Christian right," he offered. "Christianity has as much to do with this battle as religion has to do with the war in Ireland. The church was an institution that was hollow and available for use, so it was taken over by people wanting to put forth their authoritarian ideas. It's not about theology, it's about economics." The war over homosexuality, he suggested, was simply a smoke screen, obscuring more powerfully determining material forces. Had Timbertown not come on hard times, my union friend argued, there would never have been support for the antigay campaign, which was an expression of status resentment.[8]

In Oregon, attitudes toward homosexuality appeared to correlate with divisions between a declining working class that felt itself displaced and ignored, and a rising professional class, for whom the declining working class was invisible or irrelevant.[9] Young urban professionals, who teemed into the state to work in high-tech industries, tended to support abortion and gay rights. Not all working-class people opposed them, of course, and a good number of middle-class people did. Nonetheless, class differences shaped the debate in important ways.

But the more I spoke with people in Timbertown, the more I

came to believe that the clash over homosexuality in small-town Oregon was not reducible to either values, as proponents of the "culture war" notion suggest, or economics, as their materialist critics contend. It was about both of these things—and more. Claims that lesbians and gays enjoy "special rights" brought together moralistic concerns about perversity with material concerns about the decline of the family wage and resentments against affirmative action, blending secular arguments about civil rights with passionate religious injunctions against sin. Authors Sara Diamond, Didi Herman, Linda Kintz, and Suzanne Pharr capture the blend of values and interests that animate these debates, and have made enormously valuable contributions to explaining the origins, meaning, and persistence of the Christian right.

This book extends their analyses, taking a somewhat different approach. Rather than focus upon the national rhetoric of Christian right organizations and the formal, organized manifestations of these movements, it looks at a single conflict in relation to a single place, a small, not particularly significant community, tracing how a cultural conflict emerges in the context of everyday life.[10] I was inspired in part by Faye Ginsburg's book *Contested Lives,* which examines the abortion controversy in Fargo, North Dakota, and shows, through the experience of one community, the clashing social forces behind the abortion debate in bold relief. To understand why women become active on the issue, argues Ginsburg, one must understand the meaning that abortion, and motherhood, has for different groups of women at a time when women's lives are rapidly changing. To understand why people became involved in a campaign against homosexuality, I show in this book, one must understand the different meanings and associations evoked by homosexuality (and by implication, heterosexuality) in a particular place, and at a time when truths about gender, and also a host of other certainties, are being questioned.

THE MAKING OF US AND THEM

In a recent book about Yugoslavia's disintegration into warring ethnic factions, author Michael Ignatieff tells a story about a Serbian militiaman who is asked what he has against his former Croatian neighbors.[11] The man looks scornful and takes a cigarette packet out of his jacket. "See this? These are Serbian cigarettes." Over there, he says, gesturing out of the window, "they smoke Croatian cigarettes." In other words, we are Serbians because we are not Croatians. A sense of similarity among *us* rests upon a sense of difference from *them*.

What this story suggests is that in their everyday lives individuals make countless decisions about who is a friend and who is an enemy, about who should be included in a particular community and who should not. People do things because they wish to protect an image of who they are in relation to the group of which they believe they are a part. We conceptualize the world into those who deserve inclusion and those who do not. Boundaries mark the social territories of human relations, signaling who ought to be admitted and who excluded. The desire to root out others in order to consolidate a sense of self seems universal. How do human beings perceive one another as belonging to the same group while at the same time rejecting human beings whom they perceive as belonging to another group? Why must we affirm ourselves by excluding others?

A community's boundaries remain a meaningful point of reference for its members only as long as they are repeatedly tested by people who are on the fringes of the group and repeatedly defended by those within it. Sociologists tell us that in order to create a sense of social order, which all societies must establish, deviants are created and punished. "Whenever a boundary line becomes blurred," writes Kai Erikson, "the group members may single out and label as deviant someone whose behavior had previously gone unnoticed."[12] The act of naming things that are dangerous demonstrates to those in the community "just how awesome its powers really are."[13] This clarifies what is acceptable and what is not, who belongs in the community and who does not. Identities that had no political or even existential significance can acquire a genuine hold as badges of group identity overnight. Though the making of collective identities and boundaries is always inherently political, at certain moments such processes become explicitly politicized.

Symbolic boundaries become more important during periods of rapid social change—when geo-social boundaries become less central. In colonial America, as communities grew and changed, some individuals who were previously accepted as part of the group found themselves run out of it as heretics—witches. In Yugoslavia, as national unity collapsed, ethnic boundary drawing came to the fore.

The more pressure there is on communities to change, it seems, the more vigorously boundaries are symbolized and conformity demanded. Clearly, the world is changing in many different ways, and at a rapid pace. In this country, during the past few decades, an unprecedented number of women have entered the workforce; the globalization of the economy has made us less and less dependent upon a sense of place, economically and culturally. Even residents of small-town Oregon, who consume media beamed from satellite dishes and work for companies whose manufacturing operations are located in far-flung parts of the world, are subject to these and other modernizing processes.

During the past decade, huge geopolitical shifts have shaped U.S. political culture. The collapse of Communism destroyed the faceless enemy upon which our national identity had been based, and had an enormous, largely unacknowledged impact upon the nation's sense of itself. The issue of "who is American" became more and more unclear. It used to be that Americans defined themselves as not-Communists. But once Communists no longer posed a threat, the drive to figure out the meaning of America became even more urgent. Communism was no longer a threat. What would replace the "other" against which American identity was defined? "A symbolically contrived sense of local similarity," writes Richard Jenkins, is sometimes "the only available defense."

Historically, the right has drawn much of its strength, collective identity, and legitimacy from its ability to construct a coherent, visible enemy and to demonize the "enemies within" in the name of the imagined nation.[14] As the old devils—Communists, working women, the counterculture—lost their power, a new devil was needed—preferably one that embodied the worst excesses of the permissive society, that transgressed sexual respectability, that seemed sufficiently outside the community to be alien, but that simultaneously represented familiar (and therefore doubly scary) urges that were accessible to anyone. How better to construct a sense of identity, the *we,* than by articulating a clear sense of what one abhorred? How better to affirm one's purity than by getting rid of the dirt?

Sigmund Freud has noted that the compulsion to name and exclude dangerous "others" may be more virulent the more similar those others are to you; all likeness must be denied and difference exaggerated. He called this the "narcissism of small differences." Freud noticed the ease with which larger cultural groups latch on to smaller groups or groups seen as social intruders, leading the English and the Scots, North and South Germans, to turn against one another, venting their aggressive impulses. He recognized how Jews have, historically, "rendered most useful services" throughout European history by being a favorite target of violent aggression.[15] For many centuries they were the "strangers" against which Europeans defined themselves. Familiar and yet unfamiliar, visible and yet faceless—they did not fit easily into any of the established categories through which people made sense of their world. These "others" who were not quite "other" caused confusion and anxiety, which made them particularly susceptible to hateful passions, and efforts to clearly delimit "us" and "them."[16]

Do lesbians and gays play a similar role in the contemporary United States? I wondered. For many centuries, the philosopher Michel Foucault tells us, the boundaries separating the homosexual and heterosexual worlds were either weak or nonexistent; homosexual and heterosexual behavior existed side by side. There was not yet an understanding of homosexuals as a recognizable, definable category of people. With the emergence of sociosexual medical categories, this changed: homosexuals became understood as a distinct group of individuals, radically different from heterosexuals. The construction of a "homosexual role," Mary McIntosh argues, "kept the bulk of society pure.[17]

It's no wonder that a series of antigay campaigns rippled through the United States in the 1990s, when lesbians and gay men were becoming more and more fully integrated into American life and the boundaries separating the homosexual and heterosexual worlds were blurring.

SHIFTING INTIMACIES

Twenty years ago, I graduated from college, packed my bags, and moved to the West Coast, fleeing from watchful parental eyes and hoping deep down to meet the girl of my dreams. I was certainly not alone. Tens of thousands of young people had migrated there before me in search of the great gay metropolis, that "imagined community" where people could act on their same-sex desires and receive support for doing so.[18] But only a couple of decades before, same-sex behavior was confined to the margins of society, in shadowy bars in major cities, or to secret, forbidden desires. Men and women possessing attractions for members of their sex were forced to keep them under wraps lest they lose their jobs and their families.

But after years of living with the "culture of suspicion," which defined clear boundaries between the straight and gay worlds, and cast homosexuals into secretive double lives, in the 1960s and 1970s some activists vowed to overturn the prevailing notion of "homosexuality as pollution." Gay liberationists attempted to "smash the categories": the boundaries separating heterosexuality and homosexuality were, they proclaimed, social illusions. For a brief moment, these ideas caught fire. Many people, influenced by the movement, were faced with a *choice* about whether to be with women or with men. Those who had never entertained the idea of homosexuality were forced to scrutinize the nature of their attractions. The heterosexual imperative was profoundly shaken.

These cultural shifts were not limited to increasing tolerance for same-sex behavior. The twentieth century ushered profound changes in sexual and gender relations. Traditional bases of sexual authority, such as religion and family, weakened, individuals engaged in sex at earlier ages and outside of marriage, the double standard of sexuality eroded. The system of reproductive sexuality is declining. If the sixties generation affirmed the shift toward sexual liberalism, shaking the foundations of traditional sexual morality, economic changes that freed individuals from the constraints of the family economy gave individuals unprecedented freedom to pursue their desires. A sexual sea change occurred: the very nature of intimacy was transformed.[19]

Over time, gays openly intermingled with the heterosexual world, began to see themselves as the moral equivalent of heterosexuals, and demanded rights on that basis. By the time I came of age in the 1980s, the American gay rights movement had become professionalized, sophisticated, mainstreamed, and wedded to a model of gay "ethnicity." In an effort to strengthen the analogy between homosexuality and race, civil rights advocates presented scientific evidence of the immutability of sexual orientation.[20] Lesbians and gay men emerged as a distinct interest group, wielding political action committees, political clubs, and human rights organizations seeking greater social and political integration. Homosexuality, once seen as a source of pollution, was becoming normalized.

In 1960, no cities or states in this country guaranteed equal rights to gay men and lesbians. By 1997, eleven states and dozens of cities and counties had passed laws protecting lesbians and gay men (and sometimes bisexuals and transgendered people) from various forms of discrimination based on sexual orientation, and elsewhere gubernatorial executive orders and mayoral proclamations officially banned discrimination. As a result, by the end of the decade, more than one fifth of Americans lived in cities or counties providing some legal protections. Five states, including New York, offered domestic partner benefits to gay and lesbian state employees.[21]

Lesbians and gay men were also increasingly visible in American society as happy, healthy homosexuals, and even began to crop up on television sit-coms, in Hollywood films, and in popular music. By the early 1990s, the vast majority of Americans, if not sexually liberal, were at least wary of extreme efforts to legislate sexual morality. Sociologist Alan Wolfe, in a study of middle-class American attitudes, showed that while Americans are far from relativistic in their own moral views, they shrink from judging the private behavior of others and dislike moralizing when they see it practiced. At the same time, a majority of the population still disapproved of homosexuality, exhibiting what Wolfe calls "soft homophobia." They believe that gays and lesbians should have rights, but objected to the belief that homosexuality is the moral equivalent of heterosexuality.[22]

A survey that asked individuals to rank different social groups using a "feeling thermometer" revealed that feelings toward gays and lesbians are "colder" than feelings for many other oppressed groups, including blacks and people on welfare, and "warmer" only than feelings for illegal aliens—confirming Urvashi Vaid's claim that lesbians, gay men, bisexuals, and transgendered people in the United States have been granted "virtual equality"—"a state of conditional equality based more on the appearance of acceptance by straight America than on genuine civic parity."[23] Clearly, attitudes about homosexuality were in flux.

Still, speaking openly about sexuality in many parts of this country remained difficult. There were wonderful gay neighborhoods in many cities, but straight people generally stayed away from them, except when tour buses stopped to gawk at the queers. Moreover, while gay people were building a new home from the ground up, we had moved away from our families, our communities—often for very good reasons—and to varying degrees we had lost our capacity to speak their language. Perhaps that's why we had underestimated the extent to which many Americans felt threatened, and troubled, by the growing normalization of homosexuality.

AGAINST NORMALIZATION

Shortly after arriving in San Francisco, I attended my first gay pride parade. It was a beautiful, balmy day, and everywhere you could see beaming faces. A small ragtag bunch of hecklers, positioned on the sidelines, tried to disrupt the buoyant mood, holding up signs that featured quotes from the Bible and singing hymns that were drowned out by the swirling, roaring crowd of tens of thousands of gay revelers. I remember thinking that the Christian protesters at the gay pride parade seemed pathetic, even laughable. In San Francisco, we operated under the notion that lesbians and gay men were marching forward, making progress in the battle for inclusion, rights, and cultural influence. Despite the emergence of a strange, shadowy disease in the city's gay community, whose ravages would not be known for some time, for most of us it was easier to be queer than ever before.

Several years earlier, in Florida, Anita Bryant's "save our children" crusade led to the repeal of one of the country's first gay rights ordinances on the grounds that it legitimized a "perverse and dangerous" way of life. Conservative Protestants positioned themselves as the moral guardians of the family, and by implication, the nation—against the excesses of the permissive society. "For the good of America's children," they argued, "the mainstreaming of deviancy must come to an end."[24] A California state representative named John Briggs sponsored a ballot measure designed to bar self-identified homosexuals from teaching in the public schools. But by the 1980s the religious right had all but faded from view, rocked by television preacher sex scandals. Or so many believed.

Since the 1960s, Christian evangelicals have steadily increased their numbers and influence in this country. As mainline Protestant denominations lost hundreds of thousands of members—an estimated quarter of their membership—the proportion of Americans who said they regularly attended church remained unchanged—at or slightly above 40 percent of the population. Mainstream Protestant denominations, such as the Episcopalians and Presbyterians, comprised 30 to 40 percent of the U.S. population in 1960; their membership has plunged to below 20 percent today.[25] If only about 10 percent of Americans identify as evangelicals, as many as one fifth of all Americans subscribe to some form of evangelical Christianity. According to one poll, one quarter of American adults say they are "always" mindful of being Christ's representatives.[26] In the western region of the United States, evangelical churches have grown at a rate greater than in the traditional southern Bible Belt.[27]

Regardless of denomination, the more committed evangelicals are to their religion, the more likely they are to be politically conservative, particularly in relation to cultural issues such as homosexuality, abortion, and school prayer. The culture of evangelicalism encourages people to take political action, should they choose to do so.[28] In 1989, activists formed the Christian Coalition to weld the evangelical subculture into a powerful political lobby, organizing pastors, distributing voter pamphlets, and giving voice to their beliefs in city councils, school boards, and state legislatures. In many states, including Oregon, religious conservatives became active in the Republican Party.

For most of the 1980s, the fight to outlaw abortion dominated religious conservatives' attentions.[29] But abortion failed to produce the political gains they hoped for, so the Christian right turned its attention to the issue of homosexuality. Hundreds of books, videos, and special reports were dedicated to identifying the gay threat and calling Christian believers to arms; dozens of organizations devoted themselves solely to antigay activities. Early religious right rhetoric fought the normalization of homosexuality by focusing upon the immorality of private homosexual behavior. But the movement's antigay rhetoric became controversial and was widely seen as hateful and dangerous. Some pundits blamed President George Bush's election defeat on the vitriolic speeches delivered by Pat Robertson and Patrick Buchanan at the 1992 GOP convention in Houston. When the inauguration of President Bill Clinton brought a Democrat into the White House, conservatives began to devise a different strategy.

Rather than attack homosexuality on grounds of immorality, they began to attribute superior power to gays and attack the status of homosexuals as a "minority" group deserving equal rights under the law. While the national organizations of the right shied away from sexual politics, fearing it would divide their constituencies, organized homophobia moved to the grassroots level, as conservatives mobilized locally to influence school boards, city councils, and local public bodies.[30] They criticized the inclusion of homosexuality in multicultural curricula, such as New York City's Rainbow Curriculum, insisting that lesbians and gay men pose a threat to children, and that rather than constituting a legitimate cultural identity, they are simply individuals who live an aberrant lifestyle.[31]

This new modernized purity campaign distinguished between the public and the private realms—publicly, at least—echoing the U.S. military's "don't ask, don't tell policy." It suggested that what goes on between consenting adults is nobody's business—we won't tell you how to live your private life. Rather than attacking individuals as perverse it attacked the status of homosexuals as a group that deserved legal protections. Being gay wasn't like being a woman, or a member of an ethnic group, it claimed. Anyone could *choose* to be a homosexual; homosexuality is a *behavior,* not a way of being. Therefore, efforts to gain homosexual civil rights were a sham. "Special rights" became a central catchphrase as organizations prepared voter guides that were distributed to millions of churchgoers nationwide. These grassroots conservative groups ran candidates for school boards and city councils, and packed PTA meetings; and they took advantage of the citizen initiative process, sponsoring ballot initiatives that promised to deny civil rights protections to lesbians and gay men.

The citizen initiative was created by turn-of-the-century reformers in the West and Midwest to circumvent corrupt legislatures dominated by special interests. It is rooted in a model of "direct democracy" that gives citizens the right to bypass governmental structures by directly enacting legislation through a majority vote. In the name of "the people," progressive reformers in the western states reversed a century of American land policies designed to transfer public land to private individuals and began to conserve public resources, creating national parks and forests. They gutted the power of traditional political parties, added women to the electorate, and expanded the rights of citizenship to include government protections for working men and women.[32]

Most U.S. state constitutions provide for some form of direct de-

mocracy, or citizen lawmaking, usually through an initiative or referendum process. In order to place initiatives on an election ballot, proponents must file the measure with the state legislature, where officials
subject it to varying degrees of review. Once enough signatures are
gathered, the initiative can appear on the ballot; once it passes with a
simple majority, it becomes "legislation" and must be implemented
by the state government.[33] California, followed closely by Colorado
and Oregon, leads the nation in the number of voter initiatives on its
ballots.

In recent years, the initiative process has been used by organizations seeking to gain national visibility for its issues, frequently on the
right. In the late 1970s, angry Californians voted for Proposition 13, a
ballot initiative that capped local property tax rates, cutting $5 billion
in state taxes, and inspiring the growing use of initiatives, particularly
by conservative groups seeking to restrict minority civil rights, affirmative action, and bilingual education. In 1992, Coloradoans for
Family Values sponsored an amendment to Colorado's state constitution to ban civil rights protections for lesbians, gays, and bisexuals,
which passed. The Oregon Citizens Alliance (OCA), a religious right
organization, followed suit, running Ballot Measure 9, which lost
statewide but won in rural Oregon and spawned the local charter
amendment campaign which is the subject of this book.[34]

THE BOOK

Christian conservatives in a small town simultaneously publicized the
existence of sexual diversity and tried to stamp it out. They began by
circulating atrocity tales that targeted visible, politically active, and
sexually promiscuous "bad gays," as we see in the next chapter. Ironically, few if any gay Timbertowners fit this description: most tended
to be well integrated into the community and uninterested, for the
most part, in political activism. What really seemed to disturb people
was that queer people, lacking a ghettoized bar culture, lived in their
world; the strangers in their midst looked very much like them.

What conditions gave rise to the conflict? Chapter 3 documents
how, in the 1980s, the traditional economic and familial underpinnings of small Oregon communities were threatened by the decline
of the timber industry and its male breadwinner economy. As an influx of immigrants from California and other parts of the country al-

tered the composition of Timbertown, boundaries separating established families, who had been in the community for generations, from the newcomers cropped up.

As the community became more fragmented, ideas of safety and salvation took ascendance, and local citizens looked to religion to reconstruct a sense of community. Chapter 4 shows how evangelical Protestants tried to create a sense of community that replicated the idealized, male-headed family, and how their faith inspired passionate devotion but unstable institutions. Individuals joined a particular church in search of emotional depth and intensity, but churches in Timbertown came and went with the season.

Historically, evangelicals have often relied upon devils to affirm their own solidarity, and pastors have long preached that homosexuality is immoral, but until recently, few brought that message to the secular public. That changed with the arrival, in the 1980s, of a more politically savvy and well-resourced national religious right. Chapter 5 focuses upon several women who were leaders of the Christian right locally, and discusses why they became involved in the campaign, and in right-wing activism generally.

In order to win, organizers knew that the campaign would have to cast a wider net and appeal to the nonreligious. Chapter 6 looks at how the Oregon Citizens Alliance evoked such tried-and-true conservative values as moral strength and respect for authority, fusing economic and cultural conservatism with appeals to hegemonic masculinity and whiteness. It positioned minority civil rights strategies as signs of weakness, dependence, and femininity, offering white working men the possibility of imagining themselves and their families as strong and independent, in contrast to weak, shameful others. By joining the fight against gay rights, men anxious about their masculinity—and women anxious about men's manhood—could embolden themselves.

Chapter 7 documents how a group of Timbertowners rose up to oppose the measure, attempting to blur the boundaries between "insiders" and "outsiders" and to connect the protection of minority rights to a conception of the greater good of the community. To do so, they imagined sexual boundaries as solid and unchanging—essentialist understandings that were strategically useful but failed to articulate a public challenge to the OCA's core claim that heterosexuality alone is normal, natural, and beautiful. Listening closely to people's stories, however, one could hear more complex understandings of sexuality.

The suggestion that conservative Christians alone knew the truth, the word of God, discredited them as religious loonies and hateful people, and they needed a different way of representing themselves to the broader public. The Christian right began to usurp the rhetoric of victimhood, redefining itself in the language of interest group liberalism and identity politics, as we see in Chapter 7. Chapter 8 documents how this grew out of a need to play to the media, which feasts on drama, polarization, and knock-down-drag-out conflicts. The media concentrated on images of extremes, playing up the most dramatic, most radical elements of both sides, feasting on name-calling and conflict. The more they were called names—Nazis and bigots—the more the members of the OCA positioned themselves as victims and martyrs. And then they began to deliberately provoke their opponents to call them such names.

Initially, what struck many people was the imagined nature of the "homosexual threat." But once named, it quickly became a focus of people's passions, and even those who had little interest in the issue were drawn into the fray. Chapter 9 documents how many people became convinced that a rising tide of perversity was at least partly responsible for the unsettling changes they saw around them. A small, relatively homogeneous town began to understand itself in terms of boundaries defined by sexuality. Eventually, it wasn't only sexuality that divided people: the conflict spilled over to race as well, and the local high school became embroiled in a nasty feud between the few students of color and their supporters, and a group of white kids.

In conclusion, I analyze the election results and reflect upon their significance for debates about the American culture wars, the role of symbolic boundaries in the making of community, and the rise of multiculturalism in America's heartland. In the face of numerous recent defeats, including those in Oregon, the religious right is retreating from electoral politics and returning to what it does best: shaping the hearts and minds of its many believers. Against premature pronouncements of its demise, I suggest that religious conservatives will remain powerful players in American society for the foreseeable future. The right alone has publicly articulated many anxieties and desires widespread among Americans—particularly those, like sexuality, that involve intimate, personal questions. But the answers they provide are exceedingly simple. The question remains: How do we live in a contested moral order? And how do we live with the strangers in our midst?

Author's Note

It's difficult to be an activist on a controversial issue in a small town, so I assured my interview subjects confidentiality in order to get them to talk freely with me. The sole person who is referred to by his actual name is Lon Mabon, the OCA's chairman, who is widely associated with the organization. (See Appendix A for further information, including a list of people quoted in this book.)

CHAPTER 2

The Personal Is Political

A story circulated through town. It was, some said, a chilling tale. Stan Holmlund, former mayor of Timbertown, owned a coffee shop on Main Street, an old-fashioned coffee shop with formica tables and soda fountain, minus the charm. One day, two women came into the shop and in the middle of their meal, out of the blue, began to kiss each other. Holmlund asked them to stop their public display of affection and when they refused he asked them to leave. The women became upset and threatened to sue him. Kissing in public was inappropriate behavior for anyone, Holmlund said, and they "tried to intimidate me with threats of potential discrimination and lawsuits."[1]

There were other stories as well. The middle school invited two gay people to speak to their students—"practicing homosexuals with AIDS"—who presented their lives as perfectly natural and normal. When a sixth grader asked them what they did in bed, they described, in explicit detail, some of their sexual activities, including fisting— proof positive that the schools, one woman charged, were infested with "militant, avowed homosexuals" who were teaching preschoolers that "masculine and feminine roles are not a matter of anatomy but of choice."[2] "I don't particularly mind them practicing an 'alternative' lifestyle but this in-your-face attitude and demands for special rights from the queers is getting more than a little obnoxious." Sign me, she closed, "Normal and proud of it."[3]

Atrocity tales such as these claimed that lesbians and gay men, unbeknownst to most people in the community, were lurking everywhere: in the schools, in the neighborhoods, and even—if you weren't careful—in your own family, flaunting behavior that should be kept private, infiltrating coffee shops on Main Street and middle school classrooms, and assaulting public decency. It didn't seem to matter that the flamboyant street protests of Queer Nation and other groups were far away, or even that there were no visible gay people, let alone militant politicos asking people to defend their rights in the town. The Oregon Citizens Alliance had arrived.

While the shrillest spokesmen on the right proclaimed that gays are in our face, flaunting their perverted lifestyle, posing a threat to our children, what really riled them was that in Timbertown homosexuals tended to be respectable people who were fairly well integrated into the community.[4]

In the 1980s, the American gay rights movement became professionalized, mainstreamed, and wedded to a model of gay "ethnicity." In an effort to strengthen the analogy between homosexuality and race, civil rights advocates presented scientific evidence of the immutability of sexual orientation. Homosexuality, they proclaimed, was not a matter of choice; homosexuals were therefore a protected class of citizens, a conceptualization that helped lesbians and gay men to define themselves as a distinct interest group and seek greater social and political integration.[5] By the 1990s, polls indicated that the vast majority of Americans, if not sexually liberal, were at least wary of extreme efforts to legislate sexual morality. These cultural shifts, though centered in urban, middle-class milieus, reverberated even in Timbertown: the assistant school superintendent was a highly respected out lesbian; many small businesses were owned and operated by lesbians who were out in varying degrees. Once viewed as a shameful secret, homosexuality was becoming a plausible lifestyle.

Unrepentant gay people, even "good gays" who lived lives that resembled, in many respects, those of heterosexuals, upset the normative order upon which the conservative Christian notion of the ideal family was based. As conservative Christians saw it, they called into question the belief in natural gender differences and promoted a vision of nonprocreative sexuality without apologies, thereby diminishing the sanctity of heterosexual marriage. If homosexuality is affirmed along with heterosexuality, Christians believed, the meaning of heterosexual marriage is diminished.

Most Timbertowners were too wrapped up in their own lives to take notice, or they saw homosexuality as a something that had little to do with them—it was an urban phenomenon, they imagined, so the "problem" could be solved by staying as far away from cities as they possibly could. But for a small but significant minority, signs of the normalization of homosexuality were deeply troubling. San Francisco had fallen, the "domino system of sexual peril" knew no boundaries, so small-town Oregon might be next.[6] Who would take moral leadership and dare to declare what is acceptable and what is not, what is deviant and what is normal? Who would rouse people out of their complacent slumber, and remind them that homosexuality threatened to pollute their town?[7]

As conservative Christians saw it, it was up to them to do it—no one else would or could do it. In some sense, they shared the feminist conviction that the personal is political, that what we do in our personal lives has enormous political ramifications, and how we feel about pornography, abortion, sexuality, reproduction, marriage, personal morality, and family values is key to what "America" stands for. And with the cultural left they shared the belief that politics should be about a lot more than money, power, and self-interest: it's about the construction of a common culture that transcends liberal individualism. Therefore, public and private worlds should not, and cannot, be seen as separate. Conservative Christians believed that they alone could lead the reimagined community and assert the privileged status of heterosexuality. They alone could produce a different sort of politics, one that would bring the values of intimate familiarity—nurturance, reciprocity, and community solidarity—into the public realm. They alone could restore rules, order, authority—structures that give shape and meaning to a world out of bounds, and guide individual actions in a world of bewildering choices and changes. The future of the community, and indeed the nation, was at stake.[8]

This wasn't the first time religious conservatives had taken a stand on a controversial issue; there were periodic outbursts of activism in town before. Once, a group of Christian parents spoke out against sex education in the schools. "I don't know why we have to use the anatomical terms for these body parts," one man proclaimed at a school board meeting. "I've been with my wife for fifteen years and I've never used those terms." There were fights against a statewide plan to reform the schools, which some parents feared would take control away from them and place it in the lap of the state.[9] There were efforts to prevent Planned Parenthood from entering the high school to distribute contraceptive information, and campaigns to release public school children for an hour of prayer.

At times, Christian activism was more subtle, less organized, seeping into everyday interactions unannounced. A high school student told me about a biology teacher who tried to inject his religious views into a discussion of evolution. He told the students, "I have to teach you about this because it's required by law, but you don't have to believe it." There was talk among Christian students about forming a prayer club at the high school; a 1990 Supreme Court decision mandated that federally funded secondary schools permit student-led religious clubs that are not linked to the curriculum.[10]

Though religious conservatives had become more visible in Timbertown and other small communities throughout the state during the 1970s and 1980s, they had yet to really translate their numbers into political power. Part of the problem was that they didn't really possess a sense of themselves as a collective "we." They assembled each Sunday with those who shared many of their beliefs and worldviews, but once they went back into their communities, they were forced to contend with the disappointments of the secular world, a world in which marriages seemed to be dissolving as fast as they were formed, where homosexuals were gaining voice and legitimacy, and where faith and family seemed to take a backseat to just about *everything*. To make matters worse, Christians always seemed to be warring against one another. Churches split, disbanded, started up anew and then split again, often leaving behind bruised egos and hurt feelings—and a belief in the Bible wasn't enough: many evangelicals didn't really think of Pentecostals as their kindred.

The OCA campaign promised Christian conservatives a public voice, and a sense of unity. Though their churches had proliferated in Timbertown over the past few decades, attendance at Sunday services hadn't increased significantly, and they wielded relatively little power when it came to making decisions. Most high-ranking town officials from the mayor on down were moderate Catholics. Fundamentalist parents sometimes raised their voices, complaining about the school curriculum or "indecent" books in the library, but usually they voted with their feet. Christians felt that the secular establishment—teachers, principals, city councilors and their ilk—ignored them, mocked them, and sometimes victimized them. If they couldn't abolish the boundary separating church and state, perhaps, at the very least, the fight against "special rights" would energize conservative Christians and give them greater public visibility in the community. Perhaps it could serve as a religious revival, bringing the unchurched back in the fold, and uniting churches across denominational lines. By repudiating that which was evil, at least they could more clearly define what they stood for.

Joining the campaign meant that the evangelical community could flex its muscles and assert moral leadership in Timbertown, and bring religious values to the secular public sphere. Individual church leaders could become more visible in the community, unifying their congregations and disavowing Christians whom they felt did not possess the necessary degree of religious commitment. Individual activists could take a stand against the secular world and its disappointments, in favor of what is right and true. Together, they could boldly articulate their vision of the community.

ONWARD, CHRISTIAN SOLDIERS

The specter of the "crowd" haunts the image of people rising up in protest, conjuring up teeming masses hell-bent upon political battle. But social movements, if the truth be told, tend to be much more organized, much less spontaneous than such images suggest. It takes a canny organizer to help transform a series of discontents and wrongs into protest.[11] The skilled organizer is part entrepreneur, part artist, manipulating a palette of inchoate ideas, material resources, and rhetorics to fashion a message that others will embrace and follow. For conservative Christians in Oregon, forty-five-year-old Lon Mabon, a portly former-hippie-turned-missionary from California, was such a leader.

In the late 1960s, after serving in Vietnam, Mabon moved to Northern California, spent a lot of time hanging out, and fell in with a group of people who had formed a Christian commune, where he met his wife, Bonnie.[12] In the 1980s, Mabon began to dabble in Republican Party politics and learned to use direct mail to recruit members from lists of people who had purchased Christian books or religious products in Oregon. Oregon conservatives had long been of the laissez-faire, live-and-let-live variety—they believed that abortion and homosexuality were personal, not political issues and vehemently defended the separation of church and state. But Mabon and others surmised that there was a vast army of conservative Christians who could be mobilized, who felt that they weren't being represented by the party, who felt strongly about abortion, sex education, and school prayer and wanted to protect "the family" against the liberal onslaught. During this period, Pentecostal and evangelical Protestantism was growing in Oregon, as it was in the nation as a whole. The recession of the 1980s was rubbing salt in the festering wounds of widespread resentment. Social conservatism was ready to enter the political arena. The Oregon Citizens Alliance was born.[13]

If the conservative movement is divided between purists and pragmatists, between those who insist on the primacy of the pure moral vision despite practical obstacles and those want to are willing to sacrifice principles for politics, Mabon is clearly in the former camp. "If you are willing to compromise, you lessen your convictions," he says, a stance that became part of his appeal.[14] In the early 1980s, Christian fundamentalists began to challenge moderate Republicans on their pro-choice stance on abortion. Mabon and his colleagues assembled hundreds of activists throughout the state, who diligently swarmed shopping malls and churches calling Christian believers to arms, and raised 90 percent of their funds through direct-mail appeals—predominantly from working people who gave $100 or less, and small businesses like Bob's Refrigeration (Sheridan, Oregon), Two Ladies Deli (Bend), Enviro Chipper (Gold Hill), Rogue Valley Coin and Jewelry Exchange (Medford), Northwest Guns (Grants Pass), and Cascade Real Estate (Eagle Point).[15] It was, with the exception of some assistance from national right-wing groups like the Christian Coalition, a grassroots operation. As chairman, Lon ran the organization from his modest home in a Portland suburb. His wife, Bonnie, their two children, and Mabon's parents pitched in.

A mimeographed sheet filled with misspellings enumerated the OCA's principles: "For over 200 hundred [sic] years the United States of America has brought more freedom, more justice, more hope and more prosperity to more people than any other nation in history. Yet today, the principles upon which this great and good republic rests are under determined attack. In the face of this crisis, we put aside other pursuits to reaffirm, with those who have gone before us, the following truths. . . ." Human rights, freedom, the Constitution, private property, family values, the right to life, free enterprise, and compassion were among those truths. According to the document, "the goal of American civil rights policy should be a race-unconscious society," and "behaviors that are morally wrong or injurious to public health" should not be protected. It suggested that while the First Amendment "guarantees freedom from the establishment of a state religion . . . Judaeo-Christian religious values should continue to have an important role to play in shaping American values." It proclaimed that "Americans have proven themselves to be compassionate and generous people" but that "private charity should become the primary source of assistance for those who are facing difficult times." And it declared that "liberalism," with its "social engineering schemes that undermine freedom" is "antithetical to the American system of liberty designed by the Founders."[16]

In 1988 the OCA mounted a ballot initiative campaign to rescind Governor Neil Goldschmidt's ban on sexual orientation discrimination in the executive branch of state government. James Dobson made a pitch for the campaign on his national radio broadcast, *Focus on the Family,* and it won a majority, though it was later declared unconstitutional by the state's Supreme Court—which only fueled the populist fire. A couple of years later, the OCA ran a gubernatorial candidate against Democrat Barbara Roberts, which was widely credited with costing the Republican candidate, Dave Frohnmayer, the governorship. It also dabbled in environmental politics, leading an effort, bankrolled by timber companies, to recall Roberts for her support of conservation and land use restrictions. The OCA's deputy director was elected chair of the Republican Central Committee, and other activists won leadership positions in the party. An OCA-led measure to ban abortion in Oregon failed miserably in 1990, but the campaign helped the organization build a base of power within the Republican Party and laid the groundwork for the future campaign against gay rights.

Four years after its initial foray into the gay rights issue, the OCA returned with Ballot Measure 9, which proposed to amend the Oregon constitution to describe homosexuality, along with pedophilia, sadism, and masochism, as "perverse, abnormal and unnatural," and prevent gays from being granted minority status. "Lon Mabon Sets 'Em Straight," trumpeted the *Seattle Times,* in a not-so-subtle dig at the man himself.[17] The Christian Coalition contributed $20,000 to the campaign. Outspent by six to one, opposed by everyone from Oregon's U.S. senators on down to the newspapers and city councils, it still won 44 percent of the vote and twenty-one of Oregon's thirty-six counties—including most rural areas.

In the parlance of political strategists, homosexuality was a perfect "wedge" issue for the OCA, one that would make its name and consolidate a base of support. The issue seemed to cut across many of the OCA's core concerns, sanctioning the worst excesses of the permissive society: tolerance for a nonprocreative sexuality that smacked of rampant individualism; lack of respect for men and women's "true" differences; and the rise of civil rights strategies that improved the position of women, minorities, and even homosexuals, purportedly at the expense of working families. Exit polls indicated that many voters had been turned off by Measure 9's harsh language and tone, though not by the idea of limiting gay rights. The OCA announced that it would return with another statewide measure in the fall of 1994.

In the intervening months, to build momentum for the campaign, it ran toned-down local antigay rights measures on the ballot in nearly three dozen selected cities and counties statewide. If passed, the initiatives would ban antidiscrimination protections for gays and lesbians, and prohibit government spending to promote homosexuality. It was a kinder, gentler version of Measure 9, modeled after the successful Amendment 2 in Colorado, sponsored by Coloradoans for Family Values. Mabon hoped the local ballot initiatives would bring the issue of gay rights to small-town Oregon, the OCA's core constituency, relatively free of the hype and posturing of statewide, media-driven campaigns. He cultivated leaders who were known in their communities, who had broad networks of contacts that they could tap, and learned hundreds of people's names by heart, calling them and writing them personal letters to elicit their support. This "plain folks" populist style appealed to a constituency that distrusted the media, and large institutions in general. It told people that they could make a difference.

Mabon contacted individual activists who had carried petitions for OCA-sponsored antiabortion measures in the past, or who had given money to pass the statewide antigay measure, or who were identified as Republican Party activists with religious sympathies. The year before, 55 percent of Timbertown's voters expressed their support for Measure 9. In the course of the campaign, the OCA assembled a mailing list of three hundred thousand supporters throughout the state. Twenty thousand people contributed more than $1 million annually to its coffers—about twice the amount raised by the Oregon Republican Party's main political action committee in the same period—making it one of the state's most powerful political machines.

A few dozen OCA supporters lived in Timbertown. Mabon contacted a handful of them. "Do you know that homosexuals are taking over the local schools?" he asked them. That was enough to spur Jeri Cookson, the sixty-five-year-old wife of a retired carpenter and a "saved" Christian, to offer her house in the middle of town for the first meeting of the local "no special rights" campaign.

About a dozen people showed up to the meeting: Republican Party stalwarts, and members of some of the more conservative churches in town—predominantly women. There was Rosie Harrington, a woman whose husband owned a large building supply store in town, who homeschooled three small children, and who had been active in conservative politics, and John James, a machinist and longtime Republican precinct leader and active Baptist. Sally Humphries, a forty-five-year-old mother of two grown children who had dabbled in antiabortion activism, and whose big blond hair and heavy makeup made her a striking figure, was there too. Mainly middle-aged, longtime Timbertown residents, they were working folks—accounts payable clerks, seamstresses, carpenters, sheet metal mechanics, truckers, and small business owners—who had made good, who owned a little property and had some money in the bank.[18]

They began the meeting with a prayer, and then they went around in a circle and people shared their gripes. Some spoke about the loss of standards at the schools, the fact that their kids and grandkids didn't seem to be learning much. Others mentioned that there were so many restrictions on new construction—clearly the government was intervening much too much in people's lives. (As a local bumper sticker read "Why is it easier to get welfare than get a building permit?") One woman expressed her dismay that divorce was rife in society, that families had a harder time staying together, and that "men didn't know how to be men anymore." Mabon steered the discussion to the issue at hand: homosexuality. "Why is it that our natural repulsion to wrong behavior is now called 'homophobia'?" he asked them. "Does wrong behavior deserve minority status?" He read them the proposed measure. If society accepts homosexuality as normal, he said, pedophilia will achieve the same status by the end of the century. "And who has allowed this to happen?" he asked. "You and I. You and I. *They* are destroying the values we hold dear, which made our country great. *We* good Christian people must take a stand against them."

"We're the 82nd airborne of the pro-family movement," Mabon proclaimed. "We drop behind the enemy lines. We take the most casualties. We take the most hits."[19] It was a rhetoric that worked on several levels. It played on a masculinist fascination with war—what Richard Slotkin has called "regeneration through violence."[20] At the same time, it evoked the image of "good Christian soldiers" doing battle for the Lord, a biblical image that appealed to evangelical Christians who saw themselves as excluded from the culture by liberals, homosexuals, and their secular humanist cronies. And it lent an air of immediacy to the struggle: *they* were winning the battle for the hearts and minds of America. *We* must respond—swiftly and strongly. This is serious business, Mabon told conservative Christians throughout the state, we must not delay.

In order to place the initiative on the ballot, he told those who had gathered at Jeri Cookson's house, they must quickly gather hundreds of signatures. The future of their children was at stake. Were they up to the task? They went around the room and each person announced how much time he or she could commit to further the cause. Sally Humphries said she would go to church and circulate petitions, and walk up and down her street and talk to her neighbors. Cookson agreed to be chief petitioner and coordinate the local campaign, ensuring that the whole town was covered. Others signed up to circulate petitions at the post office downtown, or in their fraternal organizations. They would mobilize Christians who were sympathetic to the antigay cause though not active on the issue, along with others who lacked strong opinions but who might be influenced to take a stand. They would use the local press—two newspapers, and several small radio and television stations—to spread awareness of the issue by writing letters to the editor, appearing on radio call-in shows, and staging demonstrations in favor of the charter amendment. Mabon impressed people with his drive, his daring, and his commitment to Christian values. "He was very, very sincere," said Cookson, and people wanted to do what they could to help.

RALLYING THE MINISTERS

Mabon also attended a meeting of the local ministerial association, which included representatives of every major congregation in town, urging it to endorse the campaign. The mainly evangelical members of the association were for the most part sympathetic to the campaign's message but somewhat reluctant to involve themselves in political matters. They defined themselves against liberal congregations, such as the Presbyterians, who built low-income housing in the community, provided sanctuary for political refugees, and adapted the Scriptures to changing times, addressing, for example, demands on the part of women for leadership in the church. Evangelical churches, in contrast, had a literal interpretation of the Bible and treated salvation as a highly personal matter, which led them to focus on fashioning a relationship between the believer and God.[21] At the same time, however, they aspired to engage in the affairs of the community, believed their faith gave them a special way of seeing the world, and felt that this way of seeing could be a light unto the community.[22]

As Bob Harrison, pastor of the Mountaintop Church, the largest evangelical church in town, explained: "We're not a social gospel church. Sure we reach out in times of trouble. But it is not the reason that we come to exist. We exist to be able to grow in Christ ourselves, help other people to know Christ. We meet the needs of our community, but that is not our primary function. We don't preach the social gospel." The Presbyterians' social activism suggests, he says, that you "have only one string on your banjo, and you play it all the time." In contrast, he described his church's role in Timbertown during a regional recession in the late 1980s: "We had a message of hope, even in a time of darkness. We focused on the positiveness that God could see you through."

Harrison's church helped its members pay their bills, got them into relocation programs, held food showers for people, and collected food donations for members in need, suggesting that conservative evangelicals do indeed have a social gospel—though it is, as an observer points out, "one which places most hope in the power of the pure in heart."[23] They tend to shy away from electoral politics, preferring instead a personal approach, which emphasizes charitable giving and institution building in the community, and they dedicate themselves to helping their own.

It didn't take much to convince Ben Jaeger of the Sacred Fate Temple that the campaign would be good for the community, though. As pastor of one of the strictest, most fundamentalist churches in town, he often spoke of the evils of abortion, homosexuality, and other sins; his church required its members to renounce alcohol, gambling, homosexuality, and adultery. Because of the power of his convictions, he has often felt himself "called to rise up on political issues," incensed by the moral decline he sees around him. Jaeger promised Mabon that he would host a rally against homosexual civil rights at his church and recruit members to volunteer in the campaign. Pastor Lance White of the Christian Center said he would do what he could to help as well, and others offered material assistance: financial contributions, meeting space.

But Henry Chomsky and Harvey Silko, representing the Presbyterians and Catholics respectively, were none too pleased by Mabon's appearance at the meeting. Chomsky remembered the OCA from a conflict that exploded a few years before at a local hardware store that offered video rentals. The store had a television set, and one day a Clint Eastwood video was playing. A man shopping in the store, who happened to be a conservative Christian, saw the video flash an image of a woman's bare breast and was offended by it. He complained to the store owner, who paid little attention. Then a couple of OCA members in town called for a boycott of the store.

"It was such a stupid issue," recalls Chomsky, who vowed to stay as far away from them as he could. His stands on abortion, the sanctuary movement, and his belief that churches must involve themselves in social justice already made him an outsider in the ministerial association. Plus, he was still reeling over the way the pastors had treated an African-American Methodist woman pastor who, threatened by anonymous death threats, sought help from the ministerial association. When it gave her the cold shoulder, Chomsky became her only ally and friend. But this was the final straw.

Chomsky roundly chastised the other pastors for cozying up to the OCA. "As an association, we have no right to involve ourselves in such political movements. This is reprehensible, and I want no part in it," he told them. The ministerial association decided that as a group it couldn't speak for all of the churches in the community. As Bob Harrison recalled, "We said you need to figure out where your church stands and if you want to stand behind it one way or another, that's fine." Nonetheless, most of Timbertown's ministers, drawn largely from Pentecostal churches in town, were sympathetic to the cause. Mabon's culture war rhetoric resonated with those who shared a worldview that was stark in its contrasts. There were good people and bad people, to be sure, and in the end, during the final judgment, the sinners would be duly punished—Revelation said so, didn't it?

In the meantime, during their lives on this earth, it was up to good Christians to do their bit to stave off the onslaught of secularism. Fighting for one's beliefs was, after all, a Christian thing to do. The Bible was filled with tales of blood shed for the glory of the Lord. They recalled how black churches had played an integral role in the civil rights movement. Perhaps it was time for conservative Christians to take a stand. Despite their initial reluctance to get involved in elec-toral politics, they saw the "special rights" campaign as an opportu-nity for churches in town to unify around something they believed in. Lon Mabon's beliefs resonated with things that Pastor White talked about each Sunday: the evils of the secular society, abortion, assisted suicide. "The church should provide leadership. We should speak morally, about where God is. Evolution is a bunch of you-know-what. We're gonna suffer if we let the secular world take over." As conservative Christian leaders in Timbertown saw it, they were being victimized for their unwavering commitment to what was true and good.

Ask a Pentecostal preacher where his stand against homosexuality comes from, and he'll tell you the Bible. From the pulpit, pastors have long preached that homosexuality is immoral. They might quote a passage from the Book of Romans that distinguishes between "natu-ral intercourse" and "unnatural practices."[24] Or they might tell you about Leviticus, which decreed the death penalty for male homosex-uality: "If a man lie with mankind, as with womankind, both of them have committed abomination: they shall surely be put to death; their blood shall be upon them" (20:13). Rules for sexual behavior are in-cluded in the tenets of most religion, but Christianity has been per-haps the most proscriptive of all. Christianity inherited from the an-cient Greeks the belief, in the words of the disciple Paul, that "the flesh lusts against the spirit, and the spirit against the flesh; and these are contrary the one to the other."[25] In addition to condemning homosexuality and other nonprocreative forms of sexuality, the Bible also prescribes draconian punishments for adultery that decree that both "the adulterer and adulteress shall surely be put to death"—a teaching that even the most fundamentalist Christians would be hard-pressed to enforce today.

When you look at Bible literalism up close, it's often not very literal at all. Pastor Bob Harrison told me that there are some things that are black and white, "plain in God's words"—like "thou shalt not murder"—and some things that are gray areas in the Bible. But when I asked him to give me an example of something that is clearly set in stone in the Bible, he strained to fit abortion into his definition of murder. "If a woman is carrying a baby, and a man came up and tried to harm her, and the baby died, that would be murder. The same with abortion—that woman is carrying a life, and God says if a life was taken, take a life for it." Many of the most conservative Bible-believing pastors claimed to "simply be following the Scriptures." Yet their actual practice, as they explained it to me, suggested a high degree of reflexivity, implying a late-modern consciousness of multiple possible interpretations.[26]

Carroll Neitz, who runs a branch of the Nazarene church out of a storefront in town, says, "When you read the Scriptures, it's important to read them in the context." Some things translate to the contemporary context, and other things don't. Prohibitions against murder, for example, do translate clearly. "There's nothing," he told me, "that would make it shift because God spoke through the writers who wrote that down." But when it comes to the role of women in the church, he said, things are less clear. "When women began to find a glorious freedom in their relationship with Christ and they began to shout about it, it began to create a problem for the gospel. In the times of the Bible, men were in authority. But we don't want that today."[27]

On the issue of homosexuality, however, Timbertown's conservative pastors seemed to be in agreement: it is wrong, immoral, sinful. One could, however, "love the sinner but hate the sin." Pastors differentiated between homosexuals as persons and homosexual acts, arguing that lesbians and gay men, like alcoholics or drug abusers, are weak-willed people who have gone astray, who sacrifice self-restraint for personal fulfillment. Homosexuality represents the potential evil lurking within us all, a sin on par with adultery, suicide, child pornography, child molestation, drug or alcohol abuse, or even murder. "God loves everyone—even ax murderers," declared one woman.[28] Pastor Bob Wilson agreed. During the "no special rights" campaign, he took the opportunity to preach a sermon on the distinction between "somebody who was caught in sin, and somebody willfully leading the lifestyle that was outside of what God called for."

Undergirding such views is the belief that homosexuality is a choice. "I'm an adult child of an alcoholic, and the Lord's changed me a lot to be able to live with that," Beverly Allen, a member of the Faith Center, told me. "So I think a homosexual could change too, but only by the power of the holy spirit—you can't do it yourself." I challenged her: "What about those people who say they can't change, that their homosexuality is not a matter of choice?" She replied that it wouldn't be easy, but that "nothing's impossible." Christian "love the sinner hate the sin" talk suggested that homosexual desire was universal, that the boundary separating gay and straight was quite permeable. It rejected the "minority" model of homosexuality in favor of a more diffuse notion of sexual possibility.

In the conservative Christian view, people who choose to become homosexuals, who identify on the basis of shameful behaviors despite their capacity to change, are people who do not care about God's judgment. "We as a society don't want to be held accountable for our choices," said one woman. "Homosexuality is a matter of choice, not chance. You are responsible for what you are."[29] Ironically, this conception of homosexuality had much in common with the idea of gay liberation, arguing that pleasure could be found anywhere, sometimes where one least expected it, that the boundaries separating heterosexuality and homosexuality were social constructions, and that sexuality is infinitely complex and malleable—individuals can take control over their sexual choices. Today, paradoxically, as lesbians and gay men have all but abandoned this position in favor of a model of "essential" homosexuality, conservative Christians have taken it up to prove the fact that gays are not a legitimate minority group.[30]

At the same time, there was much more at stake than sexuality. For many Timbertowners, homosexuality conjured up the specter of encroaching multiculturalism, which they saw as a threat to Christian hegemony. "There are lots of people moving here," Lance White unabashedly told me. "Gay people are coming in, and they're gonna try to propagate themselves. People from Asia, who are nonbelievers, people with a New Age mentality, who believe they've lived two or three lives. We're gonna have clashes—spiritual, political. There's an iceberg comin' up to hit the Titanic and people don't even see it. Someone's gonna come up the winner, and someone's gonna be the loser."[31]

White was one of a number of pastors in town who had been influenced by the growing politicization of conservative Christianity in the 1970s and 1980s, when Pat Robertson railed against the power of mainline Protestantism and organized Christian citizenship campaigns. When I asked him who his heroes were, he listed Bill McCartney, the founder of the Promise Keepers; Chuck Colson, the Watergate co-conspirator-turned-Christian-talk-show-host; and Billy Graham. Following their example, he welcomed the chance to become active in the political sphere and take a stand against secular humanism. "It's up to us to direct a community and a society, and protect it," pastor Bob Harrison told me, "and part of God's protection for us was to give us some moral laws to live by."

But some conservative church leaders had reservations about bringing the church into politics, and politics into church. Historically, Pentecostal groups have steered clear of politics—most of them live in expectation of an early Second Coming, and therefore see little value in political confrontation in the here and now. Others feared that controversy might divide their congregations. Hank Cosby, of the Flowing River, a small fundamentalist church in town, described himself as conservative but opposed the Oregon Citizen Alliance: "I hate people defining Christianity as what we're against rather than what we're for."

Therein lay the challenge facing Timbertown's evangelical community at the start of the campaign against gay rights. In the face of the vast diversity of evangelicalism in town—and indeed in the nation as a whole—evangelicals' sense of identity is utterly dependent upon its opposition to others: nominal Christians, non-Christians, and sinful others. Evangelicals construct and maintain their collective identity largely by drawing symbolic boundaries that create distinctions between themselves and relevant "out" groups. They believe that they have a mission to engage society at many levels to try to exert a positive Christian influence—a fact that made them receptive to efforts on the part of the OCA to bring their views to the electoral arena. At the same time, however, evangelicals tend to be skeptical of political reform, preferring to work through personal relationships "to allow God to transform human hearts" and see this as the most effective means of social reform.[32] This tension was visible in Timbertown's evangelical community.

Once the OCA made homosexuality an issue, it was impossible not to take a stand, and most conservative pastors enthusiastically spoke out against homosexuality. But many stopped short of explicitly endorsing the OCA campaign. When Bob Harrison preached a sermon against abortion, he recalled, there was a disagreement among his churchgoers. Some were pro-choice, others were pro-life. Some of the more fundamentalist churches dictate a stand on such issues, but in his church "people have to follow their individual conscience." Harrison agreed to distribute campaign literature in opposition to abortion and gay rights, and he preached sermons that condemned homosexuality, but he drew the line when it came to recommending specific actions to his congregants. "That crosses the line to where it becomes political," he said. "We cannot say you should do this or you should do that. We call each person to say if you feel like you need to respond to this somehow personally, then you need to do that, but the church can't. I couldn't mention political things."

Irwin Callow of the Faith Center also supported the OCA campaign from "behind the pulpit," shying away from taking an active stand. When Jeri Cookson asked him if she could set up a table at the back of the church to register people to vote, Callow declined on the grounds that it wasn't proper for a church to involve itself in such a fashion. Deep down, he worried that the OCA would then campaign to change his church's particular religious practices or drive it out of town. So while they felt that they could not take political stands, church leaders could inform their congregants about "biblical imperatives."

Carroll Neitz was in general agreement with the campaign's goals as well, having been approached by a couple of his congregants to take a public stand against "special rights." But he doesn't believe that you can legislate morality. "You couldn't sit here in this chair and dictate to the world that this is against the law. In order to change somebody you have to let God change them. It's not worked out in the ballot box, it's worked out in personal relationships. If I have a homosexual friend, he's going to see Christ's likeness in me, not in the particular box I checked." He was hesitant to take a public stand on homosexuality, fearing potential repercussions—including resistance on the part of some of his congregants.

As any good sociologist could tell you, what people say and what they do are often quite different things. There were individuals who kept to themselves, who listened to injunctions against homosexuality but who refused to heed their words. I spoke with Helen Potts, a forty-five-year-old member of an evangelical church, who told me that while she had great respect for her pastor, and looked forward to his sermons each Sunday, she was a "quiet believer"; there were certain things she agreed with, and certain things she did not agree with—the church's teachings against homosexuality among them. Helen had a gay brother who lived in San Francisco to whom she was close, who shared holiday meals with her family. She didn't really tell any of her friends about him, though "they knew," she said. Although she considered herself to be a Bible-believing Christian, Helen distanced herself from her church on matters of homosexuality, in the same way Catholics who practice birth control might thus controvert church doctrine but nonetheless identify strongly as Catholics.

I met a number of members of conservative congregations in town who practiced "quiet belief"—participating in church affairs, and adhering to most church doctrine, though selectively editing out parts they found offensive, or incompatible with their own lives. While most conservative Christians believed that homosexuality was condemned by the Bible, many held, unlike the OCA, that gays and lesbians deserved equal protection under the law. Helen Potts: "Well, it's true that homosexuality is against God, in some respects at least. But does that mean that gay people should be punished? I don't think so. It's not really something that can be helped." Dissenting from the belief that homosexuality is a free choice, she embraced the "immutability" argument that suggested that "they can't help it," and that individuals who engage in homosexual acts could be loving disciples of Christ.

Though such ambivalence rumbled through many conservative congregations in town, publicly it was nowhere to be found. Ambiguity does not play well in political campaigns, which require neat, polarized oppositions—*we* believe this; *they* believe that. The closer one got to the campaign leaders, the more cut and dried the issue of homosexuality seemed. For the truest of believers, those who organized the meetings, made the phone calls, and proudly waved signs that read "Save the Children," a politics of certainty, undergirded by a belief in absolute morality, prevailed. Such convictions left little room for any doubt, for ambiguous complexity that might cloud the clarity of their worldview.

CHAPTER 3

Resentment's Roots

The West is a realm of chronic impermanence, where the camp, not the village, has been the typical settlement. Cattle ranchers, conducting their business on the hoof, on 1,300 mile drives from Texas to Montana and the Dakotas, set the tone for the loggers, miners and railroad construction gangs who followed them. People got what they needed from the land, and moved on, like grazing cows. Communities were quickly formed and quickly dismantled. The transition from a boom town to a ghost town took only days to make. The word "cabin," meaning a temporary shelter or a compartment in a moving vessel, accurately described the characteristic western home. Later on, the Airstream trailer, on or off a cinderblock foundation, would provide the West with a style of domestic architecture that nicely matched its prevailing social history.

Jonathan Raban, *Badland: An American Romance*

It's kind of like the end of an era. You know, you have your colonial era. And then you have your gold rush era. And then you have your old west era. And now you have the timber era, and that's ending. It's kind of like it's sad to see it go, but I'm curious to see what's coming.

Twenty-year-old man from the Rogue Valley, Oregon

Everyday people know the New West is inevitable. They just don't know what their role will be in it. What they don't want is to become bit players in a new economy, flipping buffaloburgers for mountain bikers from the city.

Timothy Egan, *Lasso the Wind: Away to the New West*

Conflicts in the American West seem always to lead back to the land. As a New Yorker, I grew up imagining myself first and foremost as a member of an ethnic group, defined in relation to others with whom

I supposedly shared a common history and political stake, and against those with whom I did not. In the American West, historically it is the land, not tribal loyalties, that shapes the political culture. The shifting fortunes of resource-based economies, the motions of migration, and the spirit of individualism weave flux and fragmentation into the texture of the landscape.

The Pacific Northwest is dotted with towns like Timbertown, established in the latter part of the nineteenth century as logging and lumber milling in the Northwest followed on the heels of the California Gold Rush. It is this land, with its acres of huge trees, vast rivers, mountains, and lakes, that drew successive waves of migrants here to farm, to mine, to cut timber, and to escape from it all. Writing in the early nineteenth century, Bostonian Hall Jackson described Oregon's mountains as "peculiarly sublime and conspicuous," and its land as "well-watered, nourished by a rich soil, warmed by a congenial heat," and "exactly accommodated to the interests of its future cultivators."[1] By the 1890s, as the forests of the Great Lakes region were becoming depleted, the timber industry moved westward in search of the seemingly boundless forests of the Pacific Northwest, bringing waves of Easterners who came in search of work.

There was a romance about an industry in which "thousands of loggers strove mightily in the tall dark forests," as one observer described them.[2] "Paul Bunyan is alive and living in the Pacific Northwest," wrote another.[3] Timbertown, like much of the region, defined its identity in relation to the brawny industry that dominated it, and lumbering was, even more than most other industries of the era, a male domain, characterized by "isolated, dirty, noisy lumber operations, salted with uncouth extroverts and roustabout timberbeasts."[4] The mill owners, traditional men if ever there were any, considered women to be unfit to work in the industry. No one put up much of a fight because the family wage paid to timber workers meant that their wives could stay home and raise children if they wished. "What's good for the lumber industry is good for the town," proclaimed Timbertown's local newspaper: "Steady employment in the industry has always been a stabilizing factor in [this town's] economy. Lumbering is good business for everyone."[5] As a WPA publication put it: "There is hardly a community in Western Oregon whose prosperity does not depend on timber."[6]

But the problem was that timber, like other resource extraction industries, was intrinsically unstable, and a diminishing resource—a fact that did not enter public consciousness until much later. Competition encouraged overproduction, resulting in a glutted market, depressed prices, and cyclical booms and busts.[7] Since the fortunes of lumber were tied to the historically volatile housing industry, it seemed always to be the first to feel the pinch of a downturn and the last to recover. Workers were itinerant laborers who had virtually no security; during the Great Depression, the industry practically collapsed. Timbertown, and places like it, were in many respects company towns, which meant that in good times everyone prospered, to a greater or lesser extent—but the town's dependence upon timber meant that the vast majority of its residents' fortunes were tied to impersonal market forces over which they had little control.

If the West is a place of chronic change, it is also a place that has searched for roots, stability, permanence. In the 1940s, after decades of struggling through booms and busts, the region finally seemed to achieve a level of stability. Spurred by the postwar housing boom, which created a seemingly limitless demand for lumber, the U.S. Forest Service freely sold timber rights to lumber companies, feeding more than two hundred sawmills that stretched from the Pacific Coast to the Cascade Mountains. "Timber Keeps Community Green" proclaimed the local headlines.[8] Thousands of refugees from the dust bowl streamed into the state to work in the mills—entire communities from North Carolina and Arkansas picked up and moved to the area.

Timbertown, and places like it, originally temporary settlements of workers and their families, grew to resemble other small American towns, a pint-sized metropolis for the valley's far-flung inhabitants, thanks in large part to the town's timber baron families who had profited greatly over the years. Mill camp houses gave way to private houses, and temporary schoolhouses were replaced by permanent school structures; dozens of churches were erected to fulfill every type of spiritual need; a hospital, library, and parks were established. Main Street bustled with shops; men flocked to service organizations like the Masons or the Lions Club in their off hours; and families formed webs of friendship networks, socializing at picnics, barbecues, and annual summer fairs.

Timbertown developed a strong small-town identity; to many, that was what was appealing about it. People lived and worked there, and most people knew one another, at least by sight. For a western town, in a highly mobile part of a highly mobile country, there were an awful lot of people who were descendants of old pioneer families who had been there for three or more generations. Many more people who came to work at the mills could trace their lineage at least two generations. These old families, whose names could be spotted on street signs, were the bedrock of the town, bound by bonds of emotional intimacy, including long-standing friendships and long-standing dislikes. "If you marry into one of these families," a common joke went, "you're related to half of the town." They were a relatively homogeneous group in terms of class and race. In this white working-class town, few were rich, few were poor.

When logging was going full bore, most of the mills were unionized, and mill workers earned salaries that pushed them into the middle class. Chuck Mendip, a third-generation Timbertowner, graduated from high school in 1972 and went to the local community college, intending to become a lawyer, but ended up being drafted at the end of the Vietnam War. When he returned home, there were hundreds of jobs at the mills for the taking, and they paid well, so he took one, like his father before him. In 1978, Mendip earned $12.80 an hour and had excellent health and retirement benefits. He and his wife, who was able to stay home and live comfortably on Chuck's salary, bought a nice house in the center of town and had three kids. Says Mendip, "I thought: this is fine. The rest of my life is great. This is going to be okay. I can retire here." Few kids went to college; after high school, they followed their fathers into the mills. Whole families— brothers, sons, uncles, grandfathers—were in the business, and proud of it.

For most of the century, a laissez-faire attitude whose guiding principle was "stay out of my life and I'll stay out of yours" guided relations among citizens in town, reflecting the political culture of the state, which tended toward a moderate Republicanism that suggested that government should remain at arm's length from its citizens. This was the West, after all, which prided itself, against the traditional hierarchies of the East Coast, on egalitarianism, freedom, and the myth of the individual against the frontier. It was possible to stay out of people's lives when you had a lot of space to spread out into, when land cost next to nothing, when your house was dirt cheap, and when you could grow your own fruits and vegetables, to get by in the off-season or during hard times. The seasonal, cyclical nature of the timber industry bred a kind of resilience.

But beginning in the 1970s, a series of cultural and economic shifts called that sense of expansive solidarity and small-town goodwill into question. The town, whose economy was based on that which could be extracted from the land, whose culture was based on relative egalitarianism and homogeneity, and whose citizens prided themselves on a fierce sense of independence, was giving way to a different world: one that was more mobile, more economically and culturally diverse, and more open to the world of which it was a part—developments that did not please everyone.

Writing in the late 1950s about a community in the British Midlands, Norbert Elias described the animosity that arose between the "established" members of the community, who had been there for generations and wished to maintain their superiority, and the newer arrivals, the "outsiders," who "share neither the fund of common memories nor the same norms of respectability" as the established group.[9] A similar story could be told of Timbertown in the 1970s and 1980s, and of logging towns across the Pacific Northwest, once vibrant communities where people worked and lived. As the timber industry declined, rural communities across Oregon found themselves without a clear place in the emerging order. Old neighborhood and workplace ties weakened, class and cultural differences deepened, and new social divisions emerged. The first sign of these winds of change came in the early 1970s, when the counterculture arrived.

BACK TO THE GARDEN

"Turn on, tune in, drop out." So urged the back-to-the-land movement, which spawned a series of parallel worlds devoted to self-sufficiency, simple living, and a "small is beautiful" ethic, set apart from the culture of materialism and waste. In the 1970s, young long-haired dropouts purchased parcels of land in many rural areas of the United States; inexpensive land and natural beauty made Oregon a hotbed for rural visionaries. Back-to-the-landers shunned technology, grew their own vegetables, and set up food cooperatives, stretching their meager incomes into a marginal if comfortable lifestyle.[10] In 1973, on the outskirts of Timbertown, a group of people purchased a thousand-acre parcel of land and established an experimental "eco-village" based upon principles of conservation, renewable energy, and ecological living.

Farther south, along the interstate highway, rural settlements named Stepping Woods, Rainbow's End, and Womanshare attracted devotees of feminism, who scorned technology, built their own houses, cultivated the fields, marked the changing of the seasons with ritual circles, and subscribed to the separatist ideal of creating an all-woman society. "I was part of a thriving counterculture," a women's land pioneer recalled in tones not altogether different from those of settlers in the West a century before her. "We were refugees from a culture unable to contain diversity. We took power in our own hands, we lived by rules often at odds with mainstream law. We were righteous and proud, angry and rebellious. We were striking out for new territory, seeking community and autonomy, on the fringes of a society that hated us for how we loved. We looked for cracks in the system, and used them to our advantage."[11]

In a different mold, fifteen miles northeast of Timbertown, a group of "Jesus freaks," evangelical Christians who emerged out of the counterculture, established a compound they called Shiloh. The Pacific Northwest became a hotbed for conservative Christian youth who, like their more radical cousins on the left, wanted to live on the land, apart from their families, rejected science and technology, expressed their beliefs through music, and valued expressive individualism. They also embraced a charismatic, passionate Christianity that was unconventional by middle-class, mainline standards, realigning their lives according to what they saw as God's plan.[12]

Over the next decade, others arrived, fleeing the rat race and bringing a concern for the environment, and Timbertown became well known as a center for organic farming and free-thinking.[13] June and Janice Trump, two sisters from Portland, had gone to college during the heyday of the counterculture, and were captivated by the vision of rural self-sufficiency. After they graduated, their grandfather helped them to buy several acres of farmland outside of town. They had long flowing hair and wore loose, flowered dresses and sometimes went barefoot, lived with men they weren't married to, didn't shave their armpits, and helped to organize Hiroshima Day events in town.

Robin Bergman grew up in suburban New York and moved to Santa Cruz, California, so that her partner could study ecologically based agriculture. They wanted to buy a piece of land to farm, but couldn't afford California real estate, and fantasized about living in a small town with an "alternative community" that was filled with other like-minded people who were free-thinking, committed to sustainable living, and embraced progressive politics. Timbertown seemed attractive because it seemed to offer the best of both possible worlds: it was a small town that had a liberal enclave of like-minded people. The area attracted a number of young couples like the Bergmans, who bought land outside of town, shopped in the local health food store, and gave their kids names like Harvest, Meadow, and Canyon. They were drawn by many of the same things that had drawn people to Oregon for generations: the desire to get away, to live a simpler life, to know their neighbors. They were captivated by the idea that they could create a sense of community according to their own vision.[14]

But many newcomers seemed oblivious to the fact that the very things that attracted them to a small community would be changed by their very presence. As a rule small communities expect newcomers to adapt themselves to the way things are already done. They expect them to fit in. Indeed, that's one of the things that attracts people to them: small towns offer the possibility of living in close proximity with people with whom you share basic values, and with whom you can build ties of reciprocity and exchange. So when the back-to-the-landers arrived, most Timbertowners, true to their live-and-let-live Oregonian values, tended to look the other way, but they didn't quite know what to make of the young, rather odd-looking newcomers with their funny ideas. They had been brought up to believe that everyone ought to believe in the same basic principles of strength and obedience, self-discipline, self-reliance, and respect for authority. It seemed, on first impression, that the newcomers shared few of these values.

People whispered among themselves, wondering whether the "longhairs" were witches or satanists, or drug addicts. Others imagined that they were Californians who were going to remake their small town into a mini California. Car bumper stickers that carried the slogans "SNOB: Society of Native Oregon Born" and "Don't Californicate Oregon" wore these distinctions out in the open. There was an uneasy coexistence between "the hippies" and the "townies."

When they are under threat, established groups, writes Norbert

Elias, create conceptions of "newcomers" that mark them as inferior. This strengthens the "feeling of belonging together in relation to 'inferiors' who tend to show less restraint in situations in which the 'superiors' demand it. 'Inferior' people," says Elias, "are apt to break taboos which the 'superior' people have been trained to observe from childhood on. Breaches of such taboos are thus signs of social inferiority. They often insult, often very deeply, the 'superior' people's sense of good taste, of propriety, of morals, in short their sense of emotionally rooted values."[15] Indeed, longtime Timbertowners developed images of the newcomers—that they were fast-paced busybodies, dirty drug addicts, sometimes even witches—against which they defined themselves as good, upstanding, community-minded folks.

Such tensions were not altogether new. In the pioneer days, California was said to attract the single adventurers and Oregon the sober, respectable types—pious farming families who had a bit of money. For most of its history, Oregon's relative lack of development separated it from its faster, richer, flashier neighbor to the south, and the two states were locked in a continuous warfare of boundary drawing and boundary defense. In the 1970s, Oregon's moderate Republican Governor Tom McCall urged, "Visit, but don't stay." In my conversations with Timbertowners, even among the most well-meaning folks, I often heard the claim: "My family has lived here for three generations, and I feel . . ." It gave them cachet, authenticity, a legitimacy with which to speak.

But dig down a bit deeper, and the boundaries between native and stranger, Oregonian and Californian, "established" and "outsider," seemed more permeable, the boundaries soft rather than solid. Many "native-born Oregonians" had parents who were from California, and sometimes those who were the loudest critics of the California invasion were themselves refugees from the sunny state to the south—with time, outsiders often become insiders. Plus, appearances could be deceiving: the hippies who swarmed into the state weren't all urban—many came from farming families. Some were even evangelical Christians. In the late 1970s, Shiloh, the Christian commune near Timbertown, collapsed, scattering its members throughout the area, where, joining established churches, they brought their charismatic religious doctrines with them. Strange intersections and overlaps made the dividing line between left and right exceedingly fuzzy. Antiauthoritarianism cut both ways: back-to-the-land types shared with small-town Oregonians a distrust of the federal government, a belief that the public schools might be corrupting their kids, and a yearning for pastoral simplicity.

Still, those who tried to cross the borders were sometimes in for a rude shock. Subdued hostility marked the interaction between the back-to-the-landers and the old-timers, creating in essence two towns. At the root of such tensions between "established" and "outsider" groups is the fear of contact with a group, in Elias's words, that "breaks rules which one is oneself enjoined to observe and on whose observation depend both one's self-respect and the respect of one's fellows."[16] The outsiders were an affront to the identity of the established group—by their very presence they questioned many of the values that long-term Timbertowners held dear. When jobs were plentiful, animosity was cushioned by affluence, but as the lumber industry began its steady decline, a series of unsettling changes ensued.

THIS IS THE END

A century after it emerged, the lumber industry came crashing down. For most of the postwar era, a housing boom had sustained the industry through strikes and minor recessions. But in the 1980s, depleted natural resources, increasing automation, and tougher environmental regulations, exacerbated by a sluggish national housing market, dealt a fatal blow to the industry and caused a regional recession. Rumblings of change could be heard at least a decade before, when environmentalists began to challenge the notion that federal forests, which supplied more than half of the logs used in Oregon mills, would forever be the nation's "wood basket." In antique shops, you could still find old Oregon postcards depicting muscular young men hauling huge old-growth trees off to the mills. But environmentalists shifted public opinion against the belief that the forests were there for the taking. They tied the impending extinction of the spotted owl, whose natural habitat was the rapidly diminishing old growth forest, to the logging industry. In 1991, the spotted owl was listed as a threatened species, and federal court orders banned most new timber sales on federal lands, cutting the U.S. Forest Service's supply of timber available for harvest in the Northwest by a half.[17]

When their livelihoods were threatened, Timbertowners began to blame "hippie environmentalists" for caring more about owls than about living, breathing human beings. It was true that the broader environmental movement often seemed to treat the concerns of locals with callous disregard, but it had little to do with the eventual collapse of the industry.[18] Because the largest timber companies had long fought efforts to enact "sustained yield management" of the forests, trees were becoming scarce.[19] The recession diminished demand for lumber and plywood. In 1981, the wood products industry laid off one third of its workforce in Oregon.[20] Towns like Timbertown, whose economic base was the least diversified, suffered the most.

Across Oregon, demand for semiskilled or low-skilled labor declined, and the ranks of the working poor grew. In 1982, twenty-seven thousand lumber workers in the region were laid off, and thousands more forced to work at reduced schedules.[21] By the mid-1980s, the timber harvest rose to record levels and a few mills reopened, but thanks to automation and increasing competition from Canada and the southeastern United States, they employed half as many workers as before in nonunion jobs that paid half as much. The vast majority of Timbertowners, whose livelihoods were directly dependent on the wood products industry, were among the hardest hit.[22] To many it seemed that the community was shutting down.

The figures told the story: there were seven active mills in the area in 1987, when production was at its peak; by 1990, there were only three, employing eighteen hundred; three years later, that figure was down to six hundred employees.[23] Timber giant Weyerhauser, which once employed twelve hundred, closed its laminated beam mill. Bohemia, once the second-largest employer in town, cut its workforce and sold most of its timber holdings to a huge conglomerate. Many of the industry's giants proceeded to close up their Northwest operations and shift their mills to the Southeast in search of cheaper labor.

Between 1990 and 1991 alone, the wood products industry in the West, including plywood manufacturing and logging, declined by 12 percent, and Oregon lost nineteen lumber mills—a time locals refer to as "the depression." Kids in the local schools used to have jobs waiting for them in the mills when they graduated from high school. But fewer and fewer kids stayed in Timbertown after graduation. Middle-aged men and women who had worked at the local mills had to settle for low-paying service sector jobs that paid far less than a family wage. Or they left town in search of work. In a household survey of six timber-dependent communities in 1989, 80 percent reported that at least one person in a household had been placed on indefinite layoff; 90 percent said that someone had to change jobs; 85 percent said that a household member had to move to find work. Nearly 20 percent said that they "definitely" would or "probably" would move away in the next five years.[24]

One could see the signs of poverty in Timbertown: people camping in vans, old houses falling into disrepair, the growing number of new thrift shops that sprouted up on Main Street. At the bottom of the heap were the transient, homeless people, mainly men, who passed through the area, doing odd jobs, and then moving on. A step above them were the young single mothers living in trailer parks on the outskirts of town, feeding their kids fast food, or boxes of macaroni and cheese they bought with food stamps, and new immigrants from Asia and Latin America.

"When we started to hit the skids, boy, did we go downhill," recalled Sam O'Connor, an affable fellow who was mayor during that period. "It was a tragedy. We lost people who had been in the community for years." Chuck Mendip: "A lot of our friends lost houses. People who were these proud mill-working folks were on food stamps. They were out doing minimum wage jobs, or on unemployment. Their children left the area when they saw there was no future for them." The town's population declined for a few years, and then remained stagnant. The economic downturn fractured the traditional paternalism that shaped relationships between mill owners and workers and called into question the widespread belief that "what's good for the lumber industry is good for Timbertown."

Meanwhile, Oregon's largest city, Portland, was enjoying an economic upswing fueled by high-tech industries such as Tektonics and Intel along with Nike, and *Harper's Bazaar* touted the virtues of the city as a kinder, gentler, greener Los Angeles. "When Cary Grant tried to pass himself off to Grace Kelly as a lumberman from Portland, Oregon, in Hitchcock's 1955 thriller *To Catch a Thief,* the absurdity of anyone as sophisticated as Grant coming from such a backwater made for a good laugh. Well into the 1980s Portland remained a sleepy, gray town where people watched trees grow for excitement. Who would

have guessed that it was on its way to becoming one of the hippest cities on the West Coast?"

The *Harper's* article told the stories of Jennifer Adams, who with
her husband converted their own house in a "decidedly untrendy
southeast" neighborhood into a "one-of-a-kind coffeehouse," a "hip-
torian's" shrine to thrift-shop chic, decorated with 1950s cowboy li-
noleum, a fake-log lamp, paintings of Hindu gods, and plastic fish."
The article continued: "This influx of people with more sophisticated tastes has had a dramatic effect on the city's culinary IQ. When
Greg Higgins arrived from Seattle to head the kitchen at the Heath-
man Hotel 10 years ago, Portland was a steak-and-potatoes town.
Now he is the chef of his own restaurant, which rivals Chez Panisse in
Berkeley. And then there is filmmaker Gus Van Sant . . . People who
wouldn't have a chance in New York or Los Angeles can go for it
here."[25] These hip newcomers, another writer proclaimed, are better educated, better trained than the current population. They will
help Oregon make the transition from a monolithic, extractive, third
world economy, in which earning a middle-class wage doesn't require
a college degree, to "a modern, diversified, high-tech economy
driven by a highly trained workforce that has little need for skills
learned in the woods."[26]

But the newer, hipper Oregon was only part of the story. As urban
Oregon underwent an economic renaissance, its lumber towns became the "other Oregon," the Oregon that didn't feel the economic
upswing of the mid-1980s. These timber towns "make Oregon Oregon," wrote one observer. "But the way of life that has kept them
going is changing."[27] The emotional and psychological impact was
enormous. "When you come to the realization that the heyday is
over," Chuck Mendip recalled, "that things aren't going to go back to
the way they were, you know, the world around you has changed."
People in their forties and fifties become pretty hopeless: "The mill is
gone. I've got nothing to do." Mendip's father worked in one of the
mills, and he always imagined he'd follow suit. By the time he was
ready to go to work, the industry was in a steady decline, but he was
able to find a job in town, as a journalist for the local paper. Few of his
friends were so lucky.

Timbertown embarked on an aggressive retooling plan whose rallying cry was jobs. A chamber of commerce brochure boasted, "The

local economy has begun a process of diversification and growth, particularly in the service sector."[28] Town officials, hoping to attract new development, projected a pluralistic, free-thinking image. "The community," a brochure touted, "is generally a conservative one, but there is almost total tolerance of even the radically different. There is no concentration of power. . . . Lumber executives help with community ventures when asked, but do not take much part in community decision-making. Government is independent of special interest and pressure groups."[29] With the help of state development money, the town received historic preservation funds to spruce up the Main Street.

To some extent, their efforts paid off. The town attracted small businesses—a company that builds parts for manufactured homes, one that manufactures medical labels, a massage table producer—along with chain stores such as Wal-Mart, McDonald's, Kentucky Fried Chicken. Former mill workers, now termed "dislocated workers," were encouraged to join a federally subsidized state-run program to retrain them for new employment. Some went back to school and became accountants or computer technicians. More typical, however, were the loggers-turned-recreational-vehicle-technicians, or restaurant workers—new jobs that paid considerably less than the old ones.[30]

Chuck Mendip earned twelve dollars an hour grading lumber in a mill in 1978; seven years later he was making half as much working in a pesticide plant. He eventually left, taking a succession of other jobs, all of which paid considerably less and provided no benefits. They were, he said, "crappy jobs." Gone were the old days, when good-paying "family wage" jobs were plentiful, when mill workers were thrust into the middle classes. Now, it took two working people to support a family, and even then it was a struggle. Low-wage, temporary, part-time, and nonbenefited jobs were increasing. Many families were forced to piece together an array of different jobs. Some took to foraging in the woods for ferns, mushrooms, and firewood. Others took occasional construction jobs, and their wives went to work. Low-income two-worker families became the norm.

"These layoffs change the whole pattern of living in town," reported the local newspaper. "This means not buying a new Ford every two years, not taking your family on vacation in the camper."[31] During the 1980s, 80 percent of Oregon's families lost income while the income of the top tenth soared. Historically, Oregon had a more egalitarian distribution of income, and less stark economic contrasts, than the vast majority of U.S. states. By 1990, it reflected the nation as a whole.[32]

THE GREEN RUSH

One person's hardship is another's windfall. The economic devastation of Timbertown, and of much of Oregon, was a boon to its neighbors farther south. During the period 1987–92, three hundred thousand people, one third of them from California, moved to Oregon, increasing the state's total population by more than 10 percent.[33] An earlier wave of migrants were largely countercultural types drawn by the beauty of the land and the possibility of living cheaply on it, or were low-income people looking for a change. Now, a new, more affluent group, in search of inexpensive property and a less complicated way of life, was beginning to arrive. The gentrification of Timbertown had begun.

Spurred by declining real estate values, the boom in California real estate, and the decline of California's aerospace industry, a growing number of people from cities moved to the area, drawn by its natural beauty and cheap land, and proximity to the university town of Eugene, to the north. Many of them were "equity migrants," cashing in on the California real estate boom of the late 1970s, in which the value of modest houses in Southern California doubled. They were retirees—members of the Depression generation who had bought their houses when the federal government pumped millions into postwar subsidies.[34] They were baby boomers who worked in high-end service and professional sectors who could telecommute or who saved a bunch of money to cushion a more frugal lifestyle. They weren't a monolithic group by any stretch of the imagination: some were white-flight suburbanites who saw the possibility of escaping California's racial diversity and high taxes, and were attracted to rural Oregon in large part because it seemed to have few of the overt social divisions that plagued California; others simply wanted a lifestyle change, and wanted to live in a community where they could make a difference.

Fifty-three-year-old Toby Ramsey, a retired X-ray technician who runs a consulting business, and her husband, a design consultant, moved to Timbertown in 1988 because they wanted a house on ten acres of land, in a place that was close to a hospital, so that Toby could get occasional work. They wanted to get away from the "superficiality and glitziness" of Southern California, and lead a simpler life. They bought a piece of land outside of town, in a breathtakingly beautiful setting near a lake, along with a number of rental properties in town, and proceeded to live out their country dream. With her makeup, perfectly coiffed hair, and designer clothes, Toby stood out among people in a town whose fashion sense owes more to Wrangler than Donna Karan. As she describes Timbertown, "It's not very intellectually stimulating, but that's okay. It's fun to come to a place like this." She misses her Los Angeles social circle, where her friends were artists, intellectuals, gay people, people of color. Before they moved to Oregon, she and her husband didn't know the first thing about rural life. Within days, she boasted, they found a spring on their property, and both even learned how to drive a tractor. "It's a whole other way of knowing, of doing things," she said.

"It wasn't New York City anymore. It wasn't Santa Cruz either," said Robin Bergman, another former urbanite. "Then suddenly something hits you in the face. Hey, this nice dream is not okay. You want to live in this place? You want to raise children in a place like this? When you're in a rural area and your neighbors don't understand who you are or what you're there for, it can be isolating." She felt comfortable with "the alternative community in town." The problem is, it's "surrounded by thousands of people in the community who are not people I'd be real comfortable with." Her small daughter went to a school that seemed so "mainstream, so mindless."

One day Robin happened to walk into her daughter's classroom when they were making crafts. The teacher had cut out paper plates and they made a ring for Christmas wreaths, and there were cutouts of little red and green paper. What bothered her is that "they all had to glue them on. There wasn't any choice. The kids who didn't fill it in, where there was still the white plate showing, were supposed to fill it in. They were told they had to do it." That sums up Timbertown for her: it's no different from anywhere else in America. "People just think that everybody should have to do the same thing. They all watch the same TV programs. There is just this mindlessness." Most

Timbertowners had values that were at odds with hers. They unthinkingly parroted the values of the dominant culture—follow the rules, do what you're told, and keep the peace. In her mind, they feared difference, and change.

But the newcomers seemed to have little patience for locals' lack of exposure to things they took for granted. Toby Ramsey told me a story about a conversation she had with a carpenter whose family has been in town forever, whom she described as a "real Oregonian." One day, they were talking about evolution and Toby told him about a museum exhibit she had recently seen, about Neanderthals, and was floored when the carpenter had never heard of these human ancestors. "He never knew there was another species of hominid, he thought our history began six thousand years ago." Toby began to realize that "there's an enormous gap in folks' general knowledge. It's a matter of not being exposed to these things."

Mary and Mel Skill moved to the area to live out their dream of having a small winery. They built a sprawling house on a hill and made their dream come true. Then their kids went to school, where they encountered teachers who provided disclaimers before teaching about evolution, and rubbed elbows with people in town whose first question to them was, What church do you belong to? "We had no idea it was so conservative here," said the Skills. "It seemed so odd that we could be stuck near a university town and feel like we're living on some other planet—Iowa!" They told me the story about their thirteen-year-old daughter who had some friends stay over at their house and offered them grapefruit. Of five girls, two had never eaten grapefruit before. It was, they believed, symptomatic of how sheltered and closed to new experiences people were. "We've got a Safeway here, for crying out loud!" exclaimed Mel. "There's grapefruit there! What's wrong with these people?" There was certainly a cultural divide that separated Timbertown even from the nearby university town of Eugene. In the 1990s, much of the Pacific Northwest experienced a gourmet coffee explosion—in Eugene one could buy a caffè latte on practically every block or at drive-in espresso stands in strip malls, but in Timbertown gourmet coffee was a rare commodity. Timbertown was, in essence, a working-class town. Yet its new arrivals were often middle-class, possessing in sociologist Pierre Bourdieu's terms, greater cultural capital. Their education and their travels made them open to new places, new experiences, and they believed in the importance of validating pleasure and "personal growth."

The old-timers, in contrast, did things the way they always had done them and resented being told to do things differently. "These people don't know anything about the world," said Cynthia Newman, whose husband was a logger until he lost his job. "They want to stay someplace they know. They're afraid to leave." When she began to do job counseling at the local community college, Cynthia often had to escort people to interviews in Eugene, which many considered to be a teeming metropolis. "They had no idea how to get there. They were clueless. Many had never left Timbertown before." Clearly, long-timers felt protective toward their community and feared change.

Others were even less charitable, suggesting that longtime residents were little more than gun-toting, liquor-guzzling rednecks. What exactly, I wondered, do people mean to imply when they call someone a "redneck"? Chuck Mendip, whose logger family had lived in town for generations, told me that it was originally a term locals used to describe one another, though the precise meaning varied with the locale. In Timbertown, according to Mendip, a redneck was someone "who was maybe a logger, who would cut your hair with a beer bottle." He was a simple, gruff guy, someone who had little use for niceties, who made his living from the land, and who drank beer and cursed. With time, however, the term took on an unkindly cast.

Bill Freeman, an engineering consultant who moved to Oregon in the late 1980s in search of a simpler life, listed a series of characteristics he associated with the archetypal redneck: "Values things more than people, has little regard for nature, has low self-esteem, doesn't take responsibility for his actions, views the world as either black or white (you are either for me or agin' me)." In other words, the term "redneck," once used to describe a simple, working guy, came to signify an uneducated, uninitiated bigot. The shift in meaning seemed to symbolize the growing influence of the newcomers in the town, and the vast cultural divide separating them from longtime Timbertowners.

Affluent immigrants often took jobs below their level of skills and accustomed pay, outcompeting less-educated, less-experienced local job seekers, particularly in high- and middle-range jobs. And they were on the whole, less apologetic about their middle-class sensibilities than their back-to-land predecessors had been. Restored Victorians with gleaming new windows and spanking new paint cropped up next to run-down houses with old heaps parked in the driveway. Outside of town, some newcomers bought vast tracts of land alongside pockets of rural poverty, and then agitated to maintain a 1983 ban on new residential development of prime forestland for fear that their green vistas would be threatened.

I visited some of these properties; their gorgeous green expanses, set off as far away from civilization as the eye could see, were often stunning. But longtime residents were none too happy about these "playgrounds for people from the city." Locals complained about how the town was changing. "There's much more traffic," Sarah Chase, the wife of a car mechanic, complained. Until the 1970s, she explained, "I used to ride up and down the interstate, and there would be no cars on the road. I'd take it easy, go fifty or sixty miles an hour." But beginning in the early 1980s, more and more people arrived in the area, and the pace of things quickened. "Now there are all these trucks. They speed up and down. People are in a rush." Sarah lamented these changes. "I'm kinda slow, I hate the fast life. It became more and more difficult to live like that."

Many people viewed the back-to-the-landers as urban dwellers who moved to Timbertown to live out their fantasies of country life, expecting to enjoy all of the conveniences of city living, and changing the town to suit their needs in the process. One could buy a nice house in town for $40,000 in the early 1980s; ten years later the same house had nearly tripled in value, pricing the children of longtime residents out of the housing market, and driving up property taxes. Many long-established residents were dismayed by this turn of events. Chuck Mendip: "Orange County folks who have made a bunch of money came up here and could buy a nice house. And that pissed off people that lived here, big time! Californians would sell their houses, have lots of money. It was during the recession, and people would come up here, and could buy property and a nice house for cash, basically. And, you know, people living here couldn't do it, 'cause there were no jobs, no money."

Although many longtime residents of Timbertown found themselves sitting on residential gold mines, the tax consequences made it increasingly difficult for them and their families to remain in the community. Political agitation for tax cuts led to a 1990 statewide property tax limitation initiative that froze or reduced property tax rates dramatically, squeezing local schools and social services. Chuck Mendip blamed the tax cut sentiment upon "those Californians": "People who come up here to retire don't want to vote for taxes. They don't have kids in school, and don't really care about preserving city services. They don't want to vote for anything controversial, and they're pretty much apt to be set in their ways by now, and don't want to embrace new ideas."[35] Eighty-two-year-old Tilly Hammett refused to mince words: "All those people coming up here who tell you how to run Oregon, I just wish they would all pack up and go home." But affluent refugees from California were not the only ones arriving.

THE STRANGERS IN OUR MIDST

> The most striking and off-putting trait of strangers is that they are neither neighbors nor aliens. Or rather—confusingly, disturbingly, terrifyingly, they are both. Neighborly aliens. Alien neighbors. In other words, strangers. That is, socially distant yet physically close.
>
> Zygmunt Bauman, *Postmodern Ethics*

Martha Bayles and Jan Hogan, a mixed-race lesbian couple, live in a small house on two acres of land near one of the old lumber mills on the outskirts of town. They came to Oregon in the mid-1970s to live "on the land" in a women's rural land cooperative in southern Oregon. When the community collapsed, they searched for inexpensive land of their own, where they could put down roots. Neither had much money, and they wanted to live in a tranquil place, free of the noise of the city, but close enough to a larger town and a lesbian community. Timbertown fit the bill. By the end of the 1980s, several rural communes known as "women's land" in southern Oregon had disbanded, scattering their former members throughout the area.

A number of lesbians also arrived and set up small businesses downtown; thirty-seven-year-old Cindy Barber was one of them. Barber's family had lived in Oregon for as long as anyone can remember, in a small logging town about fifty miles from Timbertown. Cindy was married to a truck driver and working in the kitchen of the Logger's Lair, a popular local dive, when she met a woman named Sammie Melton, who waited tables there. They struck up a friendship, and had heart-to-hearts about their respective failing marriages. Cindy had married her husband on the condition that he quit drugs, and "he made a solemn oath that he would do so" but he slipped up. She gave him an ultimatum: "it's either me and the kids, or drugs," and drugs won out. So Cindy left him. It was a somewhat fortuitous end, because she and Sammie, who had two kids and a fifteen-year-marriage, were falling in love. Neither one had ever imagined that she was attracted to women until they met each other. At first they wrote if off as "silly infatuation." But the feelings stuck—trying to deny them "was like stopping a runaway train."

"There was no way I could not be with her," Cindy recalls. "No way at all. I felt like my whole life ended with that moment when we finally came together. That one was gone and a new one started. It was just wonderful. We were scared shitless and totally head over heels." It was a classic Romeo and Juliet story of star-crossed lovers whose romance defies community norms—with a twist. They left their husbands, packed up their kids and all of their possessions, and took off on the interstate, not knowing where they would go. They ended up in Timbertown because it was a small town like the one they had come from, and they thought it was pretty. For several years, they lived together as "roommates"—they never used the term "lesbians" because they didn't know what it meant. "We didn't know any lesbians. We'd never even read a book about it, nothing. And so, when we moved in together, it was like two women who lived together that just happened to be in love."

Since Cindy and Sammie had always liked books, they decided to open a used bookstore in town, on Main Street. Soon they began to meet other women who owned local businesses. It was no coincidence that lesbians owned a disproportionate number of small businesses. Historically, Jews have also been small business owners: I thought of my own grandparents, on both sides of the family, who worked in the rag trades in Europe, selling material and haberdashery, and my mother's cousin Andrew, who fled the Nazis by the skin of his teeth and with only the shirt on his back, and ended up selling men's suits on New York's Lower East Side. More recently in this country, new immigrants from Southeast Asia have opened small shops selling fruits, vegetables, and inexpensive import items. It's what you do when you're landless and shut out of the centers of power. "If you're a lesbian, you don't want to work for someone else. You don't want someone else to choose your fate," says Cindy. "We're trying to protect ourselves."

The school system was also a refuge of sorts for freethinkers in town. After the timber industry collapsed, the school district, with a staff of 350, became the largest single employer in town, overshadowing even lumber giant Weyerhauser. The middle school in particular employed a number of lesbians and gay men—most of whom lived out of town, and enjoyed a certain degree of tolerance, as long as they weren't too forthcoming about their private lives. Harvey Silko, a retired high school history teacher and good Catholic father of ten kids, tells me that he has long known people on staff who were gay, even though "nobody identified them as that in the 1950s or 1960s." Then, in the 1970s, as the gay liberation movement started to brew, some of them began to rouse themselves out of their closets. "They refused to stay quiet." That public visibility didn't last all that long, however. A few "made an issue of it," started talking about it to everyone. But when the dust settled, and the cultural rebellion subsided, most went on their little lives just as they had always done. Most of the more open, politicized gay people moved away.

Perhaps the best-known lesbian in town was thirty-six-year-old Barbara Hammer, assistant school superintendent, who had joined the school district staff ten years ago, after graduating with a degree in physical education. She quickly rose up in the ranks to become vice principal and athletic director of the high school, and eventually assistant superintendent of the district. Sarah, Barbara's longtime partner, is also a teacher in the district. When we talked in her office, at the school district's headquarters, the door was open and a bank of secretaries was poised outside of the door. She spoke quietly, cautiously, never using the term "lesbian," but being quite up front about her sexuality. "Every single staff member knows about me personally," she told me. "And with few exceptions, they've been very supportive. I've had lots of opportunities to go other places, and do things that would probably be considered moves up, and all that. But the thought of going to a different community and starting all over on that particular issue isn't appealing at all when that part of me is out here and is very well established."

Like an increasing number of people who work in Timbertown,

Barbara and Sarah live out of town, which has permitted them more personal freedoms to present themselves as they pleased in their private lives. In Timbertown, Barbara would never dare to hold Sarah's hand in public, but in Eugene they can socialize freely. They've constructed separate lives. In much the same fashion, when twenty-seven-year-old Vicki Harstrup, an athletic woman in her mid-twenties, wants to "go out with the gals," she leaves Timbertown. She grew up on a farm and knows just about everyone in town, she says, but she's "more comfortable with animals than people." Vicki's house, which she shares with her girlfriend, Gloria, a slight blonde who works as a waitress in a café downtown, is lined with ribbons celebrating her achievements as a runner and her prize-winning sheep and pigs. Growing up, she was a leader in the local 4H club. Now she's a cashier in a supermarket, and her animals—and Gloria—are her closest friends. She's not out as a lesbian to everyone she knows, but she doesn't hide it either. Her double-women's symbol earring, too tiny to be noticed by many, marks her difference. "Most people never get close enough to see what it is, and if they do, they never ask. I don't know if anyone's familiar with it."

Their stories reminded me of what a man once told me about secrets and lies in small towns. In places where a certain degree of surveillance is the norm, drinking, not just social drinking but serious drinking, is frowned upon—echoes of a Puritan past. You don't want your neighbor, or your cousin, to see you alone at the bar drowning your sorrows: if they ask you what's going on, you have to tell them. So if someone wishes to drink he or she tends to go to a neighboring town where it's easier to maintain anonymity. Much the same is true of homosexuality in small-town Oregon: there's a certain degree of tolerance if you play by the rules, which you know without being told. You don't hold hands with your girlfriend in public. And you certainly don't kiss her. If you want to do that, you leave town—temporarily, or permanently. Gay people in Timbertown are private, subdued—not really closeted, but not all that visible either.

Since the early nineteenth century, social critics have imagined an opposition between the city—artificial, anonymous, and sexually licentious—and the country—the repository of nature, face-to-face relations, and tradition.[36] Small-town life was hampered by tradition, small-mindedness, and constant surveillance, but cities could be "liberated zones" where tolerance and individuality was possible. There is an undeniable truth to this story: cities afford a certain anonymity that made open homosexuality and other difference possible; tens of thousands of people knew this and flocked to cities in search of sexual freedom. Gay people in San Francisco, New York, and a handful of other cities established neighborhoods that were lively alternatives to mainstream hetero culture. San Francisco's Castro District and places like it were based on the quintessentially American notion that people could "start all over again from scratch," that they could make "new lives, new families, even new societies."[37] Results of a 1994 survey of sexual behavior and attitudes supported the notion, suggesting that homosexuality—or at least open homosexuality—was largely an urban phenomenon.[38]

Certainly, in many parts of the country, gay people live in fear of verbal threats, physical harassment, and even murder, and are forced to lead double lives. A recent *New York Times* headline announced: "Murder Reveals Double Life of Being Gay in the South," describing the life and death of a thirty-nine-year-old man in the small Alabama town of Sylacauga.[39] Such stories, while certainly horrific, erase the diversity of experiences of lesbians, gay men, and other sexual minorities living in the countryside, and portray them as universally unhappy, closeted, or duplicitous. Yet gay people have long lived in Timbertown and in other rural areas, and often quite comfortably. During the course of speaking with people, I met or heard about at least a dozen people who consider themselves lesbian or gay, and I'm certain the actual number is much higher. Unlike the lesbians and gay men I knew in San Francisco, New York, and Boston, they were, for the most part, well integrated into the community, and predominantly women—gay men tended to move to cities in higher numbers, and were less likely than lesbians, who were often drawn to "the land," to move to a rural communities and small towns.

Gay people in Timbertown, and in other small Oregon towns, typically aren't "out" in the conventional sense. Their sexuality usually isn't known to all they meet, and they have little interest in making a "big political statement" about it. They tend to talk about their homosexuality in two different ways: as what they have "always been" and have little choice over, or as situational: they fell in love with the girl next door, the boy who washed the dishes in the restaurant where they worked, the woman who changed their tires at the auto repair shop. They've barely heard of Rita Mae Brown, Adrienne Rich, or even Alison Bechdel, but you won't find them trembling in their closets either—they keep a low profile, sometimes because they're afraid of the potential repercussions of going public, but also because they're private people who don't want their sexuality to define them. Much like their neighbors, they're far more interested in spending quiet time with family and friends, gardening, and sheet-rocking their houses than carrying political banners.

Lesbians and gay men were probably invisible to all but the most savvy Timbertowners. More visible were the growing number of dark-skinned faces in town, mainly Latinos—from Mexico, as well as Honduras, El Salvador, and Nicaragua. "I saw my first black person in town twelve years ago," says fifty-two-year-old Cynthia Newman, "and you gotta stare when that happens. You're just not used to it." Now, she says, "it's not unusual to see people in the grocery store. You hardly saw Hispanics, and now there's lots of them." They were employed at a nearby chicken factory, or in restaurant kitchens, or in the forests, planting trees. To accommodate their growing numbers, the Catholic church in town added a mass in Spanish. There were also a growing number of Asian refugees from Tibet and Cambodia, who worked in the mushroom harvests, or as maids and cooks. The school system added two full-time English as a Second Language teachers to accommodate the growing influx.

A teacher in the school district who works with the immigrant population tells me that "for a community this size that has seen a huge increase in immigrants, we have done some pretty impressive scrambling." But in addition to lacking economic resources, the immigrants remained outside the established community and were therefore excluded from the emotional ties and networks of reciprocity that bound members of the community to one another. So were the handful of African Americans in town, even if they weren't new arrivals.

Perhaps the invisible, phantasmic nature of the homosexual presence in places like Timbertown is what makes it all the more anxiety-producing for some people. Thirty years ago, sociologist Mary McIntosh wrote that "the creation of a specialized, despised and punished role of homosexual keeps the bulk of society pure."[40] But in Timbertown, gay people are strangers who are not all that strange. Sometimes they are the shopkeeper, the neighbor, the assistant school superintendent, and even one's son or daughter. And while dark-skinned people are visibly alien, gay people blurred the boundaries of the securely defined world.

PERMANENT FLUX

By the early 1990s Timbertown's traditional economic base had all but vanished. If most residents once lived and worked in town, a majority were now commuting twenty miles or more to work. On weekends, they drove to one of the shiny new malls in and around Eugene to shop, to see a movie, or to go out for dinner—if they could afford to do so. Rising real estate prices meant that it was less and less possible to get by on little money, and low-income people who subsisted partly on bartering and growing their own food were increasingly reliant upon a cash economy. Those who struggled to stay in the middle class found that the price for success was speeding up—both spouses needed to work. And they could no longer pass mill work on to their sons; educational credentials were becoming more and more important. The community, once rooted in the lumber industry, made up of families who had settled the land for generations, had been transformed into a bedroom community, more diverse economically and culturally, but lacking a strong sense of itself.

Depending upon how well one was poised in relation to these changes, the gentrification of the town—its transformation from a logging town into a mecca for retirees, tourists, and small business—was either promising or foreboding. Forty-three-year-old Harry Boyle, who grew up in Timbertown, is a member of the planning commission, an entrepreneur who is quick to tell me that he holds a college degree. He is married to a woman from Japan and has two kids. "The logger noneducated mentality is declining. A lot of people have been moving in who have college degrees. That's good." He is unequivocal. "We don't have four employers controlling the town anymore. In the past, we've had booms and busts, strikes and national economic downturns. Now we're more diversified, and that's better." Certainly, for those who were able, by dint of skills, age, or personality, to move with the times, and adapt to a changing labor market, the changes were good. But for those who were less adaptable, and who found themselves in low-paying service jobs, the prognosis wasn't nearly as positive. And of course the change was about more than simply economics: it was about a way of life.

On Main Street, where there were once only hardware stores, gun shops, and a five-and-ten, you could now find a good cup of cappuccino. But since the only department store had closed down, you had to travel twenty-some miles to buy clothes for your kids. Timbertown was losing its traditional small-town identity. Seventy-five-year-old Sarah Henson, whose family arrived in the 1940s to work in the mills, complained: "You used to be able to walk up on Main Street and know everybody. Sometimes I can meet twenty people in one day and only one will say hello. Now if my granddaughter misses her bus home, I get a call and have to pick her up because she's too afraid to walk on her own." The sense of intimate familiarity linking generations of people in town, who shared a common history, was diminishing. Former mayor Sam O'Connor: "It used to be that people socialized in groups. Today, people are more and more isolated. There's less interconnectedness." Such laments tell a familiar American story of individualism and a persistent longing for community.[41]

Activist Beverly Brown, writing of logging communities in southern Oregon, described the emergence of "communities of affiliation," in which people come to associate with and trust only those "who share a similar social class or specific social values." Once, the relative homogeneity of the town, in terms of class, race, and general cultural values, created cohesiveness. But as the town's traditional economic base collapsed, and more and more Californians, lesbians, and Latino and Asian families arrived, Timbertown's identity changed. Longtime residents became more vulnerable to unemployment and family instability and felt torn between different ways of organizing the world, different meaning systems. Once there had been tensions between "established" and "outsiders." Now, with the decline of the logging industry, it had become more and more difficult to imagine longterm residents as being very established at all. As a consequence, their sympathies changed: they began to think of their own interests as ever more narrowly defined.[42]

Once stability seemed within reach. Now Timbertowners seemed to live in a permanent state of flux. As one man put it, "There's somebody telling them, they can no longer be what you desire to be. Or what you have the skills to be. You have to be something else."[43] A newspaper article entitled "Romantic View of Small Towns Ignores Troubles" foreshadowed the changes ahead: "Those little towns face some cruel choices. There's going to be this incredible social transformation for them. They will not be the same. The people will think different about themselves and about their world."[44]

CHAPTER 4

Community Reimagined

A good deal of what passes for religion is just a vague fear or
homesickness.

Archie Robertson, *That Old-Time Religion*

JESUS BELIEVER

SWPF, 40ish feels 20ish. Healthy brunette, adventurous, silly & serious.
Work hard, always busy, desire a break. Love laughter, outdoors, horses,
watching sports and worshipping Jesus. Long for a close friendship,
buddy and helpmate. Fitness trainer would be cool too. No smokers.

Personal ad, Timbertown *Advertiser*

Oregon is today the most "unchurched" state in a most religious nation: there are fewer church members per capita than in anyplace else
in the United States. While 70 percent of Americans are affiliated
with churches, only 40 percent of Oregonians are. You'd never know
this on a typical Sunday in Timbertown, where, during the past
twenty-five years, evangelical churches have flourished—as they
have in the nation as a whole. As the old bonds of community eroded,
small-town Oregonians craved a sense of authority, a set of rules, of
order, they could obey, a unitary vision of the world that would link
them with something larger than themselves. Increasingly, this security came from evangelical Protestantism, which provided a common
language and set of reference points for understanding the world, and
for reimagining a sense of community.[1]

Evangelicalism emphasizes the expressive aspects of religious belief and the capacity of the individual, once he or she is "saved," to develop a "personal relationship with the Lord." It views the Bible as the
word of God, and sees salvation as central to religious faith. These beliefs are shared in some form by one fifth of the American population—all but mainline Protestants and other nominal Christians, as

well as Catholics, Jews, and other non-Christians.[2] Eighty percent of evangelical Christians attend church services once a week or more. They believe their faith has implications for all aspects of life.[3] And despite doctrinal differences, they think of themselves as a subculture with a special "Christian" way of seeing the world.

The first white Americans were brought to Oregon by the fire of evangelicalism, intent upon civilizing the natives. By the early 1840s, the American missionaries had established seven settlements in the Oregon country.[4] Though evangelicals failed to Christianize the Native American population—unconvinced by claims that they would burn in hell if they didn't stop gambling and having sex out of wedlock, the natives rebuffed their would-be civilizers—they succeeded in extolling the virtue of Oregon to others, and more than three hundred thousand people took the Oregon Trail in search of the "land at Eden's Gate." In equal measure pious and adventurous, they prohibited swearing, obscene conversation, and immoral conduct, but they were also treasure seekers and free spirits who possessed little respect for authority.

Preachers found Oregon's "seeming incoherence of religious organization" both puzzling and frustrating. "They form[ed] the most secular society in the United States as gauged by church membership statistics," wrote one historian, "yet when questioned they claim to be religiously concerned and find religion to be important in their personal lives." Like many in the West, Oregonians were believers but not belongers.[5] The contradictory mix of moralism and libertarianism continues to this day: while most believe in God, relatively few are churchgoing—historian Patricia Limerick calls this "disorganized" religion. Generally, a longtime Timbertowner told me, "people work hard and party hard and don't care much about church." But piety thrives on the margins.

In the nineteenth century, the anti-institutional religiosity that swept across the West gave rise to a wide array of spiritual seekers and new religions. A century later, in the wake of the "Mystical Sixties," thousands of young people joined the Jesus movement, seeking a personal, charismatic alternative to mainline Protestantism, and dozens of them settled in Oregon on seventy forested acres called "the Land." Around the same time, thousands of other young, middle-class people followed a bearded guru named Bhagwan Shree Rajneesh to his communal city in central Oregon, where they built a meditation university and first-class hotel, and devoted themselves to the goal of spiritual surrender.[6] A similar impulse toward religious innovation —which appeals to those with fire in the belly but little faith in established religions—fueled the recent revival of Christian evangelicalism.

For most of Timbertown's history, mainline Protestant denominations dominated the town, as they did the rest of Oregon. In the 1930s, when its population numbered three thousand, there were Methodist, Presbyterian, Catholic, and Baptist congregations, and a smattering of small fundamentalist sects, many without church buildings. After World War II, migrants from North Carolina came to work in the mills, bringing Southern-style evangelicalism and a new religiosity. In the 1960s and 1970s, as mainline congregations declined in popularity, a series of new evangelical churches cropped up, reflecting trends in the United States as a whole. By 1972, there were twenty-four churches in town, mainly conservative Protestant.[7]

Today there are about forty churches in town, and the vast majority of them are evangelical—with a Pentecostal bent. The Conservative Baptist, Church of Christ, Assembly of God, Church of the Nazarene, Foursquare, and their ilk vastly outnumber the Methodist, Presbyterian, and Lutheran congregations—and that's not counting the small mom-and-pop fundamentalist churches. Offshoots of more established Pentecostal congregations, with names like "Latter Rain," and "Living River," they barely have a building or telephone number, yet claim that they alone possess the truth.

Making sense of the myriad Protestant denominations in Timbertown would be a challenge for anyone. For a Jew who had barely set foot into a church except for the occasional wedding or funeral, the task was especially daunting. In my universe, the only really notable religious differences were among Protestants, Catholics, and Jews. How, I wondered, could I possibly make sense of the huge variations among Protestants, even in a small town? My difficulties were compounded by the fact that churches, with few exceptions, rarely identified their affiliations, and names were often deceiving. The Sacred Fate Temple was, not so very long ago, called the Evangelical Faith Temple. The Bible Church was actually a Baptist congregation—a "stealth Baptist" church, I was told.

I had been pleasantly surprised to find that most church leaders were happy to speak with me—with the exception of representatives of the most fundamentalist churches in town, the Sacred Fate Center, and several independent storefront churches. Fundamentalism, which today is more a mind-set rather than a movement possessing a clearly definable theology, exists on the edges of evangelicalism. Fundamentalists are born-again Christians who believe in the literal truth of the Bible, which they consider to be the word of God, and the prophesied end of the world—a "rapture" that will initiate one thousand years of Jesus' rule on earth, culminating in a final judgment.

"You and they live in two different worlds," Bob Harrison explained when I told him about the resistance I encountered. "Some of those people are so fundamentalist that they have to start their own little churches because they say they're the only ones that preach the truth and no other congregations in the community can do it." Many fundamentalists home-school their children, refuse to pay taxes, and try their best to shield themselves from the harmful influences of the secular modern world. "They can be so far-out, some even have guns. They're real radical," Lance White said. That his congregation, which prohibits drinking and swearing and frowns upon divorce, was considered moderate was proof of just how conservative the faith community in town really was.

Bruce Bawer, a liberal Episcopalian, describes the principal differences between conservative and liberal Christians as follows:

> Conservative Christianity understands a Christian to be someone who subscribes to a specific set of theological propositions about God and the afterlife, and who professes to believe that by subscribing to those propositions, accepting Jesus Christ as savior, and (except in the case of the most extreme separatist fundamentalists) evangelizing, he or she evades God's wrath and wins salvation; liberal Christianity, meanwhile, tends to identify Christianity with the experience of God's abundant love and with the commandment to love God and one's neighbor. If, for conservative Christians, outreach generally means zealous proselytizing of the "unsaved," for liberal Christians it tends to mean social programs directed at those in need.[8]

Many evangelicals, who honestly believe they are creating a better world by promoting their version of Christianity, would no doubt disagree with this interpretation. But in relation to mainline Protestantism's relative doctrinal openness, evangelicalism tends to be static and legalistic. Indeed, that may account for its appeal.

By most sociological accounts, the certainties of old-time religion should have long since fallen victim to the corrosive effects of modern pluralism. But modernity has not in fact brought secularization to the United States. In fact, the opposite seems to be true: religious fervor seems deeper than ever. Some suggest that evangelicalism flourishes only in places that are relatively sheltered from contact with the modern world. But in fact Timbertown, like many other small towns, has become less and less autonomous, more and more open to the "outside world." More people travel out of town to work. Greater numbers of people migrated to the town from surrounding states, as well as from Latin America. More and more people are connected to the Internet and to other new forms of media. Indeed, what is striking is that evangelicalism rose in popularity at a time when Timbertown became less sheltered from contact with the modern world rather than the reverse. The influences of the outside world seem to strengthen the evangelical foothold.

In the past, Timbertowners strongly identified with their town and the timber industry that formed its backbone. But in recent years, the fragmentation of the community and the rise of new social divisions made it more and more difficult to think of the town in those terms. Evangelical Christianity appealed to many residents' desire for connection, community, and belonging and for a morally orienting sense of identity. It helped individuals distinguish, in philosopher Charles Taylor's words, between "what is good and bad, what is worth doing and what not, what has meaning and importance for you and what is trivial and secondary."[9]

WHAT TIME IS IT? IT'S REVIVAL TIME!

At Sacred Fate Temple, a sprawling Pentecostal church set behind a large parking lot, I pulled up beside a marquee that shouted out, in big bold lettering: "JESUS IS THE ROCK THAT WILL NOT ROLL." I was ushered in by two smiling women and greeted with warm handshakes and a query: "Is this your first time?" Having answered yes, I was led into a large chapel filled with working folks, nearly entirely white, and evenly divided among men and women. The hall, which holds about three hundred, was about two-thirds full. The average age was about forty-five, and there were few children despite the church's commitment, described in a brochure, to "reach out to children and their families." Onstage, two young men played electric guitars against a drum-machine beat. A woman greeted the crowd: "Hi y'all. Get ready to be inspired!" Song lyrics were projected on a screen so that the congregation could join in, and they enthusiastically did: singing, swaying, hands flailing, guitars twanging, drum machine beating. There was a uplifting, show biz quality to it all.

Finally, a man in his early fifties with a jet-black beard and long sideburns, appeared. He walked across the church pews and aisles, booming voice amplified, speaking of sin and salvation, of true Christians and heathen others, of the possibility of redemption— from sin, from suffering, from deprivations of all sorts. "I was once on the bottom," he proclaimed. "I was voted least likely to succeed in high school. But then I found the Lord." During the course of the hour service, he took his congregation on an emotional roller coaster ride, a performance filled with drama, excitement, and adventure. Pastor Jaeger punctuates his service with vivid portraits of suffering individuals, his voice building to a crescendo as he describes the personal transformations possible through commitment to Christ. The congregation laughed, they shouted, they hugged one another, and sometimes they cried. People joined in affirmations, waving hands, and spontaneous calling out, "Yes! hallelujah! Thank you, Jesus!"

When asked to account for the popularity of Pentecostalism, a pastor explained: "It's radical Christianity. The worship is more vocal, more spontaneous, less written down." The "old-time religion" embodies, writes Archie Robinson, a "belief in the right of the individual to interpret the Bible according to his own conscience, and in the competence of the individual, the ability of each soul to deal directly with the Creator."[10] Hierarchies are downplayed, personal experience is key, there is a "constant drive for unity through simplification," and a move away from the coldness and formality in worship.

Pentecostalism draws its members largely from dissatisfied Baptists and mainline Protestants. It was born at the dawn of the technological age, at a time when America was becoming more affluent and more urban, and it seized thousands and then millions of Americans until it became the largest Protestant body in the world. The new religion was quintessentially American in impulse, revivalist in tone and highly individualistic—a rebellion against structure and form and, particularly against the rationalistic direction of the mainstream faiths. It reaches out to its congregation with little hierarchy, stressing the right of each man and woman to interpret the Bible and the right of any man or woman to preach.

From the start, Pentecostalism was an outcast faith, a fact that strengthened its appeal. That appeal certainly persists today among the modest working poor of small-town Oregon. You don't need to be educated or have fancy clothes to participate in this faith. "We try really hard to have no big "I's" and little "U's," says a brochure for the Sacred Fate Temple. There was, to be sure, little formality in evidence. Many of those assembled were dressed in western attire—bolo ties, cowboy boots. Others wore the simple clothes of laborers—overalls and muddied work boots. One family—a mother, father, and two little girls—stood out in their Sunday best: color-coordinated black-and-red outfits.

The Sacred Fate Temple is as close to fundamentalism as established congregations in Timbertown get. Its pastor preaches the inerrancy of the Bible, warns his congregation of the end times, and offers them that the alternatives are redemption or eternal damnation. If I had examined this modest congregation of world-weary devotees alone, I might have concluded that evangelical Christianity appeals to anxious people who feel their social status threatened and yearn for security. Pentecostalism, one author explained, appeals to "the lower economic stratum, to those who, finding worldly goods denied them, have denied the world."[11] But the religious landscape of evangelicalism, even in a small town like Timbertown, is more complex and diverse than this statement suggests. For one thing, explanations for religiosity that focus on believers' need to compensate for "status anxiety" fail to account for the extraordinary popularity of evangelicalism, particularly in the West, with highly educated Americans. This is especially true since the 1980s, when a new wave of evangelicalism gained popularity, particularly on the West Coast.

Exemplifying this trend is the Faith Center, which calls itself a "spirit-filled church." Its members seek to establish a direct and highly emotional connection with Jesus as part of their worship, which sometimes includes faith healing and speaking in tongues, and they also incorporate aspects of the therapeutic, individualistic, and antiestablishment values prevailing in American culture since the 1960s. These new wave evangelicals are soft and entertaining, and they carry a message of uplift. At a Sunday service, a gathering of predominantly middle-class, well-groomed baby boomers listened to a sermon telling about how Jesus shelters people from storms, and extolling the virtues of economic success. "It looks like a family when you come and sit down," one woman described the congregation to me. In recent years, nondenominational Protestant churches like this one have spread like wildfire through the western states, including Oregon. They offer many of the features of old-style conservative Protestantism: they adhere to traditional doctrines, defend the Bible, encourage churchgoing, value personal evangelizing, and share the belief that the world is divided into two groups: the saved and the unsaved.

Sermons center on Bible teaching and frequently embrace "gifts of the Spirit" such as speaking in tongues, and the commitment to spread the gospel through conversion, but in a modernized, therapeutic fashion.[12] Congregants are allowed to be open about their hurts and also feel accepted; they are strongly encouraged to find a personal relationship with God through prayer and Bible study, and are made to feel free of "institutional" religion, especially denominational hierarchies.[13] Church sanctuaries are typically devoid of religious ornamentation, their music is contemporary—electric guitars and pop-style "praise choruses" frequently replace organs and hymnals—and they temper the older belief in the absolute authority of husband over wife with a softer patriarchalism, in which women, though rarely preachers, take active roles in their congregations.[14] Members tend to be more socially tolerant than those who embrace the old-style Pentecostalism of the Sacred Fate Temple: they smoke cigarettes, drink alcohol, and laugh at off-color jokes, all of which would be unthinkable in more traditional church contexts.

The Faith Center is part of a charismatic and evangelical denomination, the International Church of the Foursquare Gospel, which has swept through Oregon and much of the West. Thanks to its fervent evangelism, it is today among the fastest-growing Christian movements—nationally, it was the only denomination over one hundred thousand that grew more rapidly between 1971 and 1990 than between 1952 and 1971—and the county in which Timbertown is located is one of its fastest-growing membership regions.[15] The denomination is linked to the Promise Keepers, the evangelical men's movement that stages revival meetings in football stadiums, urging its participants to become better Christians and family men.[16]

The Faith Center's antiestablishment evangelism attracted a number of members who moved to the area as part of the youth-based Jesus movement of the 1970s. Beverly Allen, a soft-spoken forty-four-year-old mother of two, was among them. Allen, who lives in a small home on a dirt road outside of the center of Timbertown, told me the story of how she became involved in the Faith Center's brand of modern charismatic Christianity. In the early 1970s, she moved from a small town in the Midwest to attend a huge urban university, and was for the first time confronted with people who took drugs and were sexually promiscuous. She became confused. "The values my parents gave me only went so far," she said. And their religion, a stodgy Presbyterianism, didn't do much to help. "They always told me: this is what you should do. But they never told me why. I really needed some answers. Why am I here? What's life all about?" A woman knocked on her dorm floor and told her about the Campus Crusade for Christ. When she attended a meeting of the group, for the first time, said Allen, "the truth of the Gospel became very real to me, and things started to make sense." Her family couldn't understand what had come over her. Nor could her peers. She began to associate mainly with other saved Christians, and met a man who would later become her husband at a campus crusade picnic.

Having committed themselves to living Christian lives, the Allens moved out west to live at Shiloh, the Christian commune that was an offshoot of Calvary Chapel in California, a "new wave" charismatic church. For Beverly, Shiloh represented a different relationship to faith, "a real relationship, through the power of the Holy Spirit, with Jesus." For ten years, she and her husband lived on the religious compound near Timbertown, where Christianity became a lifestyle as well as a belief system. They spoke to their savior through prayer several times a day, believing that he intervened directly and powerfully in their lives, and engaged in charismatic prayer and group devotion. But in the late 1970s, when a host of organizational problems led to the disintegration of the group, its members scattered throughout the area, incorporating themselves into different communities. Often they brought the religious doctrines they learned with them, joining fundamentalist and charismatic churches.

Like Shiloh, the Faith Center encourages a physical kind of worship that includes the raising of hands and speaking in tongues, and other signs that the "Holy Spirit is moving in significant ways," says Allen. At the same time, she says, "it's not just a brainless faith." It is a movement that appeals to educated people such as herself. Their pastor, she says proudly, has a doctorate in theology from a prestigious seminary. "He's well versed in Greek and Hebrew and has really studied the Bible, but he preaches from his heart, like a real person." When the New Testament is taught, she says, "you don't have to check your brain at the door. We don't want somebody to come and shout in our faces the way some pastors used to preach. Or tell us, 'You just have to believe,' without telling us why. We want to know why. That's what a church like Faith Center offers."

Sally Humphries, also a regular Faith Center churchgoer, has a somewhat different take on its appeal. "It's just everyday stuff," she said. "The pastor is funny, the songs are wonderful. We do sing an old hymn, usually only one. It's biblical, but you can relax." Her words suggest that the Faith Center's success is largely due to its simultaneous construction of a strong sense of identity and its incorporation of elements of American individualistic culture. If evangelical Christianity is thriving, it seems that it owes much to modern pluralism, that force that was supposed to have made it obsolete. It has, according to sociologist Christian Smith, created a subculture that has managed to maintain "both high tension with and high integration into mainstream American society simultaneously."[17]

CREATING INTIMATE FAMILIARITY

Timbertown's evangelical Christians built a sense of solidarity upon the emotional bonds of the saved—what Linda Kintz calls "intimate familiarity." I caught glimpses of this when I attended a number of different church services through town, passing at times as a member of the congregation, or someone who was shopping around for a new congregation. I was struck by how warm, how inviting people were if they thought I was one of them, or aspired to be. At the Sacred Fate Temple I heard a lot of talk of family—"We're a family, we love one another"—and lots of talk about love—Jesus' love, the love of church members for one another, the pastor's love of his congregation. "We are like one family," he proclaims. "You don't always get along, but you always love 'em." Near the end of the service, Jaeger beckoned his congregation, "Is there anyone here who needs a bit of extra help, who's goin' through hard times?" A middle-aged woman raised her hands and walked to the front of the room, and he embraced her. "Oh, Sally, I pray that the Lord will banish your cancer." She cried, the pastor hugged her, and everyone proceeded to join in, hugging, crying, and smiling.

Evangelicals express, through words and deeds, how important they are to one another. They kiss and soothe one another's aching souls. I had never witnessed such heartfelt emotional displays among individuals who were unrelated to one another and I was often touched by them. When I was late for an appointment to meet with Beverly Allen, she expressed genuine concern and asked me if I was all right. Shortly after interviewing Sally Humphries, I received a very nice note on flowery stationery thanking me for the time I spent with her, inviting me to attend her church. "I think you would find it very friendly and inspiring," she wrote. The following Christmas, she sent me a card as well. It was difficult, even for a seasoned cynic like myself, not to be encouraged by such signs of warmth—they are in some respects a profoundly democratic impulse. Anyone, with few exceptions, can walk into an evangelical church and feel welcome, and if you don't show up the next week, someone is likely to call to find out why. If you're not already one of them, you are seen simply by virtue of your presence, as someone who potentially could be— becoming "born again" is a conscious, volitional act, a process that anyone, regardless of one's religious, racial, ethnic, or even sexual past, can embrace. It doesn't matter whether one is Presbyterian, Catholic, or even Jewish—one can convert. It doesn't matter if one is homosexual—one can renounce one's old, sinful life. Indeed, becoming born again is all about the renunciation of the old self and the construction of a new one.

When I arrived at Barney and Annie Wooten's house the first thing I saw was a maroon Cadillac parked in the driveway, with a bumper sticker depicting a Jesus fish eating a Darwin fish. Under the image was the caption "Survival of the Fittest." The second thing I saw, as I entered their suburban ranch house, was their wedding photo, next to a framed marriage certificate. Scattered throughout the living room were framed prints depicting images of submission: men bowing down and accepting the Lord Jesus Christ. Barney is a big, burly fellow in his late forties who was wearing a T-shirt emblazoned with a graphic advertising last year's local Christian crusade, which gathered thousands of like-minded evangelicals for several days of prayer and proselytizing. Barney has a bushy black beard and a deep, booming voice. He and Annie met while working for the state as scientists. When they married, and Annie couldn't find a job in commuting distance of their home, she quit her job and became a full-time homemaker and mother.

When I asked Barney how he became "born again," he told me that when he had recently divorced he was heading out to a rock 'n' rodeo bar to learn country-and-western dancing when he spotted a church marquee that read "ISN'T IT TIME TO COME HOME?" Intrigued, he ended up pulling into the church driveway. "I never did learn how to country-and-western dance, but I ended up visiting the pastor for a number of weeks and asking questions about Christian doctrine. I just found myself starting to seek, and starting to move in that direction and starting to read." That led to a career of Bible study and commitment to a "Christian life."

Conservative Christians, despite their doctrinal differences, think of themselves as a subculture with a special way of seeing the world. Barney and Annie send their son to a Christian school. In the past, they had been at odds with many of the teachers and administrators in the public school system whom they felt were insufficiently attentive to the needs of Christian parents. Barney objected to many of the novels that were taught in English classes, such as Alice Walker's *The Color Purple*. "From a Christian perspective, the content of the book," he said, "is pretty severe, pretty extreme. It says things about how God is and what God approves of. From a religious standpoint, it's blasphemous. It tries to redefine God, and what God would accept. It's very unholy."

When Barney told the school board that he objected to the inclusion of the novel in the school curriculum, he was informed that students, if they wished, in consultation with their parents, could decide to read alternative novels—a response that he considered to be unsatisfactory. "The burden it places on children is wrong. They're supposed to talk this over with their parents. Then they're supposed to defend their reasons for not wanting to read the book to the teacher. If they succeed in all of this they're excused from the class." But children are impressionable beings who need direction, he says. With time, he and his wife became convinced that only a Christian school could provide the sort of moral education his family felt was necessary. When they began to send their child to a Christian school, said Barney, "it was just like the clouds cleared away. Little problems became easy to solve because you were dealing with people of like mind, like values, and you just immediately perceive things alike." For Barney, Christianity is a "master identity" that shapes his relationship to the world at every waking moment. He feels a sense of intimacy with other "saved Christians" and feels distant from those who are not.

For evangelicals, a sense of intimacy with other "saved" Christians is often established at a very early age. A fourteen-year-old girl from a nonreligious family told me about being in a car pool with a family in town who asked her, "What church does your family attend?" She told them that her family didn't attend church, and they retorted, "Don't you have any family values at all?" When it came time for her to try out for the varsity tennis team, one of the coaches, a friend of the family she carpooled with, excluded her, despite the fact that she was as good a player as any of her friends that made it. "I wasn't Christian enough," she told me. Janice Trump, the owner of a bookstore on Main Street, told me about having met a ten-year-old boy some time ago, the child of an acquaintance. After she talked with this boy for a while, he asked her, "Are you a Christian?" She replied yes, she told me, because she wondered what his response would be. "I thought you were a Christian," the boy said, "because you seemed so nice and caring." How did this little boy know to say this? Clearly, his parents had taught him to identify other Christians and place his trust in them.

Writing about the way that Christian conservative doctrine appeals to women, Linda Kintz suggests that it is the mother whose job it is to "train children in familiarity." Children, she says, are raised "to feel and experience their own sensuality, their own bodies, in very particular ways, and to look for and find others whose feelings, values, and identities are intimately familiar to them."[18] As a case in point, Beverly Allen told me that she home-schools her children, an eight-year-old boy and an eleven-year-old girl, because she believes it will "strengthen them spiritually, socially, and academically, so that they live the life that God's called them to." She wants her children to be insulated from some of the competitive pressures of the secular world—"all the emphasis on what you're wearing, and what boys like you." Her middle-school-age daughter, she says, "is pretty sturdy," but at the same time she says, "Kids say nasty things to one another." Christian home-schooling offers the possibility of thriving in a kinder, gentler world.

In the same breath, Allen acknowledges that the world that her daughter will live in "is going to be with lots of people and lots of places. She's never going to be as sheltered as she is now." She tells me a story about her daughter, who is learning how to horseback ride at a farm west of town. She's there five or six hours a week, learning to ride, working at the farm in exchange for lessons. Some, but not all, of the people at the farm, Allen tells me, are Christians. Her daughter is old enough to pick up on things that other people talk about, and the other day one of the women started talking about crystals and other New Age paraphernalia. Sarah understands that "this is a nice person, but her beliefs are different. So she can know the difference, and handle it herself. I teach her to handle herself in that situation, and not get thrown by things. And be able to stand strong in her own faith, and when the opportunity arises, speak for herself and say, 'This is what I believe.' "

Allen tells me this story to illustrate her expansive notion of community. Some people who home-school their kids are complete "isolationists," she says, but that's not true of her family. "I don't see the outside world as a threat. That's the extreme. I don't think there are that many people who are doing that fringy thing." There are some home-schoolers, she tells me, who adopt very traditional gender roles for their girls, for example. They teach their girls to be homebound forever, that they should never work outside of the home. "I wouldn't go that far," she says. Allen's faith may separate her from secular society, but that doesn't mean she deprecates the larger society in which she lives. It's not that non-Christians are bad people, they're just *different*. Christians believe they are special: they possess a truth that others lack.

Increasingly, this Christian evangelical identity is becoming a visible presence in commercial culture as well, thanks to books, jewelry, fish symbols on cars, and other objects of Christian consumerism.

There is a burgeoning multimillion-dollar Christian rock music industry, and even evangelical tattoo artists who specialize in marking
their customers' bodies with images affirming their undying allegiance to Jesus. At a vast new Borders bookstore in my town, the religion section, one of the largest in the store, displays conservative
Christian books, many of which focus on psychological and lifestyle
issues like child rearing or alcoholism, and would barely be distinguishable from non-Christian materials if not for their message of
Christian uplift. At the Rite-Aid store near my home, I can buy books
by evangelical leaders Gary Bauer and James Dobson, but liberal publications such as *The Nation, The Progressive,* or even *Ms.* are nowhere
to be found. At the Hallmark store in my local mall, WWJD (What
Would Jesus Do) jewelry, once available only through church youth
groups, sits next to children's Sesame Street figures at the checkout
counter. Teenagers hang them from their backpacks and give them to
their friends. For the kids who wear them, these bracelets are a simple
way of being "out" as a Christian—they're not altogether different
from the rainbow symbols and lavender triangles worn by gay people.
"When you see someone wearing one, it helps to know who is related
to you in that sense, you know what I mean?" explains a thirteen-
year-old girl. "I feel instantly connected to that person."[19]

EXCLUDING THE UNFAMILIAR

As I spoke with members of Timbertown's evangelical community,
and was encouraged by the friendliness with which I was received, I
had to acknowledge that the warm welcome I received was for a censored version of my life. While I spoke openly about myself as a Jew,
and as a mother, I never mentioned my lesbianism for fear that it
would cut off the conversation. If they *really* knew me, I wondered,
would I be greeted with the same degree of warmth and affection? I
think not. If conservative Christians construct a sense of intimacy
among those very much like themselves, this intimacy is predicated
upon the knowledge that there are *unfamiliar* others. In their sermons,
preachers often play on the contrast between the warmth, familiarity,
and trust of the congregation and the cold, cruel, heathen world outside. The more fundamentalist the church, in my experience, the
more clearly these "others" are spelled out. In this sense Christians are
not unique: social groups know who they are in large measure by

knowing who they are not. Timbertown's conservative Protestants defined themselves in opposition to nonbelievers, homosexuals, radical feminists, and, in subtle ways, people of color.

The Sacred Fate Temple, emblematic of old-style evangelicalism, prohibits gambling, divorce, and sexual excess, and preaches restraint, duty, and submission. In an often quoted passage in the New Testament, Paul commands that wives submit to their husbands. At a Sunday service, Pastor Jaeger quoted Paul's message to the Ephesians, "A wife is to submit graciously to the servant leadership of her husband," a passage that provides the scriptural foundation for women's subordination, say some. Jaeger added a little extra embellishment. The Virgin Mary "had never been with a man," he told the congregation. "She had never been with a woman either," he snickered. "But if it had been the 1990s," he said with a wry smile, "who knows?" Intimate familiarity is based in large part on women's adherence to traditional roles. Masculinity and femininity are God-given, biological essences; men are protectors, women are nurturers; men's and women's roles in society, believers insist, reflect a dichotomy given in nature, and are sanctified through marriage.[20]

This is not to say that all Christian evangelicals fully repudiate feminism. "Even within the evangelical subculture," writes Sara Diamond, "gender relations are subject to change."[21] Beverly Allen's experience is a case in point. Allen has a master's in journalism, reads voraciously, and keeps up with what's going on in the world. The Faith Center incorporates much of what she liked about being a part of the Jesus movement. It is a denomination, says Allen, that "treats women as equal citizens" and permits them to assume leadership positions. The Foursquare movement was, she tells me, founded by a woman. It is true to the teachings of Jesus, who himself "elevated women." Women take active leadership roles in the Faith Center, whose members' views about gender are enlightened by conservative Christian standards. They believe that women are as capable as men, that they should be leaders in the faith, and that women possess an inner strength that men lack, that their role as nurturers and teachers in the family is as important as anything anyone could do, even if society does not recognize it as such. And rather than exhort women to submit to men, they speak instead of the "mutual submission" of women and men to each other.

But in actual practice, Allen's femininity seems quite traditional. At Shiloh, Allen and her husband learned to abide by a strict gender-based division of labor: women were responsible for child care, cleaning, and laundry, and men engaged in mechanical and construction projects. Homosexuality was strictly outlawed. The Shiloh sisters missed out on the reintegration of women into the labor force and the early surge of American feminism's second wave. They believe that women best serve Jesus by submitting to male authority, and by being models of empathy within their families. Today, Allen's family replicates that pattern. Like many members of the Faith Center, she values women's role while affirming a male-headed family. Once she had children, she quit her job. It was a sacrifice because her family needed the money, and because "society doesn't value motherhood very much." She never imagined that she would be a stay-at-home mother. But with time, she came to realize, "Yeah, this is really my primary goal, now: wife and mother. And that's okay." Her husband does paid work outside of the home, as a manager in a seed company, and Allen homeschools their two children and does most of the cooking, housework, and emotion work. She conforms to Shiloh's definition of a good wife—"modest, virtuous and obedient to God and to her spouse."[22]

When evangelical Christians speak of "the family," which they often do in the course of church services, Bible study groups, and after-church gatherings, they inevitably mean the heterosexual family, with a father at the helm. So central to the understanding of what makes up "good Christian families" is the assumption of male-dominant heterosexuality that it never needs to be uttered. It's not so much that women's sexuality is repressed. Indeed, as Linda Kintz suggests, many conservative Christians divide sexuality in two: sacred sexuality—within marriage—and sinful sexuality—outside marriage—and claim that a good Christian woman can be both a good mother and a sexual being because her sexuality has been purified. Far from associating sexuality with original sin, contemporary evangelicals reclaim sexual passion for the married couple. Marabel Morgan's best-selling 1973 book *The Total Woman,* encouraged evangelicals to think of their bodies as God-given sites of pleasure. A widely read Christian advice book followed suit, suggesting that the commandment of God "necessarily includes the strong and beautiful mating urge a husband and wife feel for each other."[23] While urging women to be obedient to their husbands, these books told their female readers that they could be sexual beings and Christians at the same time.

If good Christian families are heterosexual, they are also, at least in small communities in the Pacific Northwest, invariably white. At the Timbertown Bible Church, a conservative Baptist congregation, I sat in a pew in the rear of the sanctuary and listened to an all-white congregation sing a rousing rendition of the hymn "White as Snow," which equates whiteness with purity and redemption. "God laid our sins on Jesus," it declares, and includes the refrain, repeated over and over four times:

> Hallelujah, Jesus saves me!
> He makes me white as snow.
> Hallelujah, Jesus saves me!
> He makes me white as snow.[24]

On a brisk fall morning, hundreds of congregants had gathered to witness the baptism of six adolescent males, and they celebrated the event with a spirited burst of song. Few if any of those who were present, I imagined, saw anything problematic about a group of white people singing of the virtues of purity, salvation, and whiteness. In fact, there is nothing inherently wrong with it. Nonetheless, their apparent obliviousness to the cultural implications of the hymn, which symbolically affirms whiteness, is itself a sign of white dominance. In multiracial environments, the church is a social institution that historically has often maintained racial separation and inequality; many conservative Protestant groups that once opposed racial integration and interracial marriage on supposed religious grounds changed those views when they became socially and political untenable, repudiating biblical passages affirming slavery.[25] Today, Timbertown's churches continue to affirm white privilege and power through symbolic rather than legal means: by creating bonds of intimate familiarity among their wholly white membership.

Where do Jews fit into this religious universe? Jews and other non-Christians are certainly "other"—the few Jews who lived in town traveled for miles to attend synagogue—but they were nonetheless symbolically important to evangelicals. During my time in Timbertown, my Jewishness marked me as an outsider from the start but deemed me a relatively respectable, and sometimes even exotic, outsider. Once I revealed my Jewishness to my subjects, many of them touched upon Jewish themes even when I did not bring them up. Jeri Cookson told me that she "has nothing but admiration for what the Jewish people went through over there, and what they are still going through over there." Others suggested that Jews and Christians have a lot in common. "We both believe in Judeo-Christian values," said Sally Humphries, who proceeded to recount how when she became born again, she started reading the Old Testament, and tried diligently to observe Jewish dietary restrictions, but quickly found it to be "too difficult."

Those who had little or no previous contact with any Jews often exoticized me. Carrol Neitz, the pastor of the storefront Pentecostal church, lit up when I told him I was Jewish. When we ended our interview, he said he had always wanted to attend a service in a synagogue, and angled for an invitation from me. When I mentioned to Pastor Lance White that I was Jewish, he replied, "That's all right, our savior was a Jewish carpenter. If we Christians lived according to the Torah, our health would be many times better. Leviticus tells us not to mix milk and meat. If I didn't mix the two, my health would be better. The Bible tells us lots of things about practical living." When the interview ended and it was time for me to leave, he beckoned. "Say hello to your rabbi for me."

While I was both relieved and pleased that they were willing to speak with a nonbeliever like myself, their philo-Semitism was sometimes troubling. Jeri Cookson waxed on about her admiration for Jews and the state of Israel, and then went on to explain that without Jews there would be no hope for a final rapture for Christians, an event that will result in everlasting life for Jesus' disciples. "The creation of the state of Israel in 1948 was sort of the countdown to end time," she told me. "The Lord's gonna come down and take his people home. So I'm a sponsor of Israel, very much so." Though she is not what she calls a "hard-core" fundamentalist, Jeri is a born-again Christian who believes in the prophesied end of the world.

Like Jeri Cookson, many evangelicals subscribe to the doctrine of dispensational pre-millennialism, which breaks human history into several periods, known as dispensations, during each of which human beings lived under a different set of divine laws and criteria for salvation. According to this scheme, the present period is the "church age," or sixth dispensation, which some describe as an era marked by apostasy and the erosion of Christian morality. This period will be followed by an event called the Rapture, or Secret Rapture, when all saved Christians will ascend into the sky to meet Christ and to be safeguarded from the Great Tribulation, a time of violence and death that will eventually be succeeded by Christ's triumphant thousand-year reign on earth and his Last Judgment of humankind.[26] The twentieth century has brought the scientific possibility of destruction. Believers in "end times" seem to deal with the dread of mass death by anticipating an earthly end that only they and others will escape. Such beliefs, according to historian Charles Strozier, are "grounded in a perverse form of idealism and deep yearnings for spiritual purification."[27] Many conservative Christians see redemption in the aftermath of a horrific end. Their love of Jews is based on the bizarrely self-interested notion that while we would be there to facilitate their final rapture, Jews, like the rest of the heathen world, would be blown to bits when Armageddon came. The fact that I could avoid that fate by quickly learning to love the Lord Jesus Christ came as little consolation.

Evangelicals also construct boundaries around their subculture, reserving acts of "intimate familiarity" for other "saved" Christians. Presbyterian leader Sylvia Watkins told me a story about how she and other volunteers in the community formed an organization that consolidated all of the groups providing emergency services available in the community so that "people would not have to be sent to this church for clothes and the Elks lodge for glasses and some place else for food." The conservative churches in town objected to the plan on the grounds that "they needed to pray with the people before they gave them their food," excluding those who are not regular churchgoers from vital services. "They use the language of caring," says Watkins, "but they really only care about people like them. Wouldn't it just be better to give them the food, and then let them know they are welcome to your place of worship?" Timbertown also has a Buddhist church, Watkins told me, "which has not always been welcomed by the faith community. They just pretended they did not exist. They were not invited to join the ministerial association" with the rest of the pastors from all the churches in town. There have been times when the Catholic church was also excluded. "Our faith community is not as ecumenical as we would like to believe it is," says Watkins. "We have many, many faiths in this community that are not represented around that table when they sit down to their meetings."

Clearly, evangelical Christians draw hope and inspiration from the churches to which they give allegiance, and they find warmth and sustenance in the emotional connections forged among other believers. Like many modern individuals, they are searching for truth, for meaning, and community. But the solutions they embrace are, for the most part, inward seeking. Their culture of intimate familiarity suggests, in Linda Kintz's words, that "the only group that can be trusted is the one that tells you to trust only yourself."[28] Compassion, in other words, is reserved for those who valorize a particular notion of family—patriarchal, heterosexual, and, above all, Christian—the model for the reimagined community. One might say that one's neighbor is an object of love if that neighbor looks and acts pretty much like oneself.

COMPETITIVE RIGHTEOUSNESS

One can understand the appeal of this vision of reciprocity and trust among like-minded people. But it is a tenuous shelter, and the reimagined community contained within it a great deal of instability. Evangelical Protestantism inspires passionate devotion but unstable institutions, and churches in Timbertown came and went with the season. When I asked people why they thought there were so many churches in Timbertown—"more churches than bars" was the typical refrain—opinions varied.

Diversity, to some, is a measure of religious strength. Wasn't it true that the greater the number of different churches, the greater the possibility that one will find a church that suits one's needs? Well, yes— and no. Bob Harrison, pastor of one of the fastest-growing churches in town, says yes. "People gravitate to churches because of belief, and they find a place that comes closest to believing what they believe is the way that the Bible explains things. You have just about as many churches as you have opinions then. That's why our church has an incredible blend of people. Our church is made up of Methodists, Presbyterians, Lutherans, former Catholics, more conservative Protestant denominations, along with those who've never had any faith before they came to know Christ. We're a Heinz 57 church."

When I talked with a preacher who ministers to a charismatic Pentecostal congregation located at the end of a long dirt road to the south of town, he told a different story: religious diversity in Timbertown is not necessarily such a good thing. A few years ago, his was one of the fastest-growing churches in town. Now, he says, if he gets a hundred people to church on Sunday he's doing well. "Once you get a movement going, it becomes institutionalized," he told me, "and then it begins to crumble." Christianity, he said, is "kinda like the railroad. Once it gets too large, it has to specialize." But once it specializes, he laments, it loses some of its soul. He wonders, "Are we maintaining a structure or are we trying to save souls?" Whether or not one thinks that religious diversity is a good thing, then, depends upon how well one is doing in the competitive quest to find and keep congregants, the lifeblood of any church.[29]

All denominations deal with the tension between soul saving and organizational continuity. Mainline churches, such as the Presbyterian, typically had an institutional infrastructure, made up of staff and national organizational resources, to provide support over time. Evangelical churches, in contrast, tend to be more dependent upon a particular pastor, who often owns the building in which they are housed, for continuity. Moreover, their congregants' passionate commitment is difficult to sustain over time. Individuals join a particular church in search of emotional depth and intensity, and the very things that bring them there carry the seeds of their own demise. "There appear to be two movements in the old-time religion, toward separatism, and toward union," a journalist writing in the late 1940s noted. "As a church prospers, it sets up mission boards, colleges, seminaries, and other enterprises; often its doctrines become less 'literal,' and it moves gradually toward closer relations with others of like views. Meanwhile, somewhere in the United States a new sect is splintering off."[30]

This dynamic was clearly visible in Timbertown, where independent evangelical congregations commandeered by a charismatic preacher tended to fold once the passion subsided, or because internal squabbles split the congregation, or because a new pastor arrived in town to steal the show. The oldest congregation in town, the Church of Christ, founded a century ago, spawned a number of other congregations—once because a minister allowed girls and boys to stay together overnight on a church outing. A conservative Baptist church in town split when the male minister and the female choir director were discovered having sex in a back room. An African-American woman minister who was assigned to the Methodist church left town in 1992 because of threats on her life and her property; the all-white, male South Lane Ministerial Association offered her little support. But before she was transferred to a church in Portland, a number of people left the congregation, scattering to the other churches in town; the remaining members moved the congregation to the right.[31]

A fifty-year-old woman tells me, "When you disagree with something someone does in a church, you start your own church." A Pentecostal preacher agrees: "There's an independent mentality in this town. Everybody wants to do their own thing rather than work through problems. There's constantly a group of people moving from church to church." It wasn't so much a matter of preachers trying to draw members away from one another, according to Bob Harrison. "People move amiably from one church to another"—sometimes because one church offers something than another church doesn't. For example, his church, he says, offers "incredible children's and youth programs, and so a lot of younger families have chosen to come here because we are able to offer that to them." So while churches may not actively compete against one another, they must find their market niche in their community, particularly in a small community like Timbertown with lots of congregations to choose from, where individual loyalty to a particular church tends to be relatively weak. After all, it's the way of the West, and indeed of America: if you don't like something, leave and start anew.[32]

Despite the existence of a pastoral group whose goal it was to coordinate church-community efforts such as a food drive or Easter pageant, a competitive righteousness pitted many of the most conservative churches against one another. Some of the rivalries were historical: Baptists tended to be anti-Pentecostal; Pentecostals had little love for mainline congregations. But even among denominations whose doctrines were indistinguishable from one another, personalities clashed. The Assembly of God pastor tells me that his church and the Sacred Fate Temple are nearly theologically identical. The only difference is a relatively minor one: divorced people can't be church elders in his church, while they can at Sacred Fate. But sit in a church service, and the differences of style are apparent, proving sociologist

Jon Stone's point that the boundaries separating conservative Protestant denominations often have more to do with symbolic and ideological differences than with theological categories. Churches split more often due to personality clashes and differences between styles of worship than due to doctrinal differences.[33]

As I immersed myself in the spiritual landscape of Timbertown, I found that many of the most committed churchgoers couldn't even really tell me their church's denomination, a fact that suggested to me that feeling is believing. Sally Humphries, who attends the Foursquare church, admits, "For years I didn't even know it was a denomination. Some denominations you know right off: 'We're about this, and this is what we Baptists believe.' But they are not like that. They don't even talk about their denomination. It's just about teaching the Bible, and singing those wonderful songs. I just see myself as a plain Christian. I don't care if you're a Catholic or a . . . Whatever you are I think that there's one God and there's one Bible, and if you believe in God and have a relationship with him, we probably would agree on everything."

Pastor Lance White: "It's the flavor of the church that has a bigger pull than theology." He lamented, "A lot of us call ourselves Christian but we don't know what we believe." I asked him what he believed, and he told me the following: "(1) Jesus is savior, (2) there is only one true God, (3) the Bible is the answer to life's great questions, and (4) Jesus is there for every need." These are, admittedly, vague principles. It would be difficult to find an evangelical Christian who did not agree with all four of these points. Nonetheless, the pastor further lamented: "You need to know what you believe. Many people don't know—it's scary." It should come as no surprise, then, that denominationalism is on the wane. "It's less possible to say my father was a Pentecostal, I'm a Pentecostal, and my kids are Pentecostals," said the pastor.

The great exception to weakening denominationalism is the long-standing division between the Presbyterian church in town and its more conservative brethren. Presbyterian pastor Henry Chomsky is a handsome man in his mid-forties who grew up a military brat in Europe. He rides a motorcycle, has a master's degree in ancient religion from Oxford, and reads biblical Hebrew. When I met him in his study in the church, he told me to call him Henry, and proceeded to complain that conservative churches have taken over the community. The worst of the bunch, he says, have a "beat 'em up with Jesus" mentality: they will go to any length to prove that they alone have the truth. During the time he has been pastor, he has increasingly come to feel like an outsider in Timbertown. His church has been active in the Latin American sanctuary movement, and it has built senior housing in town. For Chomsky the most pressing problems in Timbertown are poverty and education. "It's difficult to get a decent education in this town," he says, a fact that prompted him to send his kids to a Catholic school outside of town. Time and time again, he says, conservative Christians have squelched efforts to teach important subjects in the public schools: sex education, the history of religion. He tries, in his preaching, to offer people an understanding of and appreciation for a variety of different religions, not just the Christian faith, and he regrets that many of his pastoral colleagues in town are intent upon fighting "the very thing that could lead us out of this darkness—knowledge."

Chomsky sees much conservative Christianity as the product of lack of education and exposure to the world. Its pastors have had little or no religious instruction, they take a very literal interpretation of the Bible, and "they focus on the same few passages over and over." He and other Presbyterians scoff at the "parking lot churches" that surround them. "In those churches you don't even need a degree to get up and preach," a woman architect told me. "And they certainly don't have any sense of design." A sixty-eight-year-old silver-haired man, and longtime leader in the Presbyterian church calls it "simple faith." The differences clearly have a lot to do with class. The Presbyterian church attracts the affluent, educated churchgoers in town, the professional middle classes, people who like the fact that their pastor is young, educated, eloquent.[34] You won't find any hooting, hollering, screaming, or crying at their services.

In contrast to evangelical churches, Presbyterian sermons are short, learned, and speak rarely of the devil and other nefarious threats, or of supernatural evil or punishment in general. Rather than offer rock 'n' roll and glitz, they are refined, understated. Rather than speak of end times, they invite their congregants to affirm the human future and to work for a better tomorrow. The Presbyterians count among their members one of the oldest and wealthiest families in town, the Joneses, who owned one of the mills, the golf course, and the inn. The Joneses stay involved despite the fact that their conservatism clashes with many of the values of the congregation because, a congregant tells me, "they like to think of themselves as cultured." Plus Chomsky knows how to talk to them. He comes from a Republican family. He even gets them, on occasion, to donate their money to good causes.

In their liberalism, the Presbyterians frequently find themselves out on a limb. Evangelicals see them as being on the wrong side of issues such as abortion, homosexuality—you name it. "I wouldn't want to be a Presbyterian in this town," says seventy-five-year-old Sarah Henson, a Timbertown native whom I met at the local historical society. "They're trying to do a lot of social work with pedophiles, child molesters, alcoholics, and people we don't need in our community." The Presbyterians' lone allies in town are, surprisingly enough, the Catholics, who have long been a minority in Timbertown as they are in most of the Pacific Northwest. In the Bronx of my youth, Catholics, along with Jews, outnumbered Protestants. In contrast, in the Northwest, Catholics are a distinct minority and in Timbertown they and the Presbyterians viewed themselves as outcasts in a sea of Pentecostalism.

Harvey Silko, the retired schoolteacher in his sixties, is a well-respected member of the community and an active Catholic. He told me that when he first came to the community, after World War II, there were only eight Catholic families in town. "Some parents complained that I was teaching their kids Catholicism," he recalled as I interviewed him in his small house, where a large crucifix has pride of place in the living room. In Timbertown, Silko said, "Catholics and Presbyterians speak the same language." They were both involved in the sanctuary movement, offering temporary shelter to Latin American refugees. The Catholic priest in town, who was once a Hollywood scriptwriter, reaches out to non-Catholics and is liberal on a variety of issues. He has even counseled that women whose pregnancies placed them at risk should seek abortions.

Still, some people criticize the Catholics and Presbyterians for not going far enough politically. Andrew Kenneth, a local Presbyterian leader who marched with Martin Luther King, Jr., in the civil rights movement, admits, "We don't do enough to reach out to the poor of this community. The mainline churches talk about justice but are really committed to the elite." Since controversies threaten the continuity of churches, mainline Protestant leaders shy away from them. Jody Shapiro Davie, in a book about women's involvement in American Presbyterianism, suggests that the denomination is driven by a powerful desire to unify and heal, to embrace ecumenicalism and tolerance. The unity of the denomination and of a given congregation rests less on a clear and specific agreement on beliefs than on a largely unquestioned assumption of consensus, and on the protection of a zone of personal privacy. If individuals have radical views, they tend to keep them to themselves; too much overt diversity poses a threat to the group. Consequently, says Davie, Presbyterians as a whole are concerned with social activism "yet not too vividly so, tolerant of political and theological diversity within the congregation as long as the details of that diversity are never mentioned."[35]

Since the 1970s, homosexuality—whether or not to ordain gay men and lesbians, and to permit gay marriages—has become the hot-button issue for Presbyterians and other mainline Protestants. The United Church of Christ is the only major Protestant denomination to permit the ordination of homosexuals. In the 1990s, the Episcopal Church, the United Methodist Church, and the Presbyterian Church rejected proposals to loosen church strictures on homosexuality. Activists within the Presbyterian Church (U.S.A), the country's eighth largest denomination, have sought, unsuccessfully, to overturn a 1978 policy that "self-affirming, practicing homosexual persons" could not be ordained within the denomination." In 1991, a liberal "Report on Human Sexuality" that included proposals to loosen church strictures on homosexuality was categorically rejected by the denomination's General Assembly, which voted instead for a poetic, inclusively worded, but vague Brief Statement of Faith. In June 1999, the Presbyterian Church (U.S.A.) rejected an attempt to lift a controversial ban on ordination of anyone—gay or straight—who is sexually active outside the "Covenant of Marriage between a man and a woman."[36]

This purposeful vagueness is mirrored at the level of the congregation, which tends to emphasize the fluidity of belief and the privacy of convictions. Opposing the scriptedness of Pentecostalism, and without the communal insistence on testimony common to more theologically evangelical groups, Presbyterians embrace "a kind of don't ask, don't tell spirituality."[37] Henry Chomsky doesn't shy away from talking about difficult issues like homosexuality, poverty, and even gun control in his sermons. But if the truth be told, Chomsky's congregants are far more conservative as a whole than he is. Timbertown's Presbyterian church has supported the ordination of lesbians and gays in public but counts only one openly gay couple among its members, and Chomsky admits, "If most of my members walked down Castro Street, they'd be shocked."[38]

The Presbyterians' spiritual openness means that the boundaries that separate them from the rest of the community are less stark, the criteria for what makes a "good Christian" less strict than for conservative congregations, and that the bonds among members are therefore less intense. A Presbyterian leader talks about the consequences of these different emotional styles. "A lot of people, when they first get passion in their religion," says Andrew Kenneth, "prefer to go to one of the newly formed churches. But the faith soon wears thin, and then they drift to more conventional churches, where they find depth but little passion."

But passion is clearly what many Timbertowners craved. Evangelical churches tried to reconstruct the embattled community, stabilizing the familial bonds that kept their congregations relatively intact, providing a shared symbolic universe. Intimate familiarity was constructed in the course of ecstatic rituals, and acts of warmth and kindness, when the church delivered a food basket to a family in need. It was modeled upon the traditional family, in which the father commanded respect and the mother provided nurturance, where children knew their place and people worked in harmony. Evangelicalism, in its emphasis upon the power of the individual to create his or her own relationship with God, seemed to appeal to Timbertowners' distrust of institutionalized religion. It offered its adherents a sense of community and belonging, and a connection to a shared moral universe, a sense of identity that rested in large part upon a contrast between "saved" Christians and the cold, cruel, heathen world outside. Outside, they declared, you are small, endangered, and alone; in our world, you can be nurtured, loved, and whole. Emboldened by their growing numbers, in the early 1990s evangelical Christians asserted an increasingly public presence.

CHAPTER 5

Decorating for Jesus

Sally Humphries is the motherly face of Timbertown's Christian right. She describes herself as someone who's a "nice person," who's helpful, and cares about people. When I arrived at her house, a large pink Victorian fixer-upper that sits next to the railroad tracks that cut a swath through town, she was working on her latest home-improvement project: slipcovers for a couch in pink chenille. The interior of the house, a shock of flowers and pastels, is filled with other projects in process: imitation paint-by-the-number stained glass for the kitchen windows, hand-painted chairs, including one for a grandchild not yet born, brightly colored flowered pillows for the living room, a needlework "bless this house." As she apologized to me for not being able to finish the slipcovers before I arrived, having to drape a tablecloth cover the couch, visions of Martha Stewart and Tammy Faye Bakker danced in my head. Welcoming me into her house, she offered me tea and cookies and then proceeded to tell me about her life, her activism, and her deeply felt Christian beliefs.

Sally's family originally came from the Midwest. In the 1960s, her father found a job working on the railroad, and they moved to Oregon, where they've been ever since. Her husband, Matt, a welder, coaches the high school soccer team; she was a stay-at-home mom to their two kids, who are now grown. Matt's job pays enough to allow her to be home and tend to her family, which she thinks of as both career and calling. Sally can't understand why women would want to work outside the home if they had a choice. "Well, that's great, if you want to work," she says, "but I don't feel like being liberated is working forty hours a week and then coming home and having to do all this too. I say, whoa, I feel sorry for you if you have to do that. I'm the one that's having the most fun. I just like being a woman in the old-fashioned-type way, but still having the opportunities if I wanted to do them."

In Timbertown, Sally, along with a handful of others—she modestly referred to them as "our little housewives' group"—spearheaded the ballot measure campaign. That the self-appointed spokespersons for the reimagined community were mainly women, full-time mothers and retired housewives, shouldn't be surprising: women tend to be community leaders. Historically women have been the backbone of many, if not most, community-based voluntary organizations, and they make up the bulk of "kitchen table activists," grassroots workers who are building a base for the conservative Christian political movement in communities throughout the nation.

Rather than see themselves acting on behalf of or for women as a group, Timbertown's female OCA activists saw themselves fighting for their families. "Mostly we were just people who had kids in school, or grandkids," said Jeri Cookson, "who wanted to do something to help people."[1] Explaining women's overrepresentation in the group, she added, "We had several men who were very strong supporters, but most of them worked. So, the women had more time." Sally Humphries was willing to admit that there might be more at stake. "We are women and we are nurturing and we care about the family. We're different from men, of course. These personal kinds of things are really important to us more, maybe they seem more urgent to us."

By participating in the campaign, Christian conservative women affirmed their specialness as women. While believing in the importance of a "strict father" at the family helm to which women must submit, Christian conservatives suggest that women play the essential role of nurturer of children and humanizer of men. Without wives, men's savage impulses would run amok.[2] But equally important, without husbands to play the breadwinner role, women would be cast adrift without material support for themselves and their children. The problem with America, Jeri Cookson informed me, is that "men don't know how to be men anymore. They were kinda thrown off by lots of things." She declared: "I'm not a feminist. But I understand where feminists come from. They have been mistreated by a lot of men for a lot of years. I do think that women have rights. . . . My husband is a very definite man. There are times when I could just break his neck, he's so old-fashioned. But I think that men need to be men."

OCA activists view individuals as essentially evil, self-serving, and destructive. Traditionally, through the family, societies regulated the dangerous desires that lurk within us all. Parents controlled what their kids learned in school. Women and men knew their proper place and abided by the rules. But now families have a harder time fulfilling these roles, and without these rules and structures, confusion, lawlessness, lack of discipline, and a decline in standards abounds. They believe that women play a pivotal role in countering this decline. Against the cruel predicament that families find themselves in today, women embody nurturance and familiarity—what Linda Kintz calls "sacred intimacy"—and the possibility of creating a kinder, gentler world. If men are selfish, cold, and calculating, women embody a different way of being, submitting their egos and subordinating their selfish desires to the needs of their family and their God.[3]

Whatever she does, whether it is making slipcovers, going door-to-door with a petition against abortion, or hand-painting an old thrift store chair, Sally does it for Jesus. Home improvement is self-improvement and self-improvement is God's work. For her, Christianity is a total identity; the devil's work or God's grace underlies everything she does. In the modern world, work is split into many little tasks, each performed in a different place, among different people, at different times. In each setting we merely play a role, one of the many roles we play. None of the roles seems to take hold of our whole selves, none seems to embody what we truly are as whole and unique individuals. Not so for Sally. Everything she does is an outgrowth of her faith:

> My crocheting, my upholstery, planting my flowers, everything I do, has to do with God, glorifying the Lord. Everyone has an assignment before God. Everyone has gifts and talents, every single person has a calling whether they fulfill it or not. Being a homemaker, or when I was a waitress, whatever I did I tried to do to the best of my ability, and do it in a way that glorifies God. The Bible teaches us we're ambassadors. I feel as a Christian I represent Christ, so I don't want to leave a mess out in my front yard. It doesn't glorify the Lord if I'm lazy. I don't exercise as much as I should, and I eat too much, but I'm working on it. Even if no one else really cares if you're doing something, it's sort of like a secret relationship you have with the Lord, so he's pleased. I'm just so excited about the Lord letting me learn how to make cushions for my couch.

COMING HOME

OCA activists told conversion stories that were often very vivid, painting a portrait of particular places, times, and contexts in which they found God. In high school, Sally was on the student council and "very liberal, very radical," she told me. "I spoke out about the war in Vietnam, I opposed having flags in the classroom." After she graduated, she married and had two children, worked as a waitress at a Mexican restaurant in town, smoked a lot of pot, and followed Eastern religions. "I had a water pipe and a bong. Instead of offering you tea and cookies, I would've offered you a hit!" Sally says she didn't know she was "searching for God." She was very unhappy, but didn't know why.

Sally had a friend who lived down the street. The friend came over one day and told Sally that she was "saved," and that she didn't smoke pot anymore. "I just felt sorry for her, because I thought how boring," Sally recalls. Then the woman began to tell Sally all about book she had just read, *The Late Great Planet Earth,* by Hal Lindsey. Lindsey was a Jesus movement leader who emphasized that God had chosen our times for a special purpose, and that by deciphering the signs written in contemporary events one could understand God's plans for the world. Writing in the late 1960s, he saw the current period of social unrest as the beginning of the end of time, and proclaimed that the time *right now* was eminently meaningful. He made people think that *their* world held God's secrets. Published in 1970, Lindsey's book sold over 130,000 copies during the first few months of its publication. By 1978, nine million copies were in print, making its way, alongside the Bible, into virtually every Jesus movement commune, home, and church.[4]

The rapture, end times, prophecies about the future. It all sounded fascinating to Sally, so she borrowed *The Late Great Planet Earth.* That evening her husband was watching sports on television, so she started reading the book. "I was just shocked at what I read," she recalls. "I was just bawling because it talked about Christ, and the Second Coming, and the Rapture, and it talked about drugs, and I thought whoa! I just knew instantly that I was going to hell. And that's a pretty weird thing because I was an honor student and had always been a Miss Goody Two-shoes, and all of a sudden I had this realization about myself, and I was just devastated." As she recounted this story, tears streamed down Sally's face.

She told me about how she stayed up all night reading the book and began to pray, though she had never prayed before. "In my heart, you know, I wanted to change, wanted to follow God." At four in the morning, when she finally finished the book, she went into the bedroom where her husband was sleeping and woke him. "Matt, I just read this book about Jesus, and this Rapture, and the Second Coming and all these things!" she told him. "And he said, 'Fine.' And he didn't get it. I had been saved or something . . . born again, you know, all those terms you hear. And literally changed. All I knew was all of a sudden I was reading the Bible all the time."

Born-again Christians describe their faith as an intense personal commitment that provides indispensable order and meaning. When she was saved, Sally Humphries told me, she became "a completely different person." Becoming "born again" is a process of coming to know God, of "being able to converse with the Lord," in Jeri Cookson's words. Typically, the process began with an unexpected turn, with a chance encounter coming at just the right time, to deliver the speaker out of a difficult situation. The chance, involuntary nature of these occurrences seemed to confirm their spiritual, even supernatural origins: I found God while walking down the street, and somebody tapped me on the shoulder; someone just happened to give me a book that changed my life.

When Jeri first moved to Southern California, where her husband was working, they didn't know a soul, and she was at her "wits' end." Her kids were having troubles of various kinds. One day, she said, "I was praying, and I said I've got to meet somebody that I can relate to, I just need a good Christian home. I'm just sitting there in tears praying." Suddenly, like a bolt out of the blue, her prayers were answered.

> I get this knock on the door. And I opened the door and it was a little Mexican woman, and I'm saying she's really strange, you know, making conversation about some silly stuff. And then finally she just said, "You know, I've just got to say this, I don't know how to say this, but I was driving down the street, and I had to turn around and come back here and knock on this door. I don't know why I'm knocking on your door, but I just had to knock on your door." The Lord told that woman to come and knock on my door.

She took her to a church where she met a group of passionate Christians, and shortly thereafter, "out of the clear blue sky, the Lord told me, he said, within a week, your kids will be okay, don't worry about 'em, they're going to work through this. And sure enough they did."

Jeri and Sally told me conversion stories with a gusto that reminded me of gay people sharing their coming out stories. Indeed, the religious conversion experience mirrors, to a great extent, the act of coming out—it purports to mark the beginning of a new, fulfilled self. Conservative Christians speak of the period before they became born again as a time when they felt lonely, abandoned, helpless. Similarly, gay people tend to describe their life in the closet as filled with self-loathing and hopelessness. Both narratives declare that the ultimate criterion of the validity of identity is individual choice: it is by choosing an identity that one makes it one's very own, personal, special, and meaningful—not "merely" something one inherits or assumes. Both attribute to the individual the power to re-create oneself, and to become a fully actualized human being.[5] And both affirm the importance of "witnessing"—coming out to others as lesbian or gay, proclaiming one's relationship to Jesus to others. At the same time, coming out and born-again stories work toward opposite ends. Coming out stories affirm a quest for individual self-realization, and see hiding, obedience to unjust authority, and personal dishonesty as detrimental. Christian conversion narratives, in contrast, see the act of becoming born again as a kind of purification, directing the individual to construct a sense of self based upon submission and self-control.

Christian conservatives speak of their selfless commitment to higher authorities—family, nation, God. On the face of it, they have found what many of us are searching for: a sense of community, family, and wholeness, a feeling that our actions matter in the world and serve a greater purpose. But as I listened to their stories carefully, to their words as well as the emotions they expressed, I could also hear lingering pain, self-doubt, and shame.

EMOTIONAL RESCUE

Sally Humphries wept with joy in my presence, recounting how she found the Lord, and spinning elaborate tales of apocalyptic end times.[6] It was striking that despite all her talk of certainty and truth, at one point in the middle of our interview she paused and said, "I just feel beet red. I'm not an expert on any of this stuff, you know." She seemed overly concerned with what I thought of her, and even told me at one point during our conversation that she worried that I might think she is crazy. A couple of days after our meeting, I received a note on flowery "He Loves Me, He Loves Me Not" stationery:

> Dear Arlene,
>
> It was a pleasure to meet you today. I enjoyed visiting with you. I do feel I went on a bit much! I don't know what got into me. I'm kind of embarrassed that I went on so. Please forgive me. I'm not always like that.
> Love,
> Sally Humphries

During the course of our discussions, several other OCA activists asked me if I thought they were making "any sense," whether they were "giving me what I wanted," whether they were being coherent. Often they spoke rapidly and obsessively, preventing me from getting a word in edgewise. Barney Wooten followed each of my questions with a ten-minute rambling answer that forced me to aggressively interrupt him at times, and seemed fearful that I might take control of the conversation. At the time I thought he was "just being a man," but then several of the female activists exhibited similar types of behavior. What was going on here?

It seemed to me that deep emotions were at play, emotions that went far beyond the standard feelings of stress and anxiety that accompany many interview settings. With time, I began to recognize many of these recurring dynamics as markers of shame. Social psychologist Thomas Scheff suggests that shame, a widespread, negative emotion, influences all sorts of social interactions, often in unacknowledged ways. Shame differs from guilt, which is much more specific. In shame, "criticism or disapproval seems to emanate from the other and to envelope the whole self." It is the "social emotion" that arises from the "monitoring of one's own actions by viewing one's self from the standpoint of others."[7] In shame, hostility against the self is "experienced in the passive mode," causing individuals to feel "small, helpless and childish," vulnerable, victimized, rejected, passive, and not in control.[8] The experience of shame often occurs in the form of imagery, of looking or being looked at.

There are, according to psychoanalyst Helen Block Lewis, two different types of shame: overt shame, in which an individual says, "I am ashamed," where one's emotions are relatively accessible, and therefore less potent and destructive; and "bypassed shame," where the individual is overly conscious of his or her self-image from the other's viewpoint, and imagines that the other person is highly critical of him or her. Unlike the markers of overt, undifferentiated shame, which are often flagrant and overt, those of bypassed shame may be subtle and covert. They include thought and speech that "takes a speeded-up but repetitive quality" which might be seen as "obsessive." Typically, Lewis says, "individuals repeat a story or series of stories, talking rapidly and fluently but not quite to the point. They complain of endless internal replaying of a scene in which they felt criticized or in error." And they are distracted.

Both types of shame create rigid and distorted reactions to reality, and because bypassed shame tends to be ignored it becomes exceedingly destructive. The shamed person "avoids the shame before it can be completely experienced, through rapid thought, speech, or actions." And he or she compensates for shame by displaying incessant thought, speech, and or action, and frequently by shows of "overt hostility" and retaliation.[9]

While Christian right activists speak about their activism as a quest to repair the world and transform culture, it is also an effort to repair themselves, to construct a positive sense of themselves and their families as strong and independent, in contrast to weak, shameful others. Where does their sense of shame come from?

One possible source is the emotional hurt that Richard Sennett and Jonathan Cobb have termed the "hidden injuries of class."[10] Timbertown's OCA activists were primarily working folks who made good, who owned a little property and had some money in the bank. They embrace a "middle-class morality," strive to earn enough money so that they feel that their economic fate is in their own hands, and live by principles such as individual responsibility, the importance of family, obligations to others, and a belief in something outside oneself.[11] At the same time, they live in an era of "declining fortunes," when many Americans' sense of entitlement to the trappings of middle-class life—home ownership, occupational security, mobility on the job, and a decent standard of living—is eroding.[12] Even as the stock market soars to unprecedented levels and many industries enjoy the fruits of a globalizing economy, few of the postindustrial economy's winners are to be found among these conservative activists.

Jeri Cookson described her family's changing economic fortunes. "We were poor. Very poor. My husband and I grew up in the Depression. I've been very very poor," she said. Jeri and her husband moved to Oregon from Southern California in 1968, looking for a better place to raise kids and work. Jack was a carpenter, like his father before him. Jeri was a full-time homemaker who occasionally worked outside the home—once the kids got older—as a cashier at Sears, selling real estate on the side. She asked me if I had ever seen the movie *The Grapes of Wrath*. I replied that I had, and she told me that it's the story of her family. "We had a rough life, believe me." When she was in school, she says, her mother and father paid scant attention to her progress. "They never looked at one of my report cards . . . they didn't care. I was a good kid, I worked hard, I never did anything wrong. They didn't care whether I learned to spell or not."

Nonetheless, she told me, "We were happy, and responsible, and we took care of ourselves, and we loved each other. We didn't have a little Beaver-type family, no we didn't. But we stuck together, and we were independent and we took care of ourselves." Jeri showed me around her home, a modest but pleasant bungalow that she and her husband bought on the cheap and fixed up. They recently refinished the floors and installed new kitchen cabinets. The house means a lot to them. It's their security in old age, but more than that, it symbolizes how far they've come. When Jack retired they started a small janitorial service, cleaning offices around town, working one or two nights a week to supplement their social security checks and their income from two rental properties they own. "We've been very blessed because we earned every dime we got," she said proudly.

Timbertown's conservative activists have struggled against a host of demons: poverty, drugs, family turmoil, and illness; they lack education and sophistication, misspeak, use bad grammar, and have never traveled abroad. While they acknowledge having had drug habits, checkered work histories, and relationship problems, their discussions of these problems were always accompanied by explanations of how they struggled to overcome them. A precarious sense of achievement fuels their quest for respectability. Yet shame and anxiety linger: the once-firm boundaries of their world are crumbling. It's a late-modern scenario in which the familiar structures of family, work, and community are rapidly being redefined, where women find themselves caught between competing loyalties to family and work; where communities are increasingly segmented, and where child abuse and other problems appear to be rising. Though they had come to enjoy a bit of economic security and respectability, their hold on middle-class status remains tenuous. Many held multiple jobs to make ends meet, and anxieties about future employment and about the fate of their children loom. Jeri, for example, spoke at great length about how the educational system, and its declining standards, is selling her grandchildren short, and expressed fears about the decline of her small timber community. She reserved most of her wrath for those who are "taking advantage of the system," and collecting welfare at her "family's expense."

OCA activists feel themselves to be victimized as hardy individualists who have had to pull themselves up by their bootstraps, living in a society that coddles individuals and squelches self-reliance. Jeri, for example, is firmly committed to the belief in the possibility of upward mobility for all, and the notion that individuals through hard work, strength, and family solidarity can help themselves. An old-fashioned cold warrior, she sees red when she imagines Big Government, liberals, homosexuals, and their ilk in cahoots with one another. The evidence, she says, is everywhere. "I would like to have the same country that I grew up in still be here for my grandchildren, but I don't think it will be. It will be a socialist nation. We will have health cradle-to-grave, you know. I won't say insurance, but health programs that if they decide you need an operation someone's going to let you have it, and you're going to say, 'Oh, gee, thanks, thanks, thanks.' And you're going to wait in line for that. And people won't even know that there was ever anything called freedom."

I told her that it seems unlikely that our country will ever see socialized medicine in her or my lifetime, particularly since Bill Clinton's relatively modest attempt to reform health care suffered a stunning defeat early in his presidency. But at this point, Jeri, lost in her own whirlwind of conspiracy thinking, isn't listening. It sets her off into a diatribe against liberal entitlements, "special rights," and the loss of standards.

> I think, in this country, people should be hired or fired, or rented to or not rented to, or whatever, by whether or not they are going to take care

of the property, or not take care of the property, pay the rent . . . not pay
the rent, do the job . . . not do the job. If somebody is not capable of making it at the university, I don't think they should be let in, and make a special case for them, or any special privileges because he's black, or white, or
green, or purple, or homosexual or not. He either passes the course and
he can make it in there, or he can't.

Jeri sees her family as having achieved economic independence alone,
with little help from the world beyond. She and other conservative
activists feel that all around them others face the same struggles but
suffer few of the consequences; they are being coddled by society, receiving a variety of handouts and entitlements, and this is unfair. A
system of entitlements benefits the least deserving: the lazy, the slothful, the morally suspect. It has created, in their eyes, a dysfunctional
society, filled with people who are trying to get something for nothing, who don't know the value of discipline and hard work. Individuals are no longer given incentives to work hard. Certain groups in society are taking advantage of the flaws in the system, and hardworking
people pay the price. On one level, this is fairly predictable conservative rhetoric. But on another level, it plays into feelings of unacknowledged shame and accounts for the rise of a rhetoric of victimhood that became pervasive on the right in the 1990s.

CRUEL TO BE KIND

When I visited her in her home, Erica Williams gave me a copy of the
Focus on the Family newsletter, assuring me that I would find it "very
interesting." I did. The organization is headed by James Dobson, a
psychologist, host of a nationally syndicated radio program, and author of a series of best-selling books such as *Children at Risk, Dare to
Discipline, Parenting Isn't for Cowards, The Strong-Willed Child, Love
Must Be Tough,* and *Straight Talk to Men and Their Wives.* In the 1992 re-
vision of *Dare to Discipline,* Dobson urges parents: "As long as tears
represent a genuine release of emotion, they should be permitted to
fall. But crying quickly changes from inner sobbing to an exterior
weapon. It becomes a tool of protest to punish the enemy. Real crying
usually lasts two minutes or less, but may continue for five. After that
point, the child is merely complaining, and the changes can be recognized in the tone and intensity of his voice. I would require him to
stop the protest crying, usually by offering him a little more of what
caused the original tears."[13]

Perhaps, I wondered, my subjects' sense of shame was also rooted in early family relationships and child-rearing processes.[14] In the moral traditionalist narrative, childhood is a battle of innocence against guilt or corruption. Children are to be protected from the corrupting influences of immoral adults (or from their own confused and perverse potential) and need discipline in order to internalize a sense of obedience and self-reliance. Good values develop self-discipline in children by using rewards and punishments, and teach discipline, self-reliance and respect for authority; by contrast, self-indulgence and lack of discipline lead to poverty, drug addiction, and a host of other problems—including homosexuality.[15] Love and nurturance are a vital part of a family life but they can never outweigh parental authority, which is itself an expression of love and nurturance—"tough love." Once mature, they are on their own and must depend on their acquired self-discipline to survive. Their self-reliance gives them authority over their own destinies.

Psychologists Michael Milburn and Sheree Conrad argue that denial is at the core of the conservative worldview. Protestant fundamentalists, following the biblical injunction that "to spare the rod is to spoil the child," have long believed that corporal punishment should be part of child rearing. Authoritarian child rearing traumatizes children, who are then taught to deny the frightening reality of physical punishment, and denial becomes a coping mechanism for children whose parents hurt them and for those who simply fear that they might. "By fostering a fantasy world that creates an absolute split between good and evil," Milburn and Conrad argue, "denial prevents us from entertaining any but the most simplistic solutions to our problems.[16] One can imagine that such beliefs would lead to an exaggerated tendency to repress feelings of shame rather than acknowledge them outright.

While Timbertown's Christian conservative activists see themselves as victims of forces beyond their control, they are, at the same time, firmly committed to an individualistic ethos that suggests that they hold their destinies in their own hands. To be morally strong, they believe, one must be self-disciplined and self-denying. To feel shame is a sign of moral flabbiness, which ultimately aids the forces of evil. Therefore, one would tend to repress and deny shameful feelings. Carried into the political realm, this moral system—with strength at the top of the list of values—leads to the belief that poverty, drug habits, and illegitimate children can be explained in terms of individual weakness. The problem comes down, as it always does, to morals.

"If we have good morals in this country and family values," proclaims Jeri, "and strong families with a husband and a wife, where kids can get authority, things would be different. With all these kids being raised by single parents, boys don't know the first thing about how to be a man. You look at these women, even wonderful women, trying very hard. But how do you teach a boy to be a husband and a father if they aren't around one, you know what I mean." Our troubles, conservative Christian activists suggest, stem from a loss of family values, hierarchies, standards.

Since shame is the function of a preoccupation with an "other," shame reparation or reduction involves retaliation against an "other" who, it is suggested, is the shaming agent. A sense of identity is constructed through opposition to those whom the shamed individual can triumph over or humiliate. For Christian conservatives, homosexuality has during the past fifteen years served as this "other." These Christians see gay people—affirming relationships that have no strings attached, no mutual duty, and no guarantee of duration—as the antithesis of moral individuals, the embodiment of a world in which rules, order, self-discipline, and stability are severely lacking.

When I asked Jeri Cookson why she was active against gay rights she replied, fusing a belief in moral and medical contagion, "It's a lifestyle that is harmful to our country because it tears down family values, harmful to the individuals involved because it is unhealthy." According to "reputable studies," she said, people involved in homosexual activities are twelve times more likely to develop hepatitis B. The specter haunting Timbertown's OCA activists is San Francisco, representing the twin evils of urban diversity and unabashed sexual license.

In *The Gay Agenda,* a 1992 video produced by a charismatic church in California and distributed to thousands of Christian right organizations nationwide, images of gay men at gay pride parades sporting sadomasochistic paraphernalia abound. The men scream, stick their tongues out, flaunt their naked posteriors in the camera lens, and engage in sexual activity with each other in the streets. Rather than represent gay men as limp-wristed and feminized, this video, enormously influential during the campaign, conjured images

of power, degradation, excitement, pleasure, savagery, and bachana-
lian hedonism, representing gay men as hypermasculine savages.[17]
OCA-distributed literature and videos such as *The Gay Agenda* construct "the homosexual" as male. Despite the fact that the vast majority of gay people in Timbertown were women, public discussions of
homosexuality typically referred to men—not the limp-wristed,
feminized men who were synonymous with homosexuality in the
popular imagination, but the hypermasculine gay men, the leather-
clad sadomasochists who flaunt their aggressive sexuality in public,
refusing to feel shame for their desires.

In the Christian right imagination, homosexuals represent undisciplined male sexuality, freed of the "civilizing" influence of women.
It called "normal" masculinity, founded upon identification with the
aggressive father, into question. Effeminate homosexuals could easily
be mocked and marginalized; masculine homosexuals posed a greater
challenge because publicly they outmasculinized straight guys who
were forced to repress their deepest, darkest sexual fantasies; butch gay
men got to live these fantasies out, and revel in their deviant desires
—and they weren't forced to share their earnings with anyone in
the process. Christians were excluded from the culture; homosexuals
were gaining in power.

The Gay Agenda contains interviews with antigay experts and is
largely intended to be an exposé of the lesbian and gay movement's secret plans for America; San Francisco is its awful culmination, and
provides a doomsday warning of what is in store for America if Christians delay. Its effect, along with that of much Christian right antigay
rhetoric, is to separate gay people into two groups: "good gays," who
embrace conventional gender roles, who live quiet lives, who keep
their sexuality to themselves, and who make no public demands on
that basis; and "bad gays," militant politicos who make their sexuality
public—particularly butch women, visibly macho gay men, and effeminate, sexually promiscuous men.

The public rhetoric of the OCA focused upon the latter group—
"bad gays"—whose leaders might be found in Eugene and Portland,
and who often had connections to the national movement. There was
a local audience for the antigay rhetoric as well, and it included "good
gays," people like Barbara Hammer and Cindy Barber, and their families—ideal Timbertowners, in many respects, who lived in long-

term committed relationships, conformed to relatively conventional gender roles, and abided by the rule of law and economic individualism. Timbertown's gay community was populated by these "good gays"—mainly women, and mothers to boot, who were as far from the image of egocentric, predatory gay men as one could get.

Perhaps the appearance of normalized lesbians in town was all the more disturbing to religious conservatives, for they challenged the stereotyped ways that they conceived of homosexuality, and by implication heterosexuality. Perhaps, such individuals revealed that the heterosexual-homosexual dichotomy was far less rigid and enduring than many Christian right images suggested.[18] When I spoke with them individually, several OCA activists sometimes admitted as much. Though Christian activists warned of the evils of homosexuality, they often qualified their claims with professions of sympathy for the devil, and variations on the theme "some of my best friends are gay" abounded.

"There's quite a few here in town. I've met several of them. Very, very nice people. Extremely nice people," suggested Jeri Cookson. While homosexuality is sinful, unhealthy, and abhorrent, individual homosexuals could, however, be good, decent people. Barney Wooten told me about gay people he works with, one of whom refuses to talk with him because of his religious beliefs. "He has more negative feelings about me than I do about him," he surmised. But when it came down to it, the conservative activists I spoke with don't *really* know any living, breathing lesbians or gay men, and their descriptions were shot through with stereotypes, cardboard characterizations, and distortions. Homosexuals, Sally Humphries told me, are "highly talented people, very artistic people," and since she considers herself artistic, she feels a particular affinity for them. She admits to having gay friends. "I'm drawn to them. They're into art and color. They're more caring sometimes. I know that they are very concerned about the charter amendment."[19]

These impressions seemed to be products of misunderstanding and ignorance. In diverse societies, individuals are forced to live with those who may be different from themselves but they construct defenses so that they do not have to come to really know them. Confronted with strangers on a daily basis, writes Zygmunt Bauman, we are practiced in the "art of mismeeting and the avoidance of eye contact." We create social distances that evict from our social space the others who are otherwise within reach. We deny them admittance, and prevent ourselves from acquiring knowledge about them. But the "others" continue to hover in the background of our perceptions, remaining "featureless, faceless."[20] Indeed, OCA activists' knowledge of homosexuality derived less from personal experience than from watching television, or from a onetime foray on a tour bus into San Francisco's Castro District, or from Christian right political materials. The superficiality of this contact allowed them to inflate their targets into folk devils whom they imagined were posing a threat to their conception of the good society. By constructing homosexuals as an abstract category, they were able to separate the fate of gay people as a group from gay people as individuals. The lack of sustained contact and knowledge of homosexual culture bred feelings of repulsion and subdued hostility that were ready, given the right political rhetoric, to condense into hatred.[21]

But this hate is mixed with love, and much as a parent can hate his or her children and love them at the same time, Christian "love the sinner, hate the sin" rhetoric permits activists to simultaneously hate gays and love them. While passing a ballot measure to prevent homosexual "special rights" might not change very much, the activists of the OCA believe it is a first step. They are assuming the role of parent, disciplining the moral flabbiness of those around them, affirming a sense of themselves as strong and independent—thereby assuaging their own anxieties. Good families, they believe, value strength and obedience and do not tolerate weakness and dependence. Homosexuals are wayward children who need to be led back on track, punished for their excesses—and certainly not rewarded for their bad behavior. Like a good child gone bad, they need to be shown a little discipline. If it takes a bit of tough love to do so, so be it. Sometimes you have to be cruel to be kind.

CHAPTER 6

Angry White Men and Women

To conservative Christians, homosexuality was sinful, unnatural, against God and the family. But religious conservatives made up a relatively small fraction of the state's registered voters. To the vast majority of the public, who believed that religion—and sex—should be kept private, these words sounded intolerant, overly zealous, even hateful. In Oregon, as in many states, conservatives were divided into two camps: libertarian anti-statists preoccupied with lowering taxes and trimming down government, and traditionalists who were waging religious battles against abortion and homosexuality. The OCA emerged out of the second camp and in order to be successful it would have to make inroads among libertarians ambivalent about mixing religion and politics and leery of religious zealots running their lives.

As Alan Wolfe suggests, Americans tend to take their religion seriously but "very few of them take it so seriously that they believe that religion should be the sole or even the most important guide for establishing rules about how *other* people should live."[1] They believe in morality writ small: "values capacious enough to be inclusive but demanding enough to uphold standards of personal responsibility."[2] In 1992, a poll showed that 60 percent of Oregonians held an unfavorable view of the OCA.[3]

"There's a whole section of folks in town," Chuck Mendip explained, "who don't give a rat's ass about religion. They say, 'Well, if I don't want to rent to a gay person, I shouldn't have to, and if I want to throw someone out, that's my right, because—damn!—it's my place, and my property.'" They were folks who wanted property rights, the right to own a gun and say, "Stay out of my bedroom, stay off of my property, leave my gun alone." Priding themselves on being independent, they saw state intrusion as fundamentally problematic. They didn't want anyone telling them what they should do with their property. The problem, as they saw it, was government: there was just too damn much of it. First they told you couldn't cut down so many trees. Now they're telling you who you can or can't rent your house to.

Timbertown is a macho community, a logger town where just about everyone owns a truck, and where hunting and fishing are popular pastimes. It is a place where masculinity rules. Autonomy is valued, dependence is seen as negative; father-dominant households are signs of strength, and when wives work, it reflects badly on the family. It is a traditional form of masculinity that is rapidly being challenged by an array of sweeping social changes. For religious conservatives, the problem comes down, as it always does, to morals. But for secular conservatives, it's about economics and the decline of the male breadwinner role.

In Timbertown, as in the United States as a whole, the "family wage" men once earned was fast becoming a thing of the past. An ailing timber industry meant that fewer and fewer families could exist on one salary, leading to a growing proportion of working women, which undermined the economic basis of the father-headed household.[4] The decline of the male breadwinner prompted confusion and discomfort because it called into question many of our culture's most deeply held beliefs about manhood and masculinity. If men do not share a distinctive identity based on their economic role as family providers, then what is a man? As sociologist Kathleen Gerson asks, "If men can no longer claim special rights and privileges based on their unique responsibilities and contributions, then how can they justify their power?"[5]

In the traditional masculine ideal, becoming a man entails identification with the aggressive father who possesses primary responsibility for supporting and protecting the family as well as the authority to set overall policy. In this model of the family, the mother has day-to-day responsibility for the care of the house, raising the children, and upholding the father's authority. Children are expected to respect and obey their parents, and by doing so build character, that is, self-discipline and self-reliance. Libertarian and social conservatives idealize this model of the family, sharing a belief in the importance of discipline and toughness.[6] They think of society as a collection of families writ large. A just society, like a good father, is firm, punishes those who transgress its rules, and condemns whining, and the expression of weakness—feelings of pain, grief, and confusion—in public. A healthy society also marginalizes subordinate forms of masculinity—such as male homosexuality.[7] The OCA idealized this model of the family, offering white working men the possibility of imagining themselves and their families as strong and independent. They could become the stewards of the reimagined community by standing up to the homosexual threat.

In order to expand the OCA's base beyond evangelical Christians, activists began to publicly downplay the group's Christian orientation and appeal instead to a desire on the part of many men to feel powerful again. "This is not a religious issue," Lon Mabon told a television talk show host during the charter measure campaign. In Timbertown, when a newspaper reporter asked OCA leader Sally Humphries about her religious affiliation, she replied, "I would rather not refer to my personal beliefs or talk about my ideas about God."[8] The OCA's "special rights" campaign tied the restoration of masculinity to the restoration of white dominance.

In the early 1990s, conservatives began to usurp the rhetoric of victimhood, claiming it for white men. In California, a movement had been brewing to deny health and education benefits to illegal immigrants, and to end the use of race and gender preferences in state employment, contracting, and education. "Sexual discrimination against white males is pervasive," proclaimed a leader of that campaign. "The available evidence indicates, in fact, that white males need protection against discrimination on the basis of their sex even more than they need protection on the basis of their race."[8]

But California was a very different place from its neighbor to the north. Though dark-skinned people had been steadily flowing into Oregon of late, particularly from Mexico and the rest of Latin America, they had not yet achieved critical mass or political voice. Despite the fact that the vast majority of Oregon's welfare recipients were white, the specter of the single black welfare mother evoked laziness, dirt, immorality—familiar symbols of stigma and marginalization. It suggested that efforts to redress discrimination against minorities inevitably led to handouts, preferences, and quotas, all of which undermined the position of "hardworking Americans"—read: straight white men.

Oregon Citizens Alliance activists began to downplay talk of morality, of sin, family values, and the like, positioning minority civil rights strategies instead as signs of weakness, dependence, and femininity.[9] "Special rights" symbolized what happened when arriveste groups—hippies, environmentalists, Californians, racial minorities, lesbians and gays, and elites—were permitted to freely stake out political and cultural claims and make demands upon the state, driving up taxes and regulations, and taking rights and privileges from their rightful owners: the good, upstanding citizens of Timbertown. White men paid the price.

DECLINING FORTUNES AND LEVEL PLAYING FIELDS

Sam Miller drives a large brown pickup truck with huge, oversized tires. When he pulled into the driveway of his modest detached house, the sort one can find in working-class neighborhoods all over the nation, he wore a baseball cap and a Harley-Davidson T-shirt. Thirty-six years old, Sam had the grizzled look of someone at least ten years older. The television, given pride of place in the simple, spare, carpeted living room, was blaring. I asked him to turn it off so that we could record the interview, as his thirteen-year-old son looked on.

Sam works as a machinist and welder for a local company that makes equipment for the wood products industry. His father worked as an auto mechanic in town for years, eventually leaving to work in the woods, in the timber industry. Sam's one of the lucky ones: he still has a job in the lumber industry, manufacturing equipment for the wood products industry. But "It's slow now," he says, so "who knows what could happen."

He likes his job, and likes living in Timbertown; he's a "small-town boy," he says. He refers to the university town to the north, population one hundred twenty thousand, as "the city" and says he "can't imagine anyone liking living there. It's too big and crowded, too overwhelming." He comes from a large, tight-knit family that has been in town for generations. He was a member of the largest graduating class in Timbertown High's history, but few of his classmates are around anymore. "Everybody's moved out. Not everybody. There are still a lot of hometown people and stuff like that. But the biggest majority of the folks I went to school with have moved out." They've gone to Portland, to Chicago, New York, even Sweden, in search of work, or simply a change. A lot of them are in the military.

He fears that the lack of job opportunities in town may force his sons, now thirteen and fourteen, to move away. But he would very much like them to have the option of staying if they wish, and living a small-town life surrounded by longtime friends and family. "Why should we raise up our young people and educate them in a small town just to send them elsewhere? If they want to go, like I say, that's fine. But if they have no choice, that's not right." That's why Sam supports the influx of new businesses in town like Wal-Mart. "They're creating new opportunities for the young people in town," he says. He doesn't buy local activists' claims that huge chains are swallowing up small businesses, devastating local commerce. "Sure, maybe they'll swallow a few people, but that's part of America's free market, you know?"

For his part, Sam goes to work every day at 5:00 A.M., comes home around 4:00 P.M., and then goes back out to work at the plant stand in town he and his wife, a kitchen aide at the local school district, run together, until 10:00 P.M. "I have to work for everything I get," and he pays his bills on time, he says proudly.

"You know, I learned a long time ago that I, as an individual, am not going to go and get anywhere in life unless I'm willing to work hard. And I've found some satisfaction in not only that philosophy but in doing so." Despite the fact that most of income comes from his job as a manual laborer, Sam describes himself as a businessman. He has long been active in the junior chamber of commerce in town, and dreams about quitting his day job once his plant business becomes more profitable.

Sam's faith in economic individualism extends to other areas of life: strength in one area, he believes, leads to strength in others. Speaking of the value of hard work, he says, "I think a lot of people in our country get by without those same basic beliefs. And I think more than hurting anybody else they are hurting themselves." As he tells me, he was once a drug addict who was in trouble with the law. "I've had my share of problems, and my share of downfalls in life. Been there and done that, you know. Got the T-shirt." But he's come a long way. He cleaned up his act, married, and has kept the same job for fifteen years. "Nobody reached out and grabbed hold of me and jerked me the right direction. It was something I had to find myself, and I think for the most part I've done that. And I think everyone is responsible. I don't care what color you are, I don't care what religion you are, I don't care what your lifestyle choice may be. Hey, life is not easy for anybody."

Throughout the nation, rising real estate prices, deindustrialization, and the globalization of the economy is whittling away at the much-revered American dream and creating a society of winners and losers. In the 1980s, as the top 1 percent of the population enjoyed a dazzling degree of wealth, and more and more people were pushed into poverty, the timber communities of the Pacific Northwest were among several rural regions that failed to ride the tide of prosperity.[10] Oregon's rapid growth in technology led to boom times for some parts of the state nicknamed the Silicon Forest. But twenty-five out of thirty-six counties were designated as having a "labor surplus," and rural Oregon's real per capital income in 1988 was only three quarters of urban per capital income.[11] Less than half of job openings provide a living wage for a single person; one quarter fail to provide a living wage for a family of three.[12]

At a time when the fastest-growing sectors of the economy require mental labor, Sam and men like him work with their hands. The postindustrial economy's losers, they feel, quite rightly, that they have little or no public voice. Labor unions were weaker than ever. The Democratic Party had all but abandoned their cause. And as if to rub salt into the festering wounds, minorities, it seemed, were the only ones getting attention. Conservative critic Charles Sykes suggested that America was becoming "a nation of victims."[13] Sam agreed.

"It's been said time and time again that there's no political agenda by the gays, but I see otherwise," says Sam. "They say, 'Well, the landlord's gonna kick me out because they find out I am gay.' Well, if indeed that's the kind of landlord that I indeed have, is that the kind of landlord that I want to rent from? It's real simple for me. If you don't like my business dealings, don't do business with me. I think there's far too much crying in this society."

"Part of life is learning to deal with your mistakes," Sam tells me. "There's a lot of people who are caught in a tailspin, pulled down by the wolves," he says, quoting a Garth Brooks song. "We can go on trying to protect and coddle people all we want, but until they are ready to get tough and face the realities of mother nature . . . if society throws us an excuse to grab hold of, then what kind of lessons are we going to learn from that?" Hard work, obedience to authority, strength, these are the virtues that shape Sam's values. They're classic American values. The angry white men of Timbertown listened, ad nauseam it often seemed, to blacks, women, lesbians, and gays whine about their problems. But who was talking about *their* pain? Who was talking about the fact that they couldn't support their families, that their wives had to go to work, that their houses and cars were being repossessed, that they were forced to abandon their families, their communities in search of work, and that the jobs they could find paid pitifully low wages, and offered few benefits or guarantees?

Sam is one of the lucky ones: he has managed to hold on to his job, and it's a pretty good one—it gives him health insurance and a decent wage. Despite the fact that he had achieved a certain degree of independence, there is shame in his voice when he speaks of a past that lingers, shaping his sense of self. Though he has not been forced to move out of Timbertown and break up his family, he can no longer support his family, as his father did before him, on one salary. He and his wife hold multiple jobs to make ends meet, and anxieties about the future, and about the fate of his children, loom. Sam is caught in a double bind: he sees himself as a victim of forces beyond his control, and at the same time he embraces a highly individualistic ethos. "With a bit of hard work," he says, "I can overcome the odds. I can make it.

"You know, as an individual, I'm not going to go and get anywhere in life unless I'm willing to work hard. And I've found some satisfaction in doing so. But I think a lot of people in our country get by without the same basic beliefs. And I think more than hurting anybody else they are hurting themselves. You know. I can pay tax dollar after tax dollar, and work harder and harder and harder, and people like that will just keep getting and getting and getting more of my tax money. And the people who are getting punished most are themselves. Because they can't look back and say, 'Gosh, look what I did.' They miss the thrill of the challenge." But such individualism is an incomplete answer to his situation; deep down, Sam knows that he has only limited control over his future. This leads him to harbor a series of resentments, inchoate and unnamed, against the world around him. The right alone seemed to speak to Sam's pain. The fight against "special rights," like that against affirmative action, promised to reverse a quarter decade of unjust handouts and restore a sense of meaning, purpose, and authority.

"*Little House on the Prairie*—that was one of the greatest shows on TV," Sam says wistfully. The show, a drama based on the everyday struggles of Laura Ingalls Wilder and her family in 1860s Kansas, aired on prime-time television for eleven years beginning in the mid-1970s. It told the tale of a close-knit family headed by Pa Ingalls, whose authority was firm but undisputed, evoking a time when communities were close-knit, families stuck together through thick and thin, and men and women knew their place. "If Pa Ingalls won't do it, hey, pal, I ain't gonna do it, 'cause I gotta get up in the morning and look in that mirror."

Many working-class people in Timbertown believed that a system of entitlements had cropped up to benefit the least deserving: the lazy, the slothful, the morally suspect. It had created, in their eyes, a dysfunctional society, filled with people who are trying to get something for nothing, who don't know the value of discipline and hard work. Individuals are no longer given incentives to work hard. Certain groups in society are taking advantage of the flaws in the system. Homosexuals and other minority groups are getting special rights, circumventing the channels that reward those who work hard. Why should they be rewarded for their choices? No one helped *me*. If only liberals kept their hands off the state, the economy . . . we'd have a level playing field.

"Level playing field" was a phrase I heard again and again in the course of my conversations. In the conservative view, this is how the world should work. Individuals compete against one another and the best, most skilled players come up as winners. The fittest survive. But as working-class Timbertowners see it, "special interests" like women and minorities are making demands on the state, feeding off the public trough, and winning "special rights," thereby rigging the game. Homosexuals and welfare mothers—promiscuous, unmarried, morally lax—are particularly suspect. They drive up the cost of government and create the need for higher taxes. In the end, everyone suffers.[14] Such comments reveal a diminishing faith in the "public" sphere, and of the power of government to redress inequalities built into the structure of the system. Faith in individualism makes such structural inequalities invisible. But even those for whom such inequalities are evident, the state is the problem, not the solution.

Nancy Sunday, thirty-seven years old, looks like a biker chick. She's got long blond hair and wears purple nail polish and a short leather jacket. Nancy's an air force brat who moved to Timbertown with her family in the early 1970s. Her parents had a trout farm, and raised ring-necked pheasants. She was on welfare for a time, when she was in college, and her husband left her and her kids. They lived in a car for three months and ate macaroni and cheese every night. "I didn't want something for nothing," she says, but she took the money —she was desperate. Then she was prosecuted for fraud, for not reporting some income, and had to return much of it to the state. Today she works as a coordinator of senior services at the local community college. It's a position that's part-time—her gross pay is $850 per month—and carries no benefits.

"I go to a store and see avocados for $1.38 each, and I think no way, and then I see a Hispanic woman buy two sacks of avocados for $48 and she pays for it with food stamps. That's why I'm against welfare— I see what goes on. I see the way it's structured, I see the abuse." There's abuse in the health care system as well, she says, telling me a story about her two teenage sons. One is a slacker, a "lazy, good-for-nothing kid." He's eligible for the Oregon Health Plan, a program that provides health care for the state's neediest citizens. But her other son, because of a loophole in the system, isn't eligible. He's an asthmatic and needs medication that costs hundreds of dollars a month. "That's what makes me conservative," she complains. "Abuses in the system."

The deteriorating faith in the "public" was exemplified by the frequency of complaints I heard about the local high school. "The high school is bad," Nancy tells me. "I've hung out there, my kids used to go there. Kids don't have much respect. They hang out, they're lost. The high school is a pit, it's delapidated." Most people in town, on the right as well as the left, talked about this. It was a source of shame for many people that water stains marred the high school's ceilings and that its walls were in such disrepair that urinals and sinks fell off their foundations, forcing closure of some of the bathrooms, that water frequently leaked on the gym floor, and that wet plaster fell from the ceiling and walls. Those who were able to often sent their kids to schools in neighboring towns. Janice Trump's daughter spent a year in Timbertown High School and "just couldn't deal with it anymore," she says. "It was a horrible place: bad attitudes, crumbling paint, lots of cursing, little actual work."

For conservatives, both religious and secular, the problem with the schools, and with the public sphere in general, was too much permissiveness, and a "loss of standards." As Nancy Sunday puts it, "The teachers let them do what ever they want. My son wrote a paper in high school in which every other word was 'fuck.' 'Fuck this, fuck that.' The teacher actually graded it! I couldn't believe it! It was offensive. I approached her, and asked her why she graded it, and she said for some people it was an effort to put something down on paper. It showed effort. But it was terrible, I couldn't believe it." The loss of standards, and the "dumbing down" of education is something that came up in conversations again and again—among both Christian and secular conservatives.

Sally Humphries spoke about her daughter's experiences in grade school. "She told me that kids weren't paying attention. Everyone in her history class was failing, but four. I mean, it was just unbelievable." John James agrees: "I think they've really dumbed down education," he tells me. "I think there's a lot of intellectual dishonesty that goes on. One of the things that really bothers me is the creative spelling that they now endorse. Kids don't have to learn how to spell as long as they get the idea. And, boy, try telling somebody that when they apply for a job. I think they are just really doing children an injustice by lowering the standards, and telling them they can basically do what they want to do, and it's going to be all right. The generation of kids that are coming up are very, very ill prepared to enter the workforce."

Kids coming out of high school in Timbertown can no longer count upon finding a good job working in the mills. Increasingly dependent upon education as a means of upward mobility, they are entering a workforce that is very different, and for which educational credentials and knowledge are increasingly crucial. Vice principal Barbara Hammer put it, "A lot of boys got to be sixteen, and then went out and took a job in the mills for fifteen bucks an hour, and they were out of here. Today, more boys are staying in high school. Their attitudes about their purpose for being in school have changed a lot. Before, they said, 'Hey, I can screw off, and I don't need to go to class, and I don't need to get good grades because I'm gonna get a good job at the mill.' "

Hammer told me that she and other school administrators toured a local mill and "were just blown away by how high-tech it is." Today, even the mills, which employ far fewer people in town than ever before, require high school diplomas. And more and more jobs require four-year college degrees, an option that only about 15 percent of Timbertown students have tended to pursue—about half the number that have joined the military. With the decline of the mills, and the growing influx of more affluent people, the number of students pursuing four-year degrees increased to about 30 percent.[15]

As they survey a rapidly changing world, working-class Timbertowners are justifiably anxious about their place within it. Will their children and grandchildren receive the education necessary for them to succeed in this emerging economic universe? Their talk of "loss of standards" suggests a widespread sentiment that public schools offer a patchwork of courses that ill prepare them to compete in the emerging high-tech workforce. A sense of anxiety shapes their scenario of a world out of bounds, a late-modern scenario in which the familiar structures of family, work, and community are rapidly being defined: where women find themselves caught between competing loyalties to family and work; where communities are increasingly segmented, and people, even in a small town like Timbertown, barely know their neighbors, where rates of drug addiction, child abuse, and other problems appear to be skyrocketing.

They are not alone. Anthony Giddens has suggested that the concept of risk has become central to the way people organize the moral world. "The late modern world is apocalyptic," says Giddens, "not because it is inevitably heading toward calamity, but because it introduces risks which previous generations have not had to face."[16]

The paradox is that conservative policies are the ones responsible for the deterioration of services upon which they depend, yet what riles the white working class most isn't the property tax initiatives that cut social programs and essential services, including Nancy's job in the community college system, and funding for a new high school to replace the old, dilapidated one. Numerous attempts to pass a bond measure to build a new high school to replace the old, dilapidated building had failed over the years. After complaining about how poorly the local school district is funded, Nancy told me that she had voted for a statewide property tax limitation that cut public funding for schools, and had enormous repercussions upon Timbertown and other small communities across the state. Faced with declining state funding, the school district tried on a number of occasions to pass a local bond issue, and each time voters turned it down. Nancy was one of them.

The working class's response to the sense that public services were not meeting their needs was to further withdraw. Christian conservatives placed their kids in religious schools, or they homeschooled them. Secular conservatives voted against increased school funding, opposed improvements in public transportation, and joined tax revolts, and then complained about the sorry state of the civic infrastructure and social services.

A further paradox is that though wealth is increasingly concentrated in the hands of a few in Oregon, as across the country, many working folks seem far more troubled by those at the bottom. Sam Miller told me that "the rich probably pay a lot more in taxes than you and I will ever know." When I sat in John James's small tract home in a poor part of Timbertown, whose walls were empty and furniture sparse, he told me that he worries about losing his job, but nevertheless gives money to the wealthy conservative Heritage Foundation. What gets his blood boiling is the knowledge that while he's playing by the rules, working hard, trying to get by, others—Latino welfare mothers, for example—are having an easier time of it. *They're* buying avocados. *I'm* eating macaroni and cheese. They're the ones the white working classes brush up against on a daily basis. The others are distant, shadowy, living in gated communities and on country estates, and therefore out of view.

While they acknowledge the existence of complex social problems that encompass vast economic and cultural changes, and pose substantial risks to themselves and their world, if there are social structures that stand in the way of individuals' quest for self-improvement, they are barely to be found; if there are families who, facing hardship, try their best to make things work and still fail, they are for the most part absent. For angry white men—and women —it is the state, prisoner of special interests and liberalism, that is really at fault. Minority groups have organized, placing pressure upon the state to accede to their demands, and have contributed to the creation of a bloated mess, a panoply of welfare programs that create undisciplined individuals and screw working Americans.

OWLS, GAYS, AND OTHER ILLEGITIMATE MINORITIES

"Protecting gay rights is analogous to protecting the spotted owl," a Timbertown OCA activist suggested. The "Battle of the Owl," the premier Western political issue of the late 1980s and early 1990s, led to the prohibition of logging on hundreds of thousands of acres of federal forests on the grounds that it destroyed the overall condition of the ecosystem, evidenced by the threatened extinction of the spotted owl. It created bitter conflicts between middle-class environmentalists and loggers, who charged environmentalists with being more eager to protect owls than jobs. The OCA, in its bid for support among laissez-faire conservatives, including loggers, tapped into old resentments stirred by this conflict, and the outsider-insider boundaries they called up. Hippies, environmentalists, and homosexuals became one: immoral, dirty, lacking in self-control, and a threat to the well-being of the entire community. Gay people, in short, were no more endangered than the spotted owl. They were in fact quite powerful.

"If you knew about the homosexual agenda, it would make the hairs on your neck crawl," said an OCA spokesperson testifying in favor of the initiative at a Timbertown city council meeting. "Their intent is to take over the state of Oregon and turn it into Queer Nation." Referring to the fact that Ashland, Oregon, had passed gay rights legislation, he warned that homosexuals had already taken over several southern Oregon communities. Timbertown was next.[17] Homosexuals were a secret, powerful presence, a "highly funded special interest group," one woman proclaimed as she rattled off what she considered a list of supposedly well-heeled liberal organizations: Right to Privacy PAC, No on 9 Committee, ACT-UP, Queer Nation, NOW, the NEA and the ACLU.[18] Collectively, gays had high incomes and therefore didn't need "special rights."

Though the state had yet to pass a law banning discrimination against lesbians and gays, Portland, Ashland, and Corvallis had local ordinances that did just that. Why, the OCA asked, should individuals who engage in homosexual acts receive these protections? Such rhetoric was designed to appeal to displaced Timbertowners, especially men, who were battling unemployment, a lack of purpose, a diminished sense of their own capacities. Loggers and their families were the target group: people who hated big government, whose pocketbooks were hurting, but whose "live and let live" attitude tended to stop short of taking stands on social issues.

"They say: we're here, we're queer, and we ain't going shopping. Well, I have a statement to make: I am here, I am *not* queer, and I *am* going shopping."[19] Welding resentments toward gays' supposed affluence with the belief that they take up altogether too much public space, an OCA supporter invoked a slogan used by the group Queer Nation in their actions for gay visibility in suburban shopping malls. As further proof of the fact that gays were lobbying for special rights, an OCA leader claimed there were "nine bills introduced into the Oregon State Legislature last session trying to get us to officially recognize their marriages and to force employers to extend health benefits to them as married couples." This, he suggested, would bankrupt the state's health plans. Furthermore, he added, such bills would have permitted homosexuals to allege discrimination and sue any employer who failed to hire or promote them or any landlord who failed to rent to them.[20]

While OCA rhetoric suggested that the personal is political—what gays do in their bedrooms is relevant to their character and is therefore a matter of public importance—the campaign's secular frame distinguished between what people do in the privacy of their home—which it considered their own business—and politicized homosexuality—which violates the public trust. Protecting individuals who keep their homosexuality private is one thing, said forty-five-year-old John James, a machinist in the wood products industry, but protecting homosexuals as a "special interest group" is something entirely different. "I don't believe in discriminating against anybody," he told me. "In my personal life I would no more discriminate against someone that was homosexual than I would against someone that was an adulterer. Basically it's their business when they keep it to themselves. Anytime they expect me to put a stamp of approval on it and give them what the state would consider a protected status as far as hiring and stuff like that, or keeping people like churches from being able to fire somebody . . . then I think that crosses over the line. And that is where I think it should be drawn. I agree to some sense that people's sexuality is their private thing unless it harms society."

Does it harm society? Is homosexuality actually a real threat in small, relatively out-of-the-way places like Timbertown? "Oh yes, I think it is anyplace," John James replied, and then proceeded to mention Barbara Hammer, the out lesbian vice principal, though not by name. "Ten years ago, people said, 'Well, they'll never be teaching in the schools.' And I don't have a problem if they are teaching in the schools if they are not advocating that in educational policies and stuff. When they have an open homosexual come and teach junior high boys how to put condoms on cucumbers and bananas and then talk about the gay lifestyle, that bothers me." Such claims echoed a gay conservative position critical of those who "flaunt" their gayness, shunning hypermasculine gays, effeminate queers, butch dykes, in favor of respectable, "straight looking" and "acting," assimilationist homosexuals.

The distinction between private and public, individual and collectivized, homosexuality resonated with Sam Miller, a self-described "moderate conservative." "I've got no problem with anybody that's gay. I've got a good friend of mine that's gay, and one time in my life he was one of my biggest supporters, and I love him to death. But you know he never pushed any of that stuff, and, for the most part, I think most gay people don't. I think that gays have rights, but I don't think gays should have special rights." But when I asked him what those special rights consisted of, he was curiously vague. "If I can't go down and do the same thing a gay person is being allowed to do, then what's the point. I think we need a level playing field, and everybody needs to know where the goals are, and where the boundaries are, and we need to go forward . . . play the game." Talk of fair games, level playing fields, was juxtaposed against "special rights," which connoted rigged games, threats to individual self-discipline and plain unfairness.

Nancy Sunday told me that she often goes to a bar in town that's owned by a lesbian couple. "It's a gay bar, but just a relaxed place to hang out. I bring my friends. It's not a greasy biker bar." Yet she supported the OCA measure because she objects to "labeling people so much." She hates labels, she says. "Gay issues are sex issues and sex issues are private. Sometimes I joke and say that next sadomasochists are going to be asking for special rights. If I was a gay person, I wouldn't want special rights. I'm offended by the fact that on applications we're still asking what color people are. It should be decided on the basis of how well you do the job."

One didn't have to be a card-carrying conservative to wonder whether homosexuals had gone too far. Even liberal-leaning folks like forty-three-year-old Harry Boyle, a small businessman and member of the chamber of commerce, thought so. "I'm different," he tells me. He's married to an Asian woman and is a practicing Buddhist. "Liberal in some ways, but not in others," Boyle opposes "one group telling another group how they should live," and says that most of the members of the Oregon Citizens Alliance are "uneducated people with a logger mentality who just want to work forty hours a week and then go home and get drunk." His father was a logger, he says, so he can say this. He's friends with some of the lesbian businesswomen in town. Sometimes he asks people, just out of curiosity, "Would you shop at a place where you knew it was owned by people who were gay?" and most people reply no. Then he tells them, "Well, such-and-such a place is owned by gay people. They're shocked," says Harry. He opposes the charter amendment. "I don't think you need measures like that. Civil rights already exist in the Constitution. You don't need something stronger. If judges don't interpret the Constitution the way it was meant to be read, maybe you need a new charter. But if they do, you don't need it."

Harry draws the line when it comes to giving benefits to the partners of gay or lesbian state employees. "The thing that really disgusts me," he says, "is those people who want benefits. If you're in a homosexual relationship, you're at a higher risk of getting sick—you've got more than a two-to-one chance of contracting AIDS. Why should other people have to pay for it? Now, I don't think that gay people should be discriminated against, but *that's* a special right." Harry's antipathy toward domestic partnership benefits reflected a pervasive resentment toward state employees "feeding off the public trough," linked with the conservative understanding of homosexuals as a group who, having made "lifestyle choice," were now trying to wrest unreasonable demands from the state.[21] His words suggest that "special rights" rhetoric held appeal even among those who were at odds with the OCA.

Some observers suggest that homophobic attitudes correlate with lack of knowledge of or exposure to homosexuality. People who know gay people, who acknowledge them as living, breathing human beings, are less like to objectify them and see them as the other.[22] Yet in my conversations, I found that even many of those who thought of individual gay people as sympathetic and likable were often captivated by "special rights" rhetoric, a fact that suggests that in Timbertown, as in the nation as a whole, public opinion about homosexuality is shifting, malleable. There is a large group of people who, like Harry Boyle, make up an ambivalent majority: "Americans who don't want to discriminate against gays and don't want to accept them," who wanted them to have the same rights as everyone else, didn't want them to have "special rights."[23]

OCA rhetoric differentiated between "deserving" and "undeserving" minorities:

> STOP SPECIAL RIGHTS. Comparing homosexual practices to a person's ethnic heritage is a disgrace to the trials and struggles of America's true minorities. Attempting to create a minority classification based on wrong and potentially destructive practices is an insult to the citizens of this Great Country. Granting civil rights protections for homosexuality is nothing more than SPECIAL RIGHTS. Who else is afforded SPECIAL RIGHTS based upon wrong behaviors?[24]

Using figures derived from a 1988 marketing study that surveyed the readers of several gay magazines, reported by the *Wall Street Journal,* this flyer compared the average annual income of homosexuals, Hispanics, and blacks, claiming that "homosexuals earn, on average, four times as much as blacks, three times as much as Hispanics, and nearly twice the national average." According to the flyer, "homosexuals are far from being an 'oppressed minority.'" While black Americans suffered demonstrable economic deprivations suggested by patterns of discrimination and segregation, the average homosexual actually enjoys the benefits of "the American dream" at a far greater rate than the rest of the population. "These national statistics show that almost half of all practicing homosexuals, far from living in daily fear that they will lose their jobs due to discrimination, hold either professional or managerial positions. You're talking about two people with good jobs, lots of money, and no dependents."[25]

By asking for recognition as a legitimate minority, homosexual activists, says June Bonnard, are trying to "hijack the dignity of the black civil rights movement and the legacy of Dr. Martin Luther King, Jr." If the local charter measure passes, she writes, "cities will be forced to compete with 'upper class' homosexuals for any city contracts, job quotas or housing subsidies set aside for minorities, even though homosexuals are 500 per cent more prosperous than underprivileged African Americans."[26] Homosexuality, in other words, is a lifestyle choice, different from race or ethnicity, attributes that are allegedly more stable and beyond the realm of choice.

This position, which cast race and ethnicity as "essential" attributes against "chosen" sexual behaviors such as homosexuality, ignored recent scholarship that suggests that race, like sexuality, is an unstable complex of social meanings that is constantly being transformed. A notoriously slippery concept to define, few scholars today consider race a legitimate biological or genetic category. Technically, a race is a population that differs from others in the relative frequency of a certain gene or genes, but the intermixing of populations calls into question the notion that there are distinct races, possessing clear boundaries. This does not imply that racial differences do not exist: they have meaning because people act as though they have meaning. As Stuart Hall has put it, "People are all sorts of colors. The question is whether you are culturally, historically, politically Black."[27] At certain times, black people have organized culturally and politically to assert their oneness, but such unity is a strategic accomplishment, not a natural fact.

Much the same could be said of lesbians, gay men, and sexual minorities. In an earlier study, I explored the similarities and differences among the group of women who call themselves "lesbians," and even among lesbian-identified women of a particular age cohort, I found vast differences in identities. Some women considered themselves to be "born lesbians," having always felt different, and attracted to other females at an early age. Others never considered the possibility of their being lesbian until they fell in love with another woman, or became captivated by the thought of loving women through their exposure to the women's movement. For others, it was purely a matter of flux and change, and they moved in and out of heterosexual and homosexual relationships. Sexual identity, like racial identity, defies generalization: it is an individual, cultural, and political accomplishment.[28] In other words, all cultures are historically contingent and invented. None are objective and natural.

Such nuanced arguments never appeared in OCA rhetoric, of course, which generalized wildly about the experiences of racial and sexual minorities. Race, it suggested, is an essential attribute given at birth; homosexuality, in contrast, is simply a lifestyle choice; lesbians and gay men are trying to piggyback on to racial claims in order to wrest concessions from the state in the form of illegitimate rights and privileges. This divide-and-conquer strategy was designed to pit two traditional liberal constituencies, blacks and gays, against each other, and build a broader base for religious conservatives among black Christians and nonreligious whites. Nationally, Christian Coalition head Ralph Reed urged religious conservatives to "cast a wider net" and build bridges with black churches and moderate Republicans. In Timbertown, where the population of racial minorities was minuscule, the claim that gays were "illegitimate minorities" declared: we are not racists—we know a deserving minority when we see one. It's just that gays are not a deserving minority group.

By stirring festering resentments, and distinguishing between two different homosexual populations—"good gays" who are quiet and mind their own business and "bad gays" who organize politically to push their "agendas" on others—conservative rhetoric pushed to make the familiar strange. As a common refrain went: you can keep your habits to yourself, but when you push them on me—that's going too far. The secular frame emphasized the importance of separating the public and the private—one's private life is one's own business, but homosexuality should not be considered a public, protected minority status. Yet in essence the campaign proclaimed that the personal was indeed political, that private and public blurred. Even those who kept their sexuality private, such as the vast majority of lesbians and gays in Timbertown, were inherently problematic by their very existence. When conservative activists spoke about gay people, they were distant, shadowy, strangers without real names or flesh-and-blood identities. The sexualized "others" had no human faces, no individuality, no friends, no families, no jobs or hobbies. *They* did this. *They* did that. Defined by their sexual behavior alone, they were less than human and lacked the capacity to become potentially moral selves.

But fiery rhetoric was not enough. The OCA needed a way to transform inchoate anxieties and fears into moral indignation and anger. It needed to create an incident that provoked a sense of outrage, that possessed a concrete, immediate target. The target couldn't be an individual gay person—that would be too inflammatory, and could easily be interpreted simply as the work of religious homophobes. Nor could it be a representative of the organized lesbian/gay movement, which had no public presence in Timbertown. It had to be an institution, something impersonal and bureaucratic, something that was run by elites, financed by taxes, and had homosexual sympathies. Enter Head Start.

THE HEAD START INCIDENT

Head Start is a federally funded program for preschool-aged children of low-income families that serves sixty Timbertown children.[29] Its mission, based on the principles of psychologist Jean Piaget, is to create a rich environment for the development of children, which invites them to observe, to be active, to make choices, and to experiment. Nationally, Head Start has also taken on the goals of multiculturalism, promoting an "antibias curriculum" that urges teachers to display "images of diversity in family styles," including single mothers or fathers, extended families, interracial families, adopted families, families with physical disabilities, as well as gay or lesbian families. "Our goal is to make sure each child feels good about who he or she is. We don't judge people's religion, job, or family; we respect everyone's different ways to live," says a Head Start notice to teachers, who are asked to include lesbian or gay families in family units, and represent them on bulletin boards.

A nationally distributed Head Start curriculum guide defines homophobia as "a fear and hatred of gay men and lesbians backed up by institutional policies and power that discriminate against them." Teachers are advised: "You may decide not to use the words gay and lesbian, but the child deserves calm recognition of the reality of the composition of his family. It's almost worse to have a family unit that doesn't include them, that's saying to the child: all families are okay except yours.

"We must be especially vigilant in our actions to shape the values children will attach as they learn about the people in their world," states the curriculum guide. "If we don't they will learn by default the messages that are already prevalent out there and both we and they will contribute to perpetuating ideas which we do not want to replicate in our children's future." It instructs teachers to expect criticism from parents who object to the antibias efforts, and urges them to involve them in shaping the curriculum, noting, in a not-so-veiled reference to religious conservatives, that "respecting parents does not necessarily mean acquiescing to all their beliefs."[30]

Each year, in Timbertown and across the country, Head Start parents are invited to review books before they are placed in the program's libraries. They include books about such "nontraditional" families as single-parented and stepparented families, interracial families and homeless families, families of divorce, families that are headed by grandparents, families with adopted children, families where there are children of different races and children who are "different" in other ways—such as those with handicaps, or those who have been incarcerated, and those with gay or lesbian parents.

Typically, teachers at the county Head Start's twelve sites presented a list of books for parents to review. Upon their approval, the books were placed in local Head Start site libraries. In February 1994, much like any other year, a letter was sent to the parents of Head Start children inviting them to a meeting to review books for the Head Start classroom. And much like any other year, among the possible books, three—*Belinda's Bouquet, Asha's Mums,* and *Saturday Is Patty Day*—dealt with the subject of homosexuality.

Asha's Mums is fairly typical of the bunch. Asha's mother is in a long-term relationship with another woman. Planning a field trip to a science museum, Asha's teacher requests that the children bring a signed permission note from their parents. When Asha presents her slip, which is signed by her two mothers, to her teacher, Ms. Samuels threatens to keep Asha at home unless she fills out the form properly. Her classmates are drawn into the controversy, and one responds, "My dad says you can't have two moms." By the end of the book, Asha's lesbian mothers have educated the classmates and their teacher, and the kids ask them, nonchalantly, "Are you Mommy Number One or Mommy Number Two?"[31]

Few if any Timbertowners ever participated in the curriculum review meetings, which usually passed uneventfully. But in the midst of the charter amendment campaign, thirty-five people showed up for the meeting: a dozen parents who had kids in the program, and a few OCA members, most of whom did not. It was the largest and loudest meeting Head Start had seen in Timbertown in recent memory. Bob Bowen, a bearded father of a five-year-old boy who was enrolled in the program, stood up at the meeting and told the crowd that he believes the subject of homosexuality is too advanced for preschoolers. Parents signed their kids up for Head Start "hoping they would learn colors, and learn to count to ten. We didn't expect any kind of major social conditioning on gay issues before kindergarten."[32]

Pamela Sneed, the former valedictorian of Timbertown High School who had become county leader of the OCA, charged that Head Start had been taken over by people who are pushing a radical homosexual agenda. "Head Start's antibias curriculum places a federally funded, government stamp of approval on homosexuality," she charged, describing the book *Asha's Mums* as a "mind-bending moral journey for a four-year-old," which teaches children to "reject their father's traditions in the span of one picture book."

Such books promote homosexuality, equating it with marriage, and brand dissenters as "homophobes." But preschoolers are too young to deal with "such a politically charged sexual issue," she charged. "Parents should be concerned that the values they teach their children at home will be erased and new ones instilled. . . . This is social engineering for change at its most sinister, aimed directly at our most vulnerable members—young children." Moreover, "it validates our claim that government is promoting homosexuality."[33]

Objecting to the fact that the antibias curriculum defines homophobia as the fear and hatred of gay men and lesbians, and a form of gender bias, Sneed asked, "How far should we go along this line of thinking to avoid hurting anyone's feelings? Would they include racist or white supremacist families along with the eight categories targeted for anti-bias teaching? Maybe adding a book to the library titled *My Daddy Wears a White Hood at Night?* Why is it necessary for the school to pass judgment, pro or con, on the family structure of the child? A loving teacher could give individual children emotional support without teaching that the home environment is right or wrong." She called for the removal of the entire Head Start curriculum, including the parts that deal with racism, prejudice against people with physical disabilities and other biases.

Comments like these were fairly predictable, reflecting a familiar objection of religious conservatives to diversity training on the grounds that it usurps parental control of "values education," instilling a pluralist, secular humanist worldview. Rather than teaching children how to develop as individuals, conservatives believe that it is the role of the schools to protect young children's "innocence" and promote their parents' traditional values. As the same time, Sneed distinguished between "legitimate" and "illegitimate" minorities, charging that homophobia is not equivalent to racism.

Most surprising was the participation of non-evangelicals. Bob

Bowen could be seen around town wearing a skullcap, diaphanous clothing, and sporting a long white beard. Bowen, who was in his late thirties, moved up to Oregon from San Diego in the early 1980s, drawn by its natural beauty: "Southern California was getting too polluted, too many cars, that kind of thing." When we spoke in his modest house, which had little furniture, except for a conspicuous altar with a Buddha, a cross, a Star of David, and few of the trappings of consumer culture, he told me that he is the spiritual head of a small religious sect derived from what he calls "mystical Christianity," a blend of Buddhism, Hinduism, and Christianity, and yoga and meditation, which is, he says, based on the texts of a pre-Christian sect, and talked about his spiritual practices, which include yoga and meditation.

Bowen had long opposed nuclear energy, supported peace activism, and generally considered himself liberal—except when it came to abortion. When he moved to Oregon he had little intention of becoming an activist, he said, until he found out that his son was about to be exposed to a book "with a girl's name in it, who had two moms." He is not, he assures me, "antigay or antilesbian or pro-right-wing on that issue, or anything like that." Nonetheless, he said, this is "a sensitive issue." It was "an ignorant thing for a government agency to do in a small mill town–type environment like Timbertown. You know, you do a thing like that maybe in downtown Los Angeles, or San Francisco or some big inner city, but to impose it into some little countryish town in rural Oregon without talking to the parents, without making them feel okay about it, is something else."

Bowen claimed that when he first objected to the books, he was told to "go away." So he wrote a letter to the editor of the *Gazette* explaining why he objected to the gay-themed books—using rhetoric that if not lifted from OCA materials, certainly sounded as if it were. The books are written by homosexuals with a radical political agenda, he argued. They expose kids to the politically charged topic of homosexual rights at a tender age. Homosexuals should not be classified legally in the fashion of racial minorities. The homosexual groups that have been attempting to get these books into the curricula of schools across the United States are radical groups such as Queer Nation, a radical extremist group denounced even by most homosexuals. "These books are so controversial that when the head of the school

district in New York added them to the school curriculum he was
forced to resign because of the outraged public protests by parents.
Considering that occurred in New York City, I am rather amazed that
the leadership of Head Start thinks a smaller, more conservative town
like Timbertown might passively accept these books!"³⁴

The fact that a longhaired, self-proclaimed "radical environmen-
talist," who actually looked and sounded like one too, would support
the OCA agenda gave the controversy greater legitimacy and news
value, and before long Bowen became a poster boy opposed to the
"gay agenda." When the *Gazette* ran a front-page picture of Bowen,
Pamela Sneed sent a copy of the article to local television stations,
claiming that the Head Start school in Timbertown was trying to introduce a "homosexual curriculum." Television stations sent a camera
crew to capture the story on the evening news, but by the time they
arrived, the meeting was over and they couldn't find any of the principals involved. So they pointed the camera at the *Gazette* article. This,
in turn, generated more media coverage, and further claims on the
part of the OCA that government monies are supporting the "gay
agenda." By this time, news that Head Start was introducing tender children to the not-so-tender topic of homosexuality was spread-
ing like wildfire throughout town. Head Start agreed to meet with
Bowen and other parents to try to convince them of the value of the
antibias curriculum.

"The children are our future! Diversity is our strength!" exclaimed Cindy Chavez, Head Start director, who defended the
agency's choice of books on the grounds that they were not at all sexually suggestive, and read passages from the books to prove her point.
Asha's Mums and *Heather Has Two Mommies* "simply describe families
in which the two people doing the parenting are members of the
same sex," said Chavez. The OCA had misrepresented their efforts,
she argued: sexual diversity was only a small part of a larger move toward inclusivity; it didn't promote homosexuality, but simply created
a more inclusive environment so that all sorts of children feel accepted in preschools. Besides, the books would be used as resource
material and not for classroom instruction.

Chavez refused to remove the books from the curriculum, and announced that Head Start would continue to include sexual orientation as one of the eight categories targeted for antibias teaching. That

only fueled the fire, and angry parents repeatedly interrupted facilitators of the meeting as they tried to explain their position. By the end of the meeting, parents of Head Start children voted, twenty-three to five, to omit books involving gay and lesbian parents from the curriculum.

Even the Timbertown *Gazette,* normally sympathetic to the rhetoric of diversity and inclusivity, came out against the circulation of the gay-themed books at Head Start. "We have already done enough to destroy the brief innocence of childhood," said the editorial. "School children are taught to fear strangers. We teach them about AIDS when they are still playing with dolls and toy cars. Preschool has enough to do teaching colors and numbers and such. . . . Head Start should be a politically demilitarized zone . . . if a child at Head Start comes from a family with homosexual parents, that child should not be stigmatized in any way. Nor should the family be characterized negatively. If the topic comes up (which seems highly unlikely), then it can be dealt with."

So powerful was the rhetoric of childhood innocence that even liberals were persuaded by it. But the suggestion that childhood should or could ever be a politically neutral zone flew in the face of the OCA's claim that values are always political. Even according to the OCA's logic, the issue was not a matter of taking values out of the classroom, it was a matter of *whose* values are held up as good and true: liberal ones, which encourage students to explore and evolve, or conservative ones, which encourage them to follow tradition.

Bowing to parental pressure, the chair of Head Start's governing board agreed to exclude gay-themed books from the Timbertown classroom, and promised to review the agency's policy of introducing books depicting homosexual families, stating that the policy would also be reviewed by the agency's parent advisory council, and officials at the U.S. Department of Health and Human Services, which funds the program. The county's Head Start agency admitted that the gay-themed books were "more controversial" than it had anticipated, and it had failed to "take the time to handle the situation as well as we should have."[35]

Bowen was pleased. The OCA helped him to gain attention for his cause. Without them, he said, nobody would have paid him much attention. When he approached Head Start, they treated him with contempt. "They viewed us as dumb hicks, just stupid mill town types who wouldn't understand subtle things like curriculum, so they tried to sneak the curriculum in. But you can't just impose your little pet curriculum and then try to hide it." The experience also changed his perception of the OCA:

> Before the conflict, I had this idea that all OCA people were neo-Nazis or something, but they weren't the monsters that the media had made them out to be. We were all interested in parents' rights. No, I didn't meet any that seemed like Adolf Hitler, but I met a lot of nice ladies who bake apple pies and spend quality time with their children, and nice gentlemen who coach Little League and work hard to support their families. Apple pies and Little League may sound a bit old-fashioned in the era of Amy Fisher and the Menendez brothers, but that was my impression of the supposedly scary OCA.

What was going on here? Was Bowen a longhaired dupe of the OCA? Perhaps. But it didn't take an evangelical Christian to support the OCA's patriarchal restoration project. In Bowen's terms, nostalgic references to apple pies and Little League become metaphors for "make room for Daddy" families where fathers ran the roost and mothers tended to the home fires—a family structure that has long faded away. It didn't take a conservative Christian to find masculinist values appealing. Sometimes angry white men even had beards and long hair.

CHAPTER 7

We Are All Queer—Or Are We?

"They've got a petition against gay rights in front of the post office," said a man who rushed into the bookstore on Main Street out of breath. Janice Trump, working the cash register, was taken back. "A petition against *what?*" She ran down the block to the post office, and cornered Jeri Cookson, who was perched outside collecting signatures to place the charter amendment on the ballot. "Why are you doing this? What are you scared of?" she asked, her voice shaking. Janice had never met Jeri, but knew her by sight. Pamela Sneed, a former valedictorian of Timbertown High School, was there as well. Janice shot them a harsh look. "What are you going to accomplish by all this hate?" Jeri, flustered, stammered, "It's not hateful. I'm-m-m not scared of anything," she replied. "It's just that they're trying to take over!"

Janice walked down the street, back to the bookstore, and told her sister about the incident. Instantly, the store, a hub for progressive people in town, was buzzing with the news. "Did you see what's going on down at the post office?" By the end of the day, everyone who was anyone knew about the OCA's charter amendment to prohibit "minority status, affirmative action, quotas, special class status, or any similar concepts, based on homosexuality."

"Come on, do you really think Timbertown is about to be overrun by screaming homos?" a woman asked incredulously. "It's not a local issue. I never heard sexual orientation mentioned in this community."[1] Indeed, few people in town had even met any openly gay people, which made the "special rights" claim seem all the more ludicrous. "Do homosexuals have special rights in Timbertown now? No. Have any homosexuals ever asked for any? No," proclaimed an editorial in the local paper. "I have never heard anybody of any political persuasion suggest that homosexuals in the City of Timbertown have special rights. What form could special rights take in the city? The city can't give homosexuals preference for hiring because the city never asks an applicant anything about sexual preference. . . . When we have a hoard of militant gays pressuring the city for special rights, then we can pass a change to the city's charter to stop them. In the meantime, we should tell the OCA to peddle its paranoia elsewhere."[2]

The OCA, many believed, was creating a panic over a nonissue. Chester Rideout, a physical education teacher, said it reminded him of a scene in *The Music Man,* where a band director arrived in town and "pitched a fit about a pool hall," causing public concern about its impact upon the town's youth. "So the band director says, 'Boy, I've got a solution for this, I've got a band, and if they play an instrument the kids won't be in the pool hall.' " Rideout pondered whether a similar dynamic was occurring in Timbertown. "We don't have a problem with homosexuals here, but they seem to be creating one." He was skeptical at first and thought, Who's going to sign the petition? Nobody will sign that! But he was wrong. Within weeks, OCA activists in town collected 783 signatures, qualifying the ballot for the local election. "My God! People are signing it!" Rideout realized. "How can they believe that they have to be protected, that there is something evil here?"

It didn't take a progressive mind to be put off by the OCA. Lots of people in town considered its activists religious zealots who were meddling in people's affairs and pushing a radical political agenda that was not altogether different from those "crazy lefties." These folks weren't particularly tolerant of other groups, and didn't have any higher motives for respecting human dignity—they were simply old-fashioned Oregon individualists with a streak of redneck in them. One fellow I met in a bookstore on Main Street, dressed in overalls with the rough hands of a laborer, railed against "those fundies," and then proceeded to ask me which church I belonged to. "I'm Jewish," I told him. "Oh, you're one of *them.* Where ya from?" "Eugene," I said. "Oh yeah, they're lots of them over there. The mayor, for one." When I told him that the mayor was not in fact Jewish, he replied, "He looks like one, and acts like one."

Now that the OCA had created the "problem" of "special rights," local people were faced with devising a suitable response. How would they defend the rights of gay people—without a gay community? Few people in town even knew any gay people, let alone any who were willing to be openly identified as such, and gay people from Portland and Eugene could easily be dismissed as outsiders. Timbertown's lesbian business owners, fearful of losing customers, weren't about to come out publicly. Cindy Barber, who ran a used bookstore on Main Street with her girlfriend, Sammie, was forced to make a choice: Should she come out publicly against the measure, or should she try to ignore it? She decided to place a sign opposing the measure in the store window. "Sammie didn't want the sign in the window, she didn't want me to become active, she was very concerned with what it would do to business." "Lesbians in town had a lot to lose," agreed Janice Trump. "So it was up to the rest of us to oppose the measure." Though the campaign was designed to consolidate the political base of the conservative organization, it also consolidated the progressive base in town, bringing together many individuals who did not know one another before.

The OCA had cast gay people as strangers, predators, and parasites, outsiders in the town's moral universe. With this set of images, how could citizens readmit the other as neighbor? How could they make the strange familiar? As a gay activist from nearby Eugene suggested, "You don't have to love gays to support gay rights. It's not a homosexual issue. It's just a matter of basic rights." You didn't have to love gays and lesbians to join up—you simply had to empathize with them.

Identity politics, which provided the model for most lesbian/gay organizing during the past few decades, suggests that politics should emerge directly from one's own identity. It establishes, political theorist Jodi Dean writes, "a space of belonging, a community that strengthens its members and gives them a base from which they can say to others: I am different, recognize me."[3] And it privileges members of minority groups as actors on their own behalf. In the absence of a gay community, Timbertown's progressive activists were forced to depart from the identity politics model. Their politics of empathy called on heterosexuals to include lesbians and gay men in their imagination without necessarily feeling totally comfortable with them, suggesting they could support gay rights without being gay them-

selves. The campaign to defend lesbian and gay rights would be organized, for all intents and purposes, by heterosexual women.[4]

Janice and her sister, June, called their friends, people they knew
who would be concerned: Robin Bergman, a fellow organic gar-
dener who they knew felt strongly about maintaining Timbertown as
an open, inviting community for all; Julie Caponi, who worked in
social services and also lived on a farm outside of town; Sylvia Watkins, a Presbyterian and former school board member; and Cassie
Smith, a secretary at the middle school who had two children in the
school district. They were in their thirties and forties, mothers and
relative newcomers who had been active in the community, mainly in
the schools.

Though she had lived in Timbertown for ten years, Cassie still felt
like an outsider. She moved there when her husband, an insurance
agent, was relocated by his company. Cassie is an attractive woman in
her early forties who has olive skin, smooth brown hair, and an easy
manner. Living in Timbertown has been, she says, a "learning experience." She spent most of her life in urban liberal enclaves, surrounded
by people who "thought pretty much the way I did." She was, she
says, "very sheltered." When she and her husband first moved to Timbertown, she felt very isolated, as if she had "landed on a different
planet." It was, she says, "a totally different world." Most people had
lived there for generations and were suspicious of outsiders. When
she first moved to town, with a small son, she commuted to work,
leaving her child with baby-sitters, which raised some eyebrows in
town. Still, she welcomed the challenge: living in Timbertown has
forced her to get to know people, people with conservative worldviews who were very different from her. She kept her kids in public
schools because she wants them to be exposed to "all walks of life." In
small communities, says Cassie, "if you don't want your kids to get
calls or threats, you have to live side by side with these people, without jeopardizing your own beliefs. I think we've been pretty successful in doing that, but it's been a struggle."

What she didn't say, but what I learned from talking with others
in town, was that by the time she reached her junior year in high
school, Cassie's oldest daughter, Samantha, a popular, outgoing girl
who excelled in sports, decided she was a lesbian. Cassie didn't go
around telling very many people about it. Like many parents, even

liberal, open-minded ones like herself, she was uncomfortable with the thought that her daughter might be different, that she wouldn't have a "normal" family, that she herself may not have grandchildren. Perhaps it was just a phase, she reassured herself, and Samantha would eventually change. In the meantime, why make a big public statement about it? Still, Cassie feared for her child. She knew that many people in Timbertown were threatened by those who are different: kids called each other names, parents avoided rubbing up against them. She couldn't just sit back and let a small group of religious extremists pass a law that would condemn homosexuality. Race, she thought, was an even bigger stumbling block; the growing number of Latino workers in the community who were increasingly evident around town really got people's blood boiling. But what it all came down to was a fear of change. "The OCA and its supporters were threatened by the thought that Timbertown was no longer Timbertown. But I thought: great. Change is good. I like small communities but I don't like it when they're closed to outside influence or ideas. The time was right. Things needed to happen."

Cassie offered her home, a cozy old Victorian in the center of town, for a meeting to discuss a communitywide response to the OCA ballot measure. She, Janice, and June invited everyone they could think of; much to their surprise and amazement, sixty people showed up. There were members of the Presbyterian church, and organic farmers who had been in the back-to-the-land movement, relatives of the few openly gay people in town, and young families from California. There were ministers, small business owners, people who lived up in the hills and rarely came into town, as well as people who were well-known progressive activists, some of whom knew one another from an earlier effort to block Wal-Mart from building a huge new store in town. Several worked in the school district—as teachers, teachers' aides, secretaries. There were a couple of lesbians and a few straight men, but no gay men. If few OCA members were college-educated, this group was, in contrast, a relatively educated, cosmopolitan one; if OCA members repudiated the values of the 1960s —personal self-expression, social experimentation, tolerance of difference—this group proudly embraced them. They called themselves Community Action Network (CAN).

How, they wondered, could they convince people in town that the proposed charter measure was destructive? The year before, opponents of Measure 9 spoke of the evils of "discrimination," and car bumper stickers exhorted the public to "protect everyone's basic rights." Such rhetoric worked fine for middle-class, urban liberals but across the state, in places like Timbertown, it went over like a lead balloon. In order to convince their neighbors that the measure would be bad for the community, they would have to mount a homegrown, grassroots operation. Slick media ads were out. Timbertowners shop at the same supermarket, and send their kids to the same schools. Personal contact would be key.

Lon Mabon and the OCA were committed to the belief that they were engaged in a war for the preservation of American morals. They spoke of battles, and of the necessity to defend the family against threats from immoral others. Confrontation seemed to fan the flames of righteous anger. The question arose: How would CAN respond to all the talk of sin and immorality? Sylvia Watkins argued that they shouldn't even try. "We're never going to win on those terms," she urged her neighbors. "We need to fight them on the divisiveness issue—the fact that the OCA came from outside to take over the town." The OCA campaign wasn't evidence of a "culture war" as Christians liked to suggest; the problem was that a small bunch of outside agitators had come in to stir things up and promote a vision of Christianity that relatively few shared. "It's those neo-Nazi churches, they're the problem," said Janice Trump, referring to the Sacred Fate Temple and the small mom-and-pop fundamentalist churches scattered throughout town. "Isn't Christianity supposed to be about love and service and acceptance and sacrifice, and helping one another?"

They wanted to steer clear of a negative campaign that would disintegrate into name-calling. "You can't change hearts and minds with an argument," said a divorced mother of three small children. "But how do you talk with a fundamentalist? There is a huge gap between us and the other half of the citizens of this town—and if we are ever to have a healthy, caring, and just society, we must find a way to bridge this gap."

> Anyone who has tried talking with a fundamentalist—the kind who supports the OCA, passes petitions, pickets and obstructs abortion clinics, holds hostile signs on the streets, or who just sends money through the mail to Lon Mabon—has experienced some degree of the frustration that comes from a failure to be heard. Picture yourself confronting one of these people on the street, or in your local shopping mall. There you

are, relatively calm and centered. You approach, marshalling your very best arguments, your kindest and most reasonable manner. You begin very calmly, listening politely to their rhetoric (it's exactly what you have read in the newspaper when they are quoted) and then presenting your thoughts, experiences and ideas. They repeat exactly what they have told you already, adding Bible verses, dark references to a jealous and wrathful God, and prophesying the imminent collapse of the family, nation and democracy. You find yourself becoming irritated because no matter how hard you try, you are not being heard and they keep repeating the same things over and over again. This is not a reasonable conversation—it is going nowhere except in circles. They are raising their voices and so are you. They look intense, self-righteous, maybe even smug. Eventually, you and they back off. You may feel that you made some points, or you may not. But chances are that you feel frustrated, bewildered and angry about the denseness and obtuseness you must encounter. How can these people who claim to be patriotic citizens and good Christians be so harsh, unloving and undemocratic?[5]

So, instead of trying to wage a protracted war against a small but well-organized enemy, members of CAN decided to shift the terms of the battle. "Responding to an attack with equal or greater force can only perpetuate the process of fighting and war," warned a memo on "How to Talk to the OCA" circulating among progressive community activists. "Our options are to engage in a never ending battle, or to diffuse the controversy by taking the campaign to a higher level, while at the same time contributing to positive social change."[6] It exhorted activists to "avoid using judgment language like 'You're wrong,' 'That doesn't make sense,' 'How can you be so narrow?'" and instead "Keep it open—'I don't see it that way,' 'It seems to me there's another way.' 'There are sides to the issue I would like to share with you.' Give the aggressors the chance to change their minds without losing face or self-esteem."[7]

Rather than engage in the religious right's culture war, CAN members would educate people to appreciate diversity in the community. They would sponsor multicultural community fairs where different groups could bring ethnic foods, and where cultural diversity could be spotlighted. They would counter rumor and misinformation by giving presentations to service organizations in town, by writing letters to the editor, and by making local radio talk show appearances. They would avoid confronting OCA activists face-to-face. Rather than label people as right or wrong, bad or good, they would try to get them to see things differently. As they saw it, OCA activists weren't bad people—aside perhaps from their leaders, who manipulated their unsuspecting followers—they were simply uneducated, misguided folks. Rather than simply do what it took to get votes, they would educate people for the long haul. CAN's first flyer depicted a group of townspeople huddled together in front of a covered bridge, invoking the historic heritage of the town:

> OUR COMMUNITY IS OUR STRENGTH. We are a group of community members who support individual legal privacy and cultural and genetic diversity. We honor the US Constitution and the Oregon Constitution which already states, "No law shall be passed granting any citizen or class of citizens privileges, or immunities which, upon the same terms, shall not equally belong to all citizens." DON'T ALLOW THE OCA TO DIVIDE US.[8]

EMPATHY TALES

To counter the message of division and decline, CAN members spoke of the importance of respecting difference and protecting diversity in a small town, connecting the protection of minority rights to the greater good of the community. The OCA had tried to prohibit homosexuals from claiming minority status, suggesting that homosexuality is a choice, while race or ethnicity were not freely chosen. Homosexuals, liberal activists responded, were very much a minority group that, like African Americans, Latinos, and others, deserved protection. To make this point, CAN members told stories—empathy tales—gathered from personal experience, such as this one from Marianne Woods, whose family had been in Timbertown for generations:

> I grew up and went to school in Timbertown during and after the war years. It was a pretty sheltered existence. I knew nothing of the Japanese-American internment camps. The horrors of the death camps in Eastern Europe seemed distant, foreign, and pretty much irrelevant in my life. I was taught to hate the Japanese, who were called "Japs," though of course I never knew one then. To a somewhat lesser extent, I was taught to hate the Germans. My own strong German heritage was denied, I guess because I probably would have asked too many questions. I don't remember

ever seeing an African American in Timbertown in those years. My family used terms like "nigger-toes" for Brazil nuts and "catch a nigger by the tail" and no one thought anything about it. I didn't even know the word "homosexual" until after I was married, although I undoubtedly knew people who were, may have even had relatives who were. We studied the Civil War in pretty simplistic terms: every war had a right and a wrong side. Since almost all of my ancestors came West before the Civil War it was easy to assume they were all Northern sympathizers (I know now it was very likely the other way around). The "covered wagon days" were lauded as the great Western Migration; the free homestead land claims were a great gift of the U.S. government. I didn't think to ask where the government got that land to give away. I knew nothing of "the Trail of Tears and Sorrow" that Native Americans were forced to follow. I thought they lived on reservations by choice. This was the world that people my age in Timbertown grew up in. I understand this world, and I am ashamed of it.

For Marianne, empathy with gay people grew out of an emerging understanding that, as a longtime member of the community, she contributed to marginalizing others, particularly racial others, and should therefore take a stand against such beliefs. Marianne, who traced her roots to a wagon train that arrived in Oregon in the 1840s, told her audience, "I was once a racist, a homophobe. Now I know the truth." Her words suggested that you too can overcome your blindness, you too can come to see the world differently. The longer one's family had been in Oregon, the more credibility one had to make such claims, it seemed, and I frequently heard the phrase, "as a fourth-generation Oregonian," or "as a person whose roots go back to Jesse Applegate [an Oregon pioneer], I believe that . . ." In Timbertown, and across the state, it is common to see people ride around in pickup trucks bearing bumper stickers that read "Oregon Native." Long-standing animosity toward Californians made such appeals attractive: it gave self-described natives legitimacy and authenticity, and positioned them as insiders. Even the left invoked nativist identifications, if only to decry racist nativism.

The world Marianne described in her testimonial, filled with racist name-calling and ignorant of sexual diversity, had all but passed into history. The sundown laws, which prohibited blacks from circulating freely at night, had been taken off the books, though one woman told me that as late as the 1970s a neighbor touted the virtues of the community, telling her, "The best thing about Timbertown is that we ain't got no foreigners or niggers here." Today, the town is somewhat more diverse, and if people still hold racist views, they tend to keep them to themselves. Homosexuality is no longer a dirty, hidden secret, though for many it was still a distant reality; you could now see the occasional happy, healthy lesbian or gay man on television. The name-calling, the harassment, the violence, persists today, to be sure, but when people use the N-word, or call someone a fag, they do so with knowledge of the power those words have to silence and efface the other. Willful hate and harassment had all but replaced the unreflexive racism, sexism, and homophobia of the past.

The few people of color living in Timbertown knew this all too well. They told stories about Filipino kids harassed on the street by the cops who thought they were Latino, and the struggles the black Methodist minister endured while living in town. There is, says Ann Ashihara, a clear pecking order. "Hispanics are sometimes okay, and maybe Asians, because Asians can be intelligent. But blacks are off-limits." That gives little comfort to Ann, who is from the Pacific Islands, and whose mixed-race children have often been called "niggers" even though they're not black, who has experienced the pain of watching her eldest son, when he was six years old, try to rub off his color so that he could look like everyone else. Another son came home from first grade one day and told her that a little girl hated him because he was black. A third son had a girl bar the door and say, "I'm sorry, black people can't come in here." The clearest indicator of racism, she tells me, is that few white people in town look kindly upon their children dating someone of a different race. "People have a hard time accepting people who are different." So when the Oregon Citizens Alliance came to town, Ann and her husband said, "That's enough."

Still, people of color kept a low profile during the campaign. Perhaps some were leery of drawing parallels between race and sexuality, wondering whether the two were really as equivalent as some suggested, or perhaps they feared further harassment if they stuck their necks out. It was therefore left to more established members of the community to make the case for a politics of empathy. For Chester and Martha Rideout, that wasn't very difficult at all. "You should see what our family tree looks like," Nancy told me. "There's a gay brother, and we have a mixed-race, partially black niece. We have a Jewish sister-in-law, they have two children, so that makes a Jewish niece and nephew. We have a Hispanic sister-in-law, we have a Down's syndrome nephew, and my brother has a home for three other Down's syndrome adults. You know, any of these people could be a target for somebody coming through town. We take this very personally because that's just among our brothers and sisters—and just within our generation." The Rideouts talked about the hidden diversity beneath their family's seemingly "normal" exterior, describing their vicarious experience of marginality, and their responsibility to embrace diversity. They suggested that minorities, whether or not they were visible, were deeply embedded in the community—it was impossible to draw boundaries around the community unambiguously, for nearly every Timbertowner surely had a relative or friend, or a relative of a friend who was black or Latino, or gay.

The politics of empathy embodied an understanding of childhood as a time of struggle and a model of parents as nurturers and educators in that struggle, and in the subsequent struggle of life. Conservatives understood childhood as a time of innocence; their "strict parent" morality valued moral strength, respect for authority, adherence to rules, and discipline—a style mirrored in the hierarchical structure of the OCA. Lon Mabon ran a tight ship, and local activists followed his lead. They saw themselves engaged in a war for preservation of their community, and were willing to do whatever it took to win. Liberals, in contrast, saw childhood as a time of struggle out of ignorance into knowledge, emphasizing communication and education, rather than discipline and punishment.[9] George Lakoff, describing this liberal worldview, speaks of the centrality of a particular model of child rearing that declares that "when children are respected, nurtured, and communicated with from birth they gradually enter into a lifetime relationship of mutual respect, communication, and caring with their parents."[10] Indeed, if one listened closely to the stories of CAN members, you could hear this understanding at work.

The Rideouts and other liberal supporters of gay rights saw themselves as nurturant parents whose goal was to love, empathize with, and respect others. Their faith in the redemptive power of education led them and other members of CAN to speak passionately about the importance of preserving free, quality education for all, and to see schooling as an essential component of a democratic culture. Mary Skill, the mother of two teenage girls, was wary of religious involvement in the schools because she felt that it foreclosed open communication. "Public education is the great leveler, the core of democracy. Anybody can get a good education if you have a strong public education system." Ann Ashihara agreed. "I have seen people change over the years," she said. "In the schools, we've had mothers who were very young when they had their children—they may have been in a violent relationship or whatever. I've seen some of them go back to school. And then when they become enlightened, they become a different person. Their whole aura changes. Sometimes they decide they don't want to be the kind of parent they were before, and they change." Perhaps, she reasoned, the same would be true of those who were leading the crusade against homosexuality: they simply needed to be educated.

CAN activists hoped that, once educated, Timbertowners would realize that homosexuals, like blacks and other minority groups, were normal upstanding members of the community—as "normal as you and me." A mild-mannered mother of two who heard about the initiative went door-to-door speaking with her neighbors about it. "They're no different from you or me," she said. "I have had friends who are gay and they never would have been able to get me to sleep with them—nor would they have tried."[11] A man spoke of a gay friend. "I know he is just wanting to settle down in a monogamous relationship and get on with the business of life. I also know he is a devoted Christian who believes that love of all life is the prime spiritual teaching."[12]

The Presbyterian church, under the stewardship of Henry Chomsky, became the institutional home of the politics of empathy, offering prayer services and lectures dedicated to the theme of tolerance, and galvanizing the congregation to organize against the OCA. It even sponsored a performance by Heartsing, a lesbian choir from Eugene. Speaking of that event, which brought forty out lesbian women to sing at the church, Sylvia Watkins recalled, "We enabled people to interact with those who were openly gay and show that you could still relate to them, you know, as people, and that they are just 'normal,' just people like anyone else. Just like people who have been sitting next to you every week in church, serving on committees. They hold down jobs, they pay their taxes. Their kids go to school. They are just like anyone else. You can't tell if they . . . they don't have any identifying characteristics. The church kept pushing that and pushing it. And tried to open the doors to other people. To come and hear before you make judgments. Come and meet people. And come and be together, and realize that when you are worshipping, you are all worshipping together, regardless of what your faith calls the Supreme Being. Or beings."

Empathy tales showcased wholesome, "normal" gay people who had families, attended church, worked jobs, paid taxes—"good gays." Following the logic of normalization, they substituted the OCA's image of homosexual "pollution" with the belief that homosexuals are "our neighbors" and no different from "you and me," drawing parallels between racial, ethnic, and sexual others, and suggesting that gays are "legitimate minorities" who, like other marginalized groups, are the targets of discrimination, and therefore deserve legal protection. CAN sponsored an ad in the local paper under the headline: "No Special Rights. Just Human Rights."

> Are these special rights?
> —being employed
> —buying a house
> —walking in public without being harassed or assaulted
> —owning a business
> —receiving city services
> —paying taxes
> Promote reason and justice—vote no on the charter amendment

The OCA measure proposes to prohibit the city from extending minority status, but what it really does is ban civil rights protections, claimed a flyer. It "makes it illegal for our local governments to do anything to protect your basic human rights." Additionally, it could prevent schools or libraries from getting periodicals that the OCA thinks "promote homosexuality, such as the *Oregonian, Newsweek,* or the *New York Times,*" or the works of people like Socrates, Walt Whitman, and Somerset Maugham. While the measure claims that it does "not limit constitutional rights," its opponents countered that it "violates the basic tenets of fairness and justice upon which our nation is founded."[13] Gay rights, by implication, are not "special rights" at all. "The measure is falsely advertised as preventing special rights. But what the measure actually does is prevent *equal* rights."[14] As a CAN flyer proclaimed: "It would be very wrong to pass a law to encourage discrimination against weak people, sick people, or addicts, or victims of child abuse. It's distressing that some people are asking us to consider such a thing."

CAN's politics of empathy argued for the normalization of homosexuality on the basis of an essentialist understanding of sexuality that claimed the boundaries separating the homo and hetero worlds were fixed, essential, impermeable—a position embraced most enthusiastically by parents of gay children.

"THEY JUST CAN'T HELP IT"

By chance, two out of seven members of the city council, as well as the mayor, had gay children. "To be honest with you, one of my children is homosexual," seventy-year-old Martha Jensen, a city councilor, told me. When the ballot measure was initially proposed, Martha was incensed. She couldn't imagine why anyone would make a public issue out of something that seemed so private. She had never politicized the issue, so why should others? She slowly walked me over to a corner of her living room where a dozen or so framed photographs of family members at Christmas, weddings, and different family occasions were displayed and pointed to a photograph of a nice-looking woman in her thirties, wearing hiking gear. Of her daughter's homosexuality, she says, "I've known it for at least five or six years, since my husband died." When her daughter came out to Martha, she was shocked, and yet "the minute she told me I realized that I had known that for a long time. And hadn't allowed it to come to the surface. But I think God loves us all, really I do, and I know this is not an 'acquired' relationship because this child, I can think now, many times as she was a little toddler, or a little older than that she didn't want anything to do with anything feminine. And as I told her, I love her dearly, she's my baby, but she has picked a difficult life. She didn't pick it. I think it was dealt to her."

As I spoke with Martha, I couldn't help but think of my own mother, exactly the same age, though living three thousand miles away. On my mother's bedroom dresser is a framed photograph of me and my partner, Nancy, and our young son. Though it was initially very difficult for my mother to come to terms with my homosexuality, over time she has come to love and accept me and has welcomed my chosen family into her own with unanticipated ease—except when faced with the challenge of telling friends and neighbors. She has come to terms with my homosexuality, in part, by thinking of it as a kind of disability, a congenital deformity: "She just can't help it." My homosexuality, she believes, is a biological orientation, an aberration over which I have little choice. In my mother's lower-middle-class Jewish world, homosexuality, like a physical disability, elicits both shame and sympathy. You don't go around saying nasty things about poor people like homosexuals—or quadriplegics—but you don't get too close to them either. If they happen to be members of your family, you come to terms with their "spoiled identity" and you love them, but you don't go around publicizing it. Much the same was true of Martha Jensen.

I asked Martha whether it was difficult for her as the mother of a gay child during the OCA campaign, and whether she felt moved to talk about her daughter with others. "There was nothing to talk about," she replied. "Nobody ever asked me or nobody ever suspected, or if they did, they were polite enough not to say anything." Martha did speak with Kathy Young, the mayor, her best friend, who has a gay son. But beyond her small circle of friends, she kept things quiet. She didn't even talk with Cliff Richards, who was also on the city council and who had a daughter about the same age as Martha's who was a lesbian as well. None of them ever spoke out publicly about it, preferring to keep things quiet. They loved their gay children, but they were members of an older generation that didn't speak about such things in polite company; sex, they believed, is a private matter.

That wasn't true of Bill and Diane Freeman, who were in their mid-forties. Bill, who had grown up in a small rural town in California, had been a forest service worker and a navy man before moving to Washington, D.C., to take a job as an engineering consultant. Having tired of the big city, the Freemans moved to Timbertown in the late 1980s in search of a simpler way of life. Timbertown reminded Bill of the small town of his youth. They bought a house, Diane became a therapist, and Bill a househusband. Bill soon got restless and began to yearn for some of the urban amenities he had enjoyed in D.C.—a good cup of coffee, and the *Wall Street Journal*—but they were no-where to be found. "That was a rude shock," he recalled.

Since they had saved some money, Bill decided to open up an espresso shop in town. They found an old storefront, fixed it up, and bought all the necessary equipment. It was a lot of work, but Bill be-lieved it was worth it. For the first time one could buy a cappuccino in town, and you could even read the *Wall Street Journal* while you sipped it. The store signified more than a fancy cup of coffee to the Free-mans: it meant that they were introducing something new and different to the people of Timbertown, who struck them as sheltered. But the shop required far more work than they had anticipated, and the payoffs were relatively slim; as a consultant, Bill could earn in one hour what he was making there for a whole day's work. And though he and Diane were doing their best to fit in, and create a different kind of world for themselves, they were increasingly alienated from Tim-bertown, which they referred to as "a redneck vortex." When the OCA came to town and began to organize against gay rights, that was the final straw.

Bill has a gay son, Doug, from a previous marriage. Bill loves his son, and accepts his homosexuality, though he wasn't always comfort-able with it. When he started telling a few friends about his son, they told him it was important for him to tell others, that people in town should know that gay people have families. He agreed to tell his story to the *Gazette,* and the following week, the local paper was embla-zoned with the headline "Parents of a Gay Son Tell Their Story."

> Bill Freeman had a sinking suspicion about his son. When the boy was 3, Freeman said, "I began noticing that my son didn't do what I'd considered normal boy things." The boy, Doug, preferred playing with Barbie dolls to toying with swords or rolling in the dirt, said Freeman. "He didn't do the usual go-out-and-slay-the-world boys' thing," he said. As Freeman later discovered, his son was gay. While the prospect of having a homo-sexual child was initially disturbing for Freeman, he has learned to accept his son's sexual orientation and to be proud of the boy he raised. And he wants others, especially in Timbertown, to understand what it feels like to be the parent of a homosexual child.
>
> Initially, he said, he thought he had control over his son's destiny. "I thought I could get him interested in hunting and physical things," Free-

man said. When Doug was 13, Freeman said, he had a girlfriend. Freeman breathed a sigh of relief. His suspicions, he thought, were unfounded. But when Diane, his present wife, met Doug, "She immediately recognized what he was." Freeman said looking back, he realizes now that this denial was based in large measure on fear. "I didn't want him to be gay," he said. "I lived in fear of the 'homosexual lifestyle'. I didn't want him to be a raging street queen. I know first hand, by raising a gay son, that in his case it wasn't a choice. I know that in his case he wasn't subjected to a group of homosexuals who made him 'turn' gay. I know he has no desire to try to make other young men gay, in fact, he doesn't find heterosexual men attractive. . . ."

Diane Freeman, his wife: "After doing research and listening to what was said to me while I was growing up, I learned that there are two basic stereotypes: If you talk about it with children, they can become gay, and that it's abnormal and people choose to be that way. . . . I learned that what I grew up with was incorrect information," she said. "What I found out was that being gay or lesbian was not a choice for most people and that there's not necessarily any familial patterns that 'make' someone that way like a domineering mother or an absent father."[15]

Like Martha Jensen, the Freemans distanced themselves from the developmental model, which understood homosexuality to be the product of a psychological failure rooted in family dynamics, and from the moral traditionalist model, which imagined that it was a matter of willful perversion, whether by choice or seduction. Homosexuality, they declared, was not a choice at all: it was an innate condition fixed at birth. One can understand the appeal of this narrative, particularly as a way of countering religious right rhetoric. It located the source of homosexuality in biology and the body rather than in morality and sin, and let parents off the hook: it wasn't their fault that their kids turned out gay—it was a historical accident, a product of nature, not nurture. At the same time, all the talk of kids who refuse to "roll in dirt" like "normal" boys should was highly conservative in many respects. It maintained a dichotomous notion of gender that associated boyishness with stereotypically male activities, imagining all deviations from hegemonic masculinity (and by implication, femininity) as evidence of deviations in terms of sexual object choice as well. And it implored its audience to embrace and tolerate deviations from the sex/gender system in the service of reinforcing the naturalness of heterosexuality. It was notable, for example, that the Freemans and their gay son became the poster family of the pro-gay side, rather than Cindy Barber, Sammie, and their six kids, whose lesbian family provides a more thoroughgoing challenge to the heterosexual family ideal.

In a place like Timbertown the Freemans' coming out was a radical act, and the article made a big splash. For a short time, it seemed that everyone in town was talking about it. The Freemans' next-door neighbors, who had been members of the Mountaintop Church of God, became convinced that the OCA measure was a good thing after hearing a sermon by Bob Harrison in church one Sunday, but they were touched by the Freemans' story; they respected their neighbors and did not want to hurt them, and they decided to oppose the OCA. Personalizing the issue made it harder for people to distance themselves from the fact the campaign was targeting flesh-and-blood individuals.

The Freemans' boldness was not universally appreciated, however. Some of the older, more established parents of gay people, including Martha Jensen, resented the publicity. Sure, they faced many of the same struggles as the Freemans faced, but why make a big issue of it? They were members of a different generation, a generation who didn't identify with the sixties, and they had lived in Timbertown longer and had a larger web of close connections to negotiate, and therefore had more to lose. To Martha, the Freemans were like other California transplants: they were anxious to alter the town. "They talked like all the people from Southern California. Wanted to change everything to the way they had been accustomed to . . . even though they had come up here to get away from that." When I asked Martha whether she ever considered coming out as the parent of a gay child, she replied, "No, never would've ocurred to me. It's a personal issue—unless they make fools of themselves, and parade downtown, and wear women's clothes that are exaggerated." Could coming out publicly as the parent of a gay child be a positive step, one that would educate people, I asked? "There will be some people who will never be tolerant, and so who needs them? You know, people don't like me because my daughter happens to be a gay person, I don't need that person. I have plenty of other people to choose from, to live with."

Rather than connect the personal to the political, Martha chose to wage her battle solely in the public arena, arguing that the ballot would hurt the town economically. Though the OCA's base was made up largely of small business owners, most businesspeople in town opposed the initiative, fearing that it would stigmatize the town, repelling out-of-town customers and potential property buyers. Amendment 2, the anti-gay amendment passed in Colorado the year before, triggered a nationwide boycott of the state which cost millions of dollars in convention business. Timbertown was already facing an economic crisis, triggered by the collapse of the timber industry, and the passage of a property tax cap. Like other towns, it was struggling to provide rudimentary services such as education and public transportation, and the high school had already reduced its course offerings and eliminated some sports and extracurricular activities.

"When we have pressing needs like building our local economy and assuring a quality education for our children, why do we want to succumb to outside agitators with their own agendas?" a group of concerned citizens wrote to the chamber of commerce opposing the OCA. A couple from Sacramento, California, who had purchased a building site in town where they planned to retire, wrote to the local paper: "We do love the area and have been looking forward to the day when we could could make the move. But, we are deeply saddened by the apparent growth and strength of a local group known as the Oregon Citizens Alliance."

Most local elites, including elected town officials, refused at first to take a stand, fearing it would further divide the community. But once the community became clearly divided, Timbertown's chamber of commerce came out against the OCA initiative.[16] The mayor and city council, including Martha Jensen, followed suit, proclaiming that the ballot measure would violate their oath to uphold the state and federal constitutions by limiting free speech and equal protection guarantees. The mayor, a grandmotherly woman, stood up before the city council and addressed the assembled citizens:

> I do not believe, in any way, that the OCA initiative benefits our community. Rather, this whole ugly business has torn our city apart, causing a state of divisiveness not known to me in the almost quarter of a century that I've called Timbertown home. To believe that your truth is the only truth is an insult to the god of variety and versatility, to quote author Taylor Caldwell.
>
> I do not believe that any of our citizens wish to destroy Timbertown.

Rather, I believe that the local proponents of the initiative have been led down the garden path, so to speak, by those who stand to benefit from this campaign.

I do not believe that anyone here approves of bigotry, or of hate mongering, or of class division. Rather, I think that hate, bigotry and the old caste system have no place in our pleasant little town. . . . We are all citizens of this beautiful little city. We have always lived in the spirit of harmony, and all the while living together, free and equal. That is, always until now.

In the spirit of Timbertown first, in the strong belief that this initiative is unconstitutional, and because of the OCA-induced pain that is infecting our community, I will not vote to put this measure on the ballot.[17]

In response, Jeri Cookson asked the city council to reject the mayor's resolution on the ground that "it intimidates people" and "further divides the city," reading a prepared statement on behalf of the OCA:

Timbertown is not an isolated community. What happens in Salem and elsewhere in Oregon does affect us. If a majority of the citizens of our town want to establish the premise that we are against giving the homosexual community minority rights, we cannot see how the City Council or our elected representatives can declare the wishes of the majority as unnecessary. . . . We are defending our ideals in the only way we know how—through the electoral process. . . . There is nothing in this proposal that causes any discrimination against anyone. All we are asking is that they not be given minority status, which will in fact discriminate against somebody else.

A city councilor responded that the movement was dividing the community, to which Jeri replied that she didn't understand what she meant by "dividing the community." Sally Humphries, sitting with her husband, Matt, stood up and said, "The amendment is not about discrimination," adding:

We have everyone coming up here saying we want to discriminate and we want to isolate certain people in the community but that just is not true. We want to protect the community. This is not a concern that is frivolous or fanatical or not based on reality. It is very much based on reality and very much happening everywhere around us and will soon be coming here. It's not a hate issue. I hope the City Council will remain neutral and realize that it is not an outside effort coming into this community.

Then five OCA supporters rose to speak on behalf of the charter measure. Rudy Ramsey retorted: "The activities of the OCA create a great deal more fear than any homosexual activity. We do not have a sexual problem in this community. However unpleasant we may view homosexual activities they are not a threat to us." City councilor Cliff Richards, the father of a lesbian, said: "I do not believe in, support, or advocate homosexuality, but I resent those who take their own personal religious beliefs and put them into a very divisive type of program. I particularly don't like minority race issues being brought up under the guise of something else." Martha Jensen took a different tack: "We have an issue here that we're not giving enough attention to and that issue is not homosexuality, it's not heterosexuality, it's the issue of promiscuity that started in this country in the midst of the sixties and continues. It doesn't just concern homosexual people, it concerns heterosexual people."

When the discussion ended, the council unanimously passed a resolution that stated: "The city of Timbertown grants no special privileges to any class of citizens. The community's energy should be focused on issues of common concern such as education, the economy, quality of life, and public safety. Therefore the City of Timbertown opposes efforts of the Oregon Citizens Alliance and other special interest groups to unnecessarily amend the Charter of the City of Timbertown."[18]

Meanwhile, the American Civil Liberties Union pursued a series of town-by-town legal challenges to municipalities that had already passed local charter amendments, and an even greater challenge was brewing in the state legislature: a bill designed to preempt the ballot measures by prohibiting local governments from enacting laws or policies granting "special rights, privileges or treatment" to any citizen or group of citizens, which would also prohibit those governments from enacting or enforcing any laws or politics that single out citizens or groups of citizens because of sexual orientation. It was supported by the mayors of four cities in the county, and praised in an editorial in the *Gazette* that suggested that the "tyranny of the majority" posed a threat to democracy, and that citizens' rights should be limited. "Voters cannot, for example, vote to take the right to vote away from African Americans, Jews, cat owners or people who score below 500 on the verbal portion of the SAT exam."[19] When House Bill 3500 was approved by the state legislature, the ACLU asked Oregon's secretary of state to cancel the antigay rights votes set for September and November, and local communities followed suit.

CAN tried to convince the Timbertown city council to prevent the measure from appearing on the ballot. "Our small community can be spared the further economic and social expense of this divisive (and now pointless) initiative," it declared. "If our city decides to proceed with this election at this time, the community of Timbertown will be labeled an Oregon community which supports and defends discrimination. You have one more opportunity to interrupt the OCA's misuse of the initiative, referendum and recall process."[20]

But the OCA was none too happy about this challenge, and cast the issue in terms of voters' rights, charging that HB 3500 "violates the natural right inherent in the people to alter the government in such a manner as they may think proper," as provided in the Oregon constitution.[21] "The bill effectively erases . . . six legally and properly conducted elections," said Pamela Sneed of the OCA. It "burns your constitutionally guaranteed rights to use the initiative at the city and county level on the homosexual rights issue."[22] Hundreds of citizens had signed a petition qualifying the charter measure for the city ballot. Now, OCA supporters proclaimed, local and state elites were standing in the way of "democracy": "The State Legislature has with one stroke—HB 3500—done away with the people's right to majority vote and said their wishes mean nothing. . . . When any group goes to the people and gets their honest opinion on paper, then the majority had better have that decision upheld. We're really making it up as we go along in this new age of the Gay Nineties and Cultural Diversity, whatever that means!"[23]

Meanwhile, throughout the state, towns were passing the charter amendments right and left. Voters in Douglas, Linn, Josephine, and Klamath counties easily passed the initiative while ten of twelve school bond proposals failed. The next month, all but one of the six OCA measures on the ballot passed easily. The OCA reported a 20 percent increase in membership across the state, and a formidable mailing list of 265,000, thanks to local organizing efforts. Timbertown's paper assessed the results:

> These returns demonstrate that many Oregonians are deeply troubled and offended by homosexuality and by the gay rights movement. There can be no doubt about that (not that there was before the election). Beyond that, this is another example of a deep division in our culture. . . .

We live in a house deeply divided. Can we find some compromise in all this division? . . . If only we could call a truce now. If only the OCA would declare a moral victory and stop there. What if they win in Timbertown in the spring? Flowers will still bloom. Rain will still fall. The OCA will have its charter amendment. They will feel better. City government will go on policing and sweeping the streets and pumping water to our houses and treating the sewage that flows from them. We could go back to living next door to each other without worrying how our neighbors and shop owners feel about homosexuality. Wouldn't it be nice?[24]

Buoyed by supporters across the state, the OCA decided to take legal action against the Timbertown city council for "dragging [its] feet on putting the anti-gay charter amendment on the ballot," and filed a complaint with the state, alleging that it violated Oregon election laws. The complainant, Jeri Cookson, asked that civil penalties be imposed against the city councilors, and against the ACLU.[25] The OCA also targeted fourteen state legislators who had voted for HB 3500 for recall, including a Democratic state representative from Timbertown. At a rally at the Sacred Fate Temple, Lon Mabon exhorted OCA activists: "I think you are really getting the run-around by your city councilors. It sounds like some of them need to be replaced. You need to recruit good candidates—good solid people who believe in morals and values."[26] Outside, nearly fifty demonstrators chanted, "Lon Be Gone" and "Go Away OCA," holding placards denouncing bigotry, hate, and holocaust.

Timbertown's city council vacillated for months about whether or not to place the OCA measure on the ballot. "It's a can of worms," said Councilman Cliff Richards, "which is all going to end up in the courts" while diverting attention from the city's pressing economic needs. "We've got too many damn things going on in this community," he said. But soon the state informed the city council that it would be prosecuted if it failed to place the amendment on the ballot. "The initiative power is quite broad," declared the state's attorney general. "It includes the ability of voters to initiate and vote on measures that are blatantly illegal or unconstitutional. The courts are the ones empowered to make those judgments, but only after voter passage of a measure." So, with ambivalence, Timbertown's city council agreed to comply with the state's request, and the vote was finally scheduled. The measure would be called "City Charter Amendment to prohibit minority status for homosexuals."

While the campaign was being waged in the city council, CAN continued to educate the community about homosexuality, drawing increasingly upon language derived from the medical model: homosexuality is not a choice, gay people were born that way, "they can't help it." Such images were buttressed by a scientific study, which emerged at the time, linking homosexuality in men to a chromosomal abnormality. At points, such claims included assertions of homosexual superiority. Gays are the answer to the country's overpopulation problems, one man argued: since they were rarely involved in violent crimes, rape and child molestation, they actually saved taxpayers' money. What's more, gays, with their exquisite decorating sense and disposable income, could pretty up any fading neighborhood. "Want proud homeowners with high incomes? Formerly rundown areas of historical merit have been gentrified by the gay. The tax base is raised, and the redevelopment is free of cost to taxpayers."[27] This argument was often embraced by gay people themselves, particularly by men. "Gays [don't] differ from straights only in the bedroom," said a letter to the editor. "The facts are, gays have differently structured brains and different genders and exhibit vastly different behaviors and abilities than their straight male counterparts. For instance, I don't indulge in ultra-aggressive behaviors (fighting, sports, armed conflicts), regard women as property (like the men of Tailhook, the Apostle Paul, and most cavemen), define my worth in terms of material and/or social prestige, or spend much of my time and money 'proving to the boys' that I'm straight."[28]

The essentialist model of homosexuality was appealing because it drew upon commonsense notions of sexuality as innate, rooted in biology and bodies rather than choices and understandings of the world. It was attractive, too, because it allayed people's anxieties about collapsing sexual boundaries. The OCA campaign proclaimed that homosexuality was a matter of choice, and raised the possibility that the boundaries separating the homosexual and heterosexual worlds were far less secure and stable than people had previously imagined. Essentialist understandings of homosexuality restored a sense of certainty, surety, stability. To parents with small kids in school, it said: don't worry about gay teachers imposing their ideas on impressionable children: homosexuals can't recruit. You either are one or you aren't one. To parents of gay children, it said: don't worry, it's not your fault that your child is gay—some people are just born that way.[29] To liberals, it provided a framework for talking about homosexuality that allowed them to simply substitute "lesbian and gay" for "African American" or "Latino" or "Asian American," and speak of the importance of tolerance, understanding, and equality, making the messy subject of sexuality far less threatening.

CHALLENGING HETERONORMATIVITY

Essentialist understandings of homosexuality were strategically useful as a means of presenting homosexuality to a community with limited knowledge, but they failed to articulate a public challenge to the OCA's core claim that heterosexuality alone is normal, natural, and beautiful. Countering the conservative effort to equate homosexuality with pollution, CAN presented it as a sexuality that was normal and natural. But it did so by confining homosexuality to particular individuals and conceiving of homosexuals as a tightly bounded minority group that posed little challenge to the heterosexual norm. Yet at times, if I read between the lines, and listened closely to people's stories, I could hear more complex understandings of sexuality, ones that grappled with individual differences, understood that homosexuality challenges the way that most people "do" gender, and acknowledged that even many straight people find heteronormativity to be restrictive.

One could hear this more complex understanding of sexuality in the stories of Janice and June Trump, the two sisters who ran a bookstore, who remember the taunts they received when they first moved to town with their boyfriends, and had kids out of wedlock, the way that people stared at their long flowing hair and unshaved legs in the 1970s and called them "lesbian witches" behind their backs. Twenty years later, during the OCA campaign they were often "gay baited" because they lived together. Some people really thought they were lesbians, imagining that they took the same last name because they were married to one another, when they were actually sisters who had never taken married names. They have always felt a kindred spirit with gay people because they have often felt like gender outlaws, and they believe it's important to challenge normative heterosexuality. "Homosexuality isn't simply a gay issue. You have to take a stand—it affects *your* sexuality," said Janice. "You have to think about what it really means. Even if you're straight, it means that you have to make that decision for yourself. You can't just sort of not think about it. It means you have to think about what it really is. It scares people."

Rather than see homosexuality as diametrically opposed to heterosexuality, which is arguably the dominant view, some members of CAN embraced the view that heterosexuality and homosexuality were on a continuum. Among them, no doubt, were those who harbored bisexual desires at some point in their lives, who questioned the homo-hetero binary as a result, though I never met anyone who was out as a bisexual. But several women living visibly heterosexual lives spoke passionately about their feelings for homosexual men. Sometimes this passion extended to a deep sense of identification that defied existing categories. Thirty-five-year-old Linda Mabley, who grew up in Timbertown and had four children in the elementary school, was an unlikely activist for gay rights, at least on the surface. She is a stout woman who has thick glasses and long straight brown hair, and wears matronly dresses that make her look older than her age. She had never been involved in a political campaign before, but when the OCA politicized the issue of homosexuality, it felt "really oppressive in a way that different political issues didn't." She explained, "Everybody has their pet issues. For some people it's the environment, for others it's peace issues." For her, the campaign was about "labeling and judging groups of people, assuming that you knew something or even everything about them on the basis of a label that was kind of arbitrary to start with."

Linda knows firsthand about the limitations of labels. She told me, in confidence, that for the past decade, she has been involved in the subterranean subculture of *Star Trek* devotees who create 'zines, homemade magazines featuring stories about an imagined homosexual love affair between the two stars of the series, Spock and Kirk. Linda attends conventions where hundreds of people, mainly heterosexual women who live a very active, often homoerotic fantasy world, meet and exchange these publications.[30] Linda clearly feels a close affinity with gay men, and with gay male culture. Several years ago, she read the book *Borrowed Time,* an AIDS memoir, and was deeply touched by it, so much so that she wrote to the author, Paul Monette, with whom she had an active correspondence for a short time before his death. Linda describes herself as someone who has "always had this kind of humanistic, open liberal view of people."

Liberals like Linda see childhood as a time of struggle out of ignorance into self-knowledge. Many gay activists suggest that self-knowledge culminates in the coming out process, when one throws off stigma and secrecy, comes to terms with one's homosexuality, and self-identifies on that basis. But what if self-knowledge defies categorization? As I spoke to her, it seemed to me that Linda was queer—not necessarily queer in the narrowly sexualized sense of being attracted to members of the same sex, which may or may not be true—but queer in terms of the range of her identifications. On the surface she may be heterosexual, but deep down, there's a lot more going on: unwieldy desires and identifications that defy simple description, which lead her to identify with queer people in a more profound fashion than many of those around her, and know that they are not simply a minority group "over there." "I felt like I was sort of tailor-made for this issue when it came up," Linda says of her opposition to the OCA. "I was able to step into it already having a lot of information and feelings. It's an important and personal issue for me." On the face of it, Linda was the last person I would have imagined to be queer. I strained to find kind words to describe the impression she conveyed, but all I could think of was "frumpy housewife." It's no wonder she felt personally threatened by effort to "label and judge" groups of people—she was proof positive that the labels were a lie.

When she became involved in the campaign, Linda was worried that people "wouldn't want their kids to play with my kids anymore." Her parents, who also lived in town, worried about it too. "They felt that I shouldn't get involved in this, it wasn't my fight. Leave it to other people to do. But it just felt too important to me. It didn't feel like something I could say only involved a certain group of people. I don't think that anything is really like that. It's all systemic, it's all connected. You can't ever say, 'Well, that's just a black issue,' 'that's just a gay issue,' 'that doesn't concern me.' How could it possibly touch me? It just didn't feel that way to me." Linda's politics of empathy blurs the homo-hetero binary, and suggests, in a way, that "we are all queer." The OCA had emphasized the strangeness of gay people, their foreignness, the anxiety they caused, and tried to set up barriers so that straight people avoided contact with gays. Supporters of gay rights responded by welcoming gay people back into the community, claiming that they are a clearly bounded group that poses little threat to heterosexual families. This position, they imagined, would allay people's fears, and in the process allow some to know the "other." They were only partially successful in doing this.

For all their good intentions, many liberal Timbertowners were ambivalent about gay rights, or felt ignorant about gay life, as are most Americans. While disavowing discrimination and calling for tolerance, they admitted some gay people into the community—those who remained quiet, conventional, and who didn't create waves—excluding those who posed a more radical challenge to the heterosexual norm. Countering right-wing claims that homosexuality is a choice, a potential that exists in all of us, liberal gay rights supporters suggested that sexual boundaries are solid and unchanging, that homosexuals are a fixed group of individuals who are born gay, who keep sexuality out of the public sphere—healthy, upstanding taxpayers who pose no threat to the community, but who are a legitimate minority group entitled to civil rights protections. While extending empathy to those unlike themselves, they imagined lesbians and gay men as a minority group possessing clear boundaries. They were willing to readmit homosexuals into the community as long as they were "good gays" who didn't draw public attention to themselves, or question the sanctity of the heterosexual family form. They privileged lesbians and gay men people who posed little challenge to the self-conception of the community as a whole. In doing so, they reworked but did not abandon a conservative familialism that rests upon heterosexual privilege and power.

It was simpler to speak of homosexuality utilizing familiar notions—genes, chromosomes, race, ethnicity—than to force people to question the dominance of heterosexuality and the straightforwardness of their own sexual selves. Many liberal Timbertowners were, after all, ambivalent about homosexuality because they lacked the vocabulary to speak about sexuality in complex ways—or were fearful of doing so. As Marianne Woods of CAN admitted, "We felt that we could not speak for gay people. And we didn't know enough about homosexuality to refute the OCA." But a more complex understanding of sexuality was needed in order to fully admit lesbians and gay men into the community. "Real knowledge of the Other," writes Zygmunt Bauman, "comes when one imagines the Other as one self, imagines the boundaries blurred, barriers broken." In the interstices of the campaign, some embraced a more radical critique, blurring the boundaries between insiders and outsiders, lesbians/gay men and "true" Timbertowners, proclaiming "we are all queer."[31] While the CAN campaign gestured toward this politic, it maintained that lesbian and gay experience had little to do with "us." It held the "other" at bay.

CHAPTER 8

I Shout, Therefore I Am

I shout therefore I am is the neotribal version of the cogito. . . .
Postmodern tribes are brought into their ephemeric being by explosive
sociality.

Zygmunt Bauman, Postmodern Ethics

Cultural conservatives and progressivists alike are far better at
articulating what they are against rather than what they are for. . . .
The culture war is not so much a conflict of cultures but a competition
of anti-cultures, for rarely does one ever hear articulated an integrated,
coherent, and affirming moral vision that encompasses the nation as a
whole in all of its glorious and irreconcilably messy diversity.

James Davison Hunter, Before the Shooting Begins

Timbertown is a place where face-to-face relationships, though
weakened in recent years, still predominate; so even if few CAN activists had close relationships with OCA activists, many knew them
and their families. Toby Ramsey, who had moved from California in
search of acreage and a simpler way of life, employed a couple of enthusiastic OCA supporters as occasional laborers on her land, describing them as "typical Oregonians, people who are kinda slow." But
they're not, she assured me, hostile or hateful. "They just want to keep
doing what their parents did. They're afraid of change." When I
stopped into their bookstore, June and Janice Trump often told me
tales of the latest activities of OCA activist Erica Williams whom they
referred to as "a bit of a nut." Robin Bergman poked fun at Sally
Humphries's Dolly Partonesque style, calling her a "man in drag."
There was a patronizing tone to these words, certainly, but it was tempered by a genuine affection born of a shared history in a small town.
OCA activists, most believed, weren't really bad people; they were
just bored housewives and retired folks who were a little overzealous.
Theirs was a liberal variant of "love the sinner hate the sin" rhetoric:

you could like OCA activists as people—they were uneducated but basically decent people who had gotten involved with an unsavory organization—and hate what they were doing to the community.

At their worst, Timbertown's liberals saw OCA activists as troubled, somewhat hypocritical individuals. Rumors about preachers kicked out of congregations for sexual indiscretions abounded, and many people seemed to think that evangelical families were even more likely to transgress sexual and other norms than others. As Chester and Martha Rideout described a neighbor: "Oh, she was all for protecting her children, but she's divorced. Her oldest son has been in the very worst kind of trouble that he could possibly be in, including possession of drugs, and has been in jail. His younger brother is pretty much like him. And the daughter is a hooker. So here's a mother who has *got* to protect her children." Some even suggested that antigay activists' fervor was fueled by their desire to compensate for their own homosexual desires, and the notion that "Lon Mabon is a closet case" was a popular refrain. Certainly, sexual desires call up emotions—love, rage, shame—that are repressed in our sex-obsessed and sex-repressed culture. Advertising images and other forms of popular culture draw upon and elicit sexual feelings, and at the same time banish them from critical scrutiny and public discussion. Conservative Christians, like all Americans, experience wayward sexual desires in a society that condemns their open expression. Torn between conflicting impulses, prominent evangelicals such as Jim Bakker and Jimmy Swaggart crusade against premarital sex and are caught with their pants down.[1]

Still, personal ties seemed to keep the debate about gay rights, which was carried on largely in the letters to editor column of the *Gazette,* on fairly civil terms, and CAN activists did their best to conceal their contempt for those they believed were dividing the town. They smiled cordially when they saw OCA activists walking down the street, or cracked jokes about them privately.[2] "We never called the other side names," June Trump assured me. "We very consciously didn't say they were hateful in public. It was a real effort sometimes! We tried to portray them as extreme without going so far as to say hateful extremists." Occasionally, though, people slipped up. When Lon Mabon came through town and spoke at the Sacred Fate Temple, CAN members were there, holding placards that read "Lon Be Gone," or "OCA—No Way." And one woman, with a devilish grin

on her face, held a sign that read "If you liked the KKK, you'll love
the OCA." One day Joe Carson, who wore his OCA button openly,
was confronted by a CAN supporter at the local video store who
informed him that "only scared or ignorant people would vote to
change the city's charter." So he smiled and said, "That's a matter of
opinion, you know." The following week, he parked his car at a shopping mall and returned to find a young woman scraping his OCA
sticker off with a key, and threatened to have her arrested to make
her stop.

These and other incidents did not go unnoticed by OCA activists
in town, who were quick to tally up a litany of street confrontations,
describing in great detail the myriad ways their neighbors mistreated
them. "I'm not as open about who I am with people I'm not familiar
with," Janice Henry told me, echoing the feeling common among
many conservative Christians that they could only trust their own.
Members of CAN felt much the same.

"Anyone who opposes the OCA is subject to such unjust, ignorant, ludicrous parallels, characterizations and generalized accusa-
tions," said a CAN supporter. "We're 'pro-sodomy liberals,' we're
against family values, we're anti-Christian, anti-religion, dangerous
to children, immoral, promiscuous, proponents of 'special' rights—
the list goes on and on. Some of us who stand up for human dignity
and oppose legalized discrimination also feel hurt, angry and resentful
when these ludicrous labels are put on us. We don't like it either when
such characterizations and generalizations are made about who we
are."[3] During the campaign, the Presbyterian church received several
pieces of anonymous hate mail, and messages tacked on the door that
said "We're praying for you" and "We've got to stop people like you,"
advising the congregation to finally see the light and rise up against
"queer-loving" Pastor Henry Chomsky. "We'd come to volunteer at
the church and wonder, what nasty message is going to be on the answering machine today?" recalled Sylvia Watkins. It led her and others to conclude that OCA activists actually enjoyed sparring with
their liberal neighbors. A former fundamentalist-turned-progressive
activist tried to explain the "fundamentalist mind-set":

> When they walk away from you and your attempts to communicate, they
> are most likely feeling a mixture of relief (they were nervous, too) and
> elation. Their goals in this encounter were very different from yours.
> They want to maintain the gap. . . . You are probably better educated,

more intellectually sophisticated and have better social skills than the people you just faced. They know that they feel inferior. They are convinced that if they try to reason with you, or match your opinions and arguments, they will "lose." They don't expect to convert you to their way of thinking because they know you are more knowledgeable. They view you as being "worldly wise," and worldly wisdom comes from Satan, the devil. They view you as an agent of Satan, sent to test them and their commitment to their faith. The more reasonable, gentle and caring you are, the cleverer Satan is being in testing them. The more you raise your voice and lose your temper, the more glory to them and to God when they hold firm against you. All that is required of them, by their church and their fellow fundamentalists, is that they state what they believe and hold to it, refusing to let anyone argue them out of those beliefs. If they do that, they have won a victory. They return to their Bible classes and share what happened, and they receive praise and support for their courage in facing you. Probably you never dreamed that you hold such power.[4]

Suggesting that the ballot measure campaign was really a symbolic means of identity building, and only secondarily about taking legal action against lesbian and gay "special rights," many liberals believed that conservatives were using them as foils in order to construct a sense of themselves as individually and collectively powerful. If confrontations with secular humanists helped OCA activists construct a sense of identity with other "saved" Christians, the predominantly heterosexual pro-gay activists of Timbertown had fewer incentives to engage in open combat: their sense of identity did not rest so much upon negating the other.

But the local campaign did not exist in the vacuum. It operated in a region where the issue of homosexuality was highly politicized, in relation to a national "culture war," and within a mass-mediated world. The farther one got from Timbertown, the less shared personal history there was, the less restraint people exercised. Radical gay activists in Eugene and Portland—especially those who came from conservative Christian backgrounds themselves—often seemed to relish confrontations as much as their opponents. So did gay spokespersons such as Dan Savage, a nationally syndicated Seattle-based writer of a sex advice column called "Savage Love." "Hopeful in Chicago" sent the following letter to Savage:

> I wouldn't tell my relatives this, but I am an Evangelical Christian who likes your column. . . . For a while I have been wondering about the hos-

tility between Evangelicals and gay people. The venom strikes me as unnecessary in both directions. We have had some halting attempts toward
interracial dialogue lately. I wonder what would happen if small groups
of evangelicals and gay people were to start meeting too.

To which Savage replied savagely:

> Look, all Evangelicals need to understand is that your opinions about ho-
> mosexuality—however you justify them, whatever deity's mouth you
> stuff them into—are only your opinions. So while I appreciate your good
> intentions, HIC, and while there may be queers out there interested in
> chatting up Evangelicals, I'm not one of them. Because as I see it, a dia-
> logue is not really necessary. All that has to happen for hostilities between
> queers and Xtian fundies to cease is for you guys to stop fucking with us:
> stop telling lies about us on your idiotic TV shows; stop opposing equal
> rights for lesbians and gays . . . and stop having a shit fit every time we stop
> by Disneyland. . . . Think we're going to Hell? Fine. Whatever. We don't
> care; just don't fuck with us. We aren't hung up on your approval, and
> we're not waiting for your okay. We can get through the day knowing that
> there are people out there who disapprove of us, just as I assume you can
> get through the day knowing that Islamic fundamentalists disapprove of
> you, or that those mean ol' Hindus believe all you misguided Christians
> are coming back in the next life as hamsters."[5]

Timbertown's progressive activists refrained from portraying
OCA activists as kooks or creeps, practicing a kind of passive resistance that opposed vitriol with messages of community solidarity.
But their efforts were subverted by forces beyond their control: by
Christian conservatives who seemed to thrive on conflict, who vehemently believed they were engaged in a culture war for the preservation of American values; by radical gay activists for whom Christian
conservatives represented hate, fear and loathing, and even radical
evil; and by the media which played up the most dramatic, radical elements of both sides, focusing upon street protests and confrontations,
amplifying the acrimony. Collectively, these forces rubbed salt into
the wounds of a festering conflict.

THEY'RE NAZIS

During the Measure 9 campaign in 1992 the OCA distributed a cartoon entitled "A Streetcar Named Perversion" depicting a gay man
manipulating the strings of the government and the economy—a

virtual copy of a 1941 Nazi cartoon showing a hook-nosed Jewish puppeteer controlling Churchill, Roosevelt, and Stalin; in place of the Jewish puppeteer was a fresh-faced gay clone. "Some things never change," suggested a left sectarian group, which juxtaposed the OCA and Nazi cartoons, declaring, "NO NAZIS, NO OCA, NO FAS-CIST USA!!"[6] The Christian right film, *The Gay Agenda,* also closely resembled the 1940 Nazi propaganda film *The Eternal Jew,* and echoed traditional anti-Semitic propaganda that deliberately inflated the power of Jewish bankers and international Jewish conspiracies.[7] Measure 9 seemed reminiscent of several aspects of National Socialist legislation, feminist/queer theorist Gayle Rubin warned; if passed, the measure would "deprive sexual minorities of equal citizenship, make them inferior by law and public policy, mandate teaching such inferiority in all state-supported educational institutions, and suppress the promulgation of opinions or evidence that would contravene such legally dictated inferiority."[8] The Holocaust "frame" was even invoked by Governor Barbara Roberts. "It is 1993 in Oregon, not 1943 in Europe," she told the Linn County Human Rights Coalition, a gay rights group. "But the signs of bigotry and growing intolerance are again with us, and we would be foolish to ignore these signs and their significance." Noting that law enforcement agencies had received 545 reports of hate crimes around the state, she criticized the OCA initiatives for "reducing people to a simple category." History, she said, "teaches us the outcome of such thinking."[9]

Oregon is very far away from Europe, and World War II has long ended. Nonetheless, during the course of the OCA campaign, references to the war, fascism, Hitler, the Holocaust, and its Jewish victims were in abundant evidence. It wasn't the first time the Holocaust frame was deployed by lesbian/gay activists. In the early 1970s, gay liberation activists in the United States and Europe adopted the pink triangle, the symbol worn by homosexual concentration camp prisoners during World War II, as a symbolic marker. In the mid-1970s, as the Christian right mobilized to defend the "moral majority" against the supposed homosexual/feminist threat, lesbian/gay rhetoric frequently drew parallels between American conservatism and European fascism. In a 1977 op-ed article in the *Los Angeles Times,* a gay rights supporter compared singer Anita Bryant to Adolf Hitler. "Just as Hitler viewed the Jews as a powerful force that was polluting and destroying society, so do Bryant and her followers view homosexuals as social defilers. There's a whole new cadre . . . around who are smart enough not to wear swastikas. They join the Klan now or create churches . . . but they're Nazis just the same."[10] By drawing parallels between contemporary lesbians and gay men, and the homosexual (and, by implication, Jewish) victims of Nazi genocide, activists suggested that homosexuals were innocent victims of generalized prejudice, and warned of the dangerous consequences of categorizing and stigmatizing groups on the basis of sexual differences.

Clearly, the Holocaust is an "atrocity tale" of wide cultural resonance. For social movements seeking to define themselves, it represents both evil and victimhood in its most radical and horrible form. Perhaps it is not surprising, then, that social movements on the left align themselves with its victims and imagine their enemies as perpetrators. Groups mobilizing to protect the rights of oppressed minorities have often embraced a sense of victimhood; casting itself as victim permits a group to dramatize its essential innocence, gaining sympathy points.[11] And how better to do so than by identifying oneself with the twentieth century's preeminent victims, the Jews? In our late modern age, when the moral boundaries separating good and evil are often amorphous, when the mass-mediation of political discourse results in the dominance of image-based politics, and when Communism no longer exists as a clear-cut, visible enemy, the Holocaust stands out as an indisputable instance of immorality. Increasingly, groups who have little or direct relationship to either the victims or perpetrators are embracing the Holocaust as a universal symbol of injustice.[12]

For many liberals in Oregon, the Holocaust "frame" offered a simple, shorthand way to articulate the emergence of scapegoat politics. It symbolized the fact that though people are created equal, social movements, and entire nations, could be mobilized to deny that basic fact. Letters to the editor flooded the *Oregonian* and the *Eugene Register-Guard,* the state's largest circulation dailies, evoking a coming Holocaust, drawing parallels between the tactics of OCA and the Nazi Party, warning Oregonians of the dangers of creeping fascism, and arguing that homosexuals are the contemporary equivalent of Jews on the brink of extinction.

> In his rise to power, Adolf Hitler strengthened his political position by creating a non-issue enemy, the Jews. In 1938 he ordered the burning of synagogues. In 1994 what will Mabon burn? Hitler ordered the burning

of books. The OCA is attempting to ban certain materials. These are two examples of an obvious path to create a political power base using misleading, divisive and underhanded tactics to rally a group of people around an issue that they have had no experience with so that they can be manipulated easily.[13]

This and other letters to the editor, which represented the views of many gay activists and their sympathizers, claimed that Oregon in 1992 bore close resemblance to pre–World War II Germany. It overstated the historical parallels to make its point, urging Oregonians to look beyond Mabon's folksy demeanor and see a cunning demagogue leading unthinking people astray.

Early in the local campaign, Holocaust metaphors were rarely used in Timbertown. If CAN activists sometimes harbored such thoughts, they rarely spoke them in public—the words were too incendiary. Eventually, however, the Holocaust frame made its way into the Timbertown *Gazette* as one letter writer argued that the OCA's Nazi-like authoritarianism logically leads to the extermination of those who oppose them.

> The OCA [tries to] remove from power anyone who opposes their views. . . . People, don't fall into this old trap. If you remember your history those are the same methods used by Hitler and the Nazi party and all the other despots throughout civilization. The first step is to strip them of their power; the second step is extermination. . . . How could any Oregonian not see the similiarity with the OCA when one reads that the Nazis asserted in the 1920s that the Jews, as sinners, undermined the morality of Germany, planned to lead good German children and youths astray, were attempting to gain greater rights than others, and had a calculated agenda by which they planned to achieve their goals?[14]

Hitler and his followers used deception to lull an unsuspecting German citizenry into supporting their genocidal plan. The same, some argued, could happen in Oregon. Even mild-mannered Martha Jensen, the Timbertown city councilor, invoked the comparison. "Most of the [OCA supporters] I saw at the City Council meeting were sincere and frightened folks, scared that their children are going to be indoctrinated by gays and lesbians in an effort to swell their ranks," she declared. "After all, Adolf Hitler perfected the lie, and bragged that if you repeat it often enough it will come true, and this is a proven theory. Works just great!" Like many Timbertowners, she distinguished between OCA leaders, whose motives, she suggested, were evil, and followers, who were led down an authoritarian path.

When I heard these claims, I couldn't help but think to myself: I know what the Holocaust was, and this is not a Holocaust. When people use the words "Nazi," "Hitler," and "extermination" loosely, it sends shudders down my spine. Though the war years fade further and further from view, the trauma burns well after the fact. Like many survivors of the Holocaust and their families, I have long been concerned with preserving our particular claims to memory, lamenting the trivializing of the Holocaust that is rife in the mass media and popular culture. As Irena Klepfisz writes, "The Holocaust has [become] a fad, a rock group . . . it has been commercialized, metaphored out of reality, glamorized, been severed from the historical fact."[15] When the Holocaust becomes just another object of popular culture, it loses its ability to shock. Are social movements that utilize Holocaust rhetoric another instance of such trivializing? Efforts to associate contemporary social movements with Holocaust memory, or any attempt to compare the Holocaust to other events in human history, some suggest, relativize and thereby undercut the specificity and uniqueness of that horrific and in many respects singular historical moment.[16]

Jewish Holocaust survivors understandably wish to preserve their version of the truth, or at least claim a special understanding based upon experience. From their standpoint, political actors on the right and the left may be equally guilty of appropriating the Holocaust. Some suggest that any effort to compare the Holocaust to other historical events constitutes, in effect, historical revisionism; the episode stands alone as the Ultimate Evil for which there is no comparison. By comparing the Holocaust to other instances of inhumanity, they de-Judaicize the Holocaust, transforming it into an instance of inhumanity bereft of special Jewish significance. For if everyone is a victim, then no one is. Contemporary social movements that appropriate Holocaust memory are, in effect, universalizing such memories.

Social movements seeking to appropriate Holocaust memory for progressive ends are thus caught on the horns of a difficult dilemma. While they may appreciate the particularity of the Holocaust, its special significance to world Jewry, and its uniqueness, by appropriating the Holocaust for their own political purposes, they are, in effect, challenging Jewish "ownership" of Holocaust memory. Yet it seems inevitable that the historical memory of the Holocaust will be made and remade, appropriated and re-appropriated. Particularly as we move further and further away from firsthand memory, and as subsequent generations are entrusted with keeping memory alive, the stories that will be told about the Holocaust will be second- and thirdhand ones. Moreover, the Holocaust is both unique *and* comparable. It belongs to Jewish history, but it also belongs to human history. The Nazis mobilized modern technology to destroy, for all intents and purposes, the unique cultures of European Jewry. But genocides continue to occur around the globe, albeit on a smaller scale. And even in this country, the genocidal mentality is present, in much milder form, in the effort to exclude whole groups of people—including gays and lesbians—from enjoying economic, political, and cultural resources.

Efforts to compare the OCA and the Nazis, while highly exaggerated, were not altogether unfounded. The OCA appealed to authoritarian impulses and played to preexisting demonologies. Historically, the right has drawn much of its strength, collective identity, and legitimacy from its ability to construct a coherent, visible enemy and to demonize the "enemies within." Jews and homosexuals have been frequently central to this demonology. After World War II, political anti-Semitism and the belief in a Jewish-Communist conspiracy were publicly discredited—Joseph McCarthy, for example, went to some length to avoid association with anti-Semitic anti-Communism, and the homosexual frequently replaced the Jew as a central figure in right-wing demonology.[17] Other demonologies have certainly found a comfortable home in this country as well. But widespread belief in American exceptionalism—"it can't happen here"—obscures the nation's history of racial exclusion.

Like many Americans, I grew up thinking of institutionalized racism as largely a southern problem; it was only much later that I learned that racism cuts through the heart of the American experience—even in the lily-white Pacific Northwest. The 1848 Territorial Exclusion Act forbade people of color ("this most troubling class of population") from settling in the entire Oregon Territory, which included parts of Washington, Idaho, Northern California, and Nevada. The act eliminated access to land rights, and made African Americans (and by association, other people of color, except Native Americans, who were acknowledged through federal law) personae non grata—people with no legal standing under the law. When Oregon became a state in 1859, it was the only free (nonslavery) state with an Exclusion Act, which remained law until 1926.[18] Laws also prohibited the marriage of whites with Asians, blacks, and Hispanics. Even after racial prohibitions were formally outlawed, organizations such as the Ku Klux Klan kept the dream of racial separation alive. In the 1920s the entire Portland city council were KKK members, and the Ladies of the Invisible Empire (LOTIE), a women's auxiliary of the Klan, which fought to return the Bible to public schools, advocated stringent immigration restrictions, opposed racial equality and interracial marriage, and sought to "cleanse and purify the civil, political and ecclesiastical atmosphere of the nation," recruited more than a thousand women to its Portland chapter in a single month.[19]

There were striking parallels between OCA and Ku Klux Klan rhetoric, to be sure: they both appealed to a predominantly Protestant constituency that idealized the purity of the family and feared change, and warned of government corruption, the proliferation of vice, and the threat of social disintegration and sexual defilement, particularly of women and innocent children. The KKK, like the OCA, attracted many female devotees, recruited primarily in churches, who hoped that they could participate in the effort to cleanse and purify America. Indeed, as sociologist Kathleen Blee explains, the leaders of the Klan in its heyday in the 1920s "did not preach hatred and intolerance" but "sought only to defend traditional moral standards against the seductive allurements of modern society."[20] Describing the OCA, one Timbertowner said: "They are much more like their holy brethren the KKK than they are like the Nazis. . . . They have introduced class hatred as acceptable in the Oregon political arena. In the beginning the KKK supported the Nazis in many ways. The German American Bund was formed, and they waved the American flag alongside the swastika. When America went to war with Germany this all dissolved. But the underlying bigotry in the name of Christianity still existed. No, the OCA does not compare to the Nazis—yet!"[21]

To make their case against the OCA, progressive activists in Oregon frequently spoke of the existence of interlocking networks among the Oregon Citizens Alliance and far right groups such neo-Nazis, Ku Klux Klan, Christian Patriots, and Christian Identity. An anti-OCA campaign flyer, for example, depicted photos of Lon Mabon, his wife, his children, and his mother and read "This is what they look like by day." Inside, a picture of Ku Klux Klan members in white robes and pointed hoods declared "This is what they look like by night." Early in its formation, one could find Holocaust revisionist literature alongside antiabortion pamphlets at the headquarters of the Oregon Citizens Alliance, and at least one OCA leader was known to have attended meetings of the Common Law Court, a far right patriot organization in Oregon. Before the firebombing murders of an African-American lesbian and a gay man by skinheads in Salem, Oregon, skinheads marched in Albany with signs proclaiming "OCA has got it right!"[22] In the 1970s and 1980s, as the Pacific Northwest became a magnet for white supremacists who wore their racist allegiances openly, it also attracted those whose racism was softer and less ideological, people who didn't want to exclude people of color but didn't want to live side by side with them either—a good number of whom had fled multicultural California.[23]

If there were continuities between the radical right and the OCA, there were also vast differences. For one thing, the OCA was not explicitly racist or anti-Semitic; if anything, its public rhetoric was at times antiracist and philo-Semitic. For all their homophobia, few if any OCA members favored eliminating homosexual persons.[24] And unlike the radical right, few if any Christian conservatives suggested that the Holocaust did not happen. If anything, my conversations with OCA activists suggested that they were drawn to Holocaust rhetoric, and felt a kindred for its victims. Jeri Cookson told me that she had "nothing but admiration for what the Jewish people went through over there, and what they are still going through over there." For Jeri and other OCA activists who saw themselves engaged in a battle against the forces of evil surrounding them, much like Jews on the brink of destruction, the image of a Holocaust has spiritual and emotional resonance with the end times, in which the end of the world is seen as a prelude to the Second Coming of Christ.[25] Many Christian conservatives interpret the Holocaust as confirmation of their belief that people are essentially evil, and that those who fail to accept Christ into their lives (including unrepentant Jews) will burn in hell. This effort to imagine the Holocaust in apocalyptic terms in highly problematic. For one thing, it imposes a Christian reading upon the genocide of a group of people who were mainly Jewish. Moreover, this Christian reading imagines the Holocaust in redemptory terms, suggesting that Jews died for their sins, that they are martyrs who will be redeemed in the afterlife, and that Jews' "sacrifice" is part of God's plan for his people, the followers of Jesus. It also lets Christians off the hook for complicity in the Holocaust and in racist and anti-Semitic practices today.

If OCA activists incorporated Holocaust imagery into their end times worldview, they also went to great lengths to distance themselves from those they considered to be the "real" purveyors of evil—the far right. Jeri Cookson made a point of telling me about a fellow who came to an OCA meeting during the charter amendment campaign. "We'd never seen him before, and he looked a little strange," she recalled. They invited him to come in and sit down, and he just sat there and listened. Every once in a while, she said, they would try to include him in the proceedings. "We kept impressing the idea that we don't hate the people—we just think the lifestyle is sinful. We do pray for the people and we love the people." In the middle of the meeting, the newcomer started saying things that were "off color," according to Jeri. "He was very hateful. He said he thought that these people should be completely eradicated. You people are too nice." So Jeri and the other OCA members talked with him, about the Bible, and they tried to impress upon him that it was important to "love the sinner," but he rebuffed their efforts. They asked him to leave. Later, she said, they found out that he was a member of the Ku Klux Klan. If extremists like the Ku Klux Klan were the *real* bigots, OCA activists suggested, they were, in contrast, reasonable, loving folks. To prove this point, an OCA campaign brochure depicted a group of predominantly white citizens, along with a smattering of darker faces—though I never encountered an OCA member who was a person of color, nor had anyone else with whom I spoke.

The belief that racism is "over there" resonated with a widespread belief among local people that one could find racism in the South back in the old days, or in extremist groups like the KKK or neo-Nazis today—but not in their nice little town. Timbertown residents frequently traced their roots to the South, proclaiming that *that* was where racism was rampant, not in the friendly Pacific Northwest. Cynthia Newman, the wife of a displaced mill worker, talked about growing up in Oklahoma during segregation and seeing separate drinking fountains for blacks and whites. But it wasn't until the late 1980s that she saw a black person in Timbertown. Then more and more Hispanics started moving into the area. Before that, she said, there was no evident racism. How, she asked, "could you have racism without colored people?" Since white people rarely think of themselves as being raced, it is easy for them to hold racist attitudes that go unmarked, and unchallenged. This was certainly true in Timbertown.[26]

Lost was the memory of Oregon's not-so-distant racist past. If the truth be told, Timbertown was a "heavy, heavy-duty KKK town," Cindy Barber reminded me. "Very, very traditional, and very steeped in the old kind of ugly, ugly ways." The fact that there are few people of color today—fewer than 10 percent of the Pacific Northwest's population, and a much smaller proportion of Timbertown's population—is rooted in this history of racial exclusion. Because the OCA never thematized race explicitly it could preserve a sense of itself as nonracist, in contrast to the far right, for whom the protection of racial purity was an explicit politic.[27]

There were, then, continuities as well as differences among the authoritarian populism practiced by the OCA and the radical right. But it was a mistake to conflate the two, as the editor of the *Gazette* suggested: "The opponents of the OCA are fond of finding parallels between Nazis and the OCA. In some ways this is unfair. Surely, the vast majority of Oregonians who support the OCA are not people who would kill millions who are different." The OCA members were not ideological racists, and most of them were not evil people. Many did not even hate homosexuals and they honestly saw their activism as being motivated by love, not hate. "But then," he warned, "most Germans in the 1940s were not rabid racists either."[28] But subtlety did not make for good newspaper copy, and the "OCA as Nazis" frame stuck.

THE WHOLE TOWN IS WATCHING

The media and the OCA were mutually dependent upon each other. In small towns like Timbertown, where little happens day to day, the

OCA ballot measure campaign generated a clearly defined, down-home conflict, replete with great visuals of foaming-at-the-mouth middle-aged ladies fighting for what they believed in. During the campaign, Timbertowners picked up the *Gazette,* published weekly, wondering who would be on the front page, and who would have a letter to editor that week. The campaign offered Timbertown residents one of the few opportunities they had to express their views on a controversial national subject in public. The OCA, in turn, needed the media to publicize its activities, and to be a secondary target in the course of the campaign; it used the press to cover its activities and then railed against liberal bias in news, balking at the fact that it tended to paint religious conservatives in a poor light.

In 1992, newspapers across the state came out solidly against Ballot Measure 9, characterizing it, at various times, as "bizarre, demeaning, hateful, poisonous" and calling OCA activists bedroom police, peeping toms, redneck jingoists, gay bashers and, of course Nazis and fascists. During the Measure 9 campaign, newpapers in the state often published anti-OCA editorials that incensed Lon Mabon and the OCA leadership, and they declared boycotts of the papers in question. For two years the OCA refused to speak to the *Salem Statesman-Journal,* citing misrepresentation; over time it refused to talk to papers in Portland, Medford, and Astoria as well.[29] As the local ballot campaigns emerged, the same general pattern persisted. Most of the state's major newspapers condemned the measures on the grounds that they were asking voters to act against nonexistent dangers. As the *Oregonian* declared: "Our schools and governments are not promoting homosexuality; no affirmative-action quotas exist or are proposed to threaten heterosexuals with losing their jobs or promotions to homosexuals; there is no homosexual conspiracy to recruit children into 'the homosexual lifestyle'; Oregon governments are not lining up to give homosexuals 'minority status' and nobody is asking them to do it."[30]

In Timbertown, much the same was true. In terms of its editorial policy, the *Gazette* sympathized with CAN's social liberalism; several of the reporters were friends with CAN activists. Week after week, the paper's editorials, which refused to mince words, came out solidly against the OCA. The *Gazette* consistently ran editorials that condemned OCA organizers as religious zealots; one editorial criticized fundamentalism, grouping Maoists, the people who blew up the

World Trade Center, and the present government of Israel, with fundamentalist Christians, and called for a "kinder, gentler, Christian fundamentalism." As the charter measure campaign arrived in Timbertown, Simon Perez proclaimed, in an editorial entitled "We Don't Need an OCA Fix for Our Charter," that the measure was a sham.

> Some wise philosopher once said, "If it ain't broke, don't fix it." I wonder what the OCA is trying to fix in Timbertown. . . . Don't get me wrong. I don't want any special rights for homosexuals. (As a rule, I am opposed to special rights for anyone except me, members of my immediate family and perhaps a very few friends). . . . What form could "special rights" take in the city? The city can't give homosexuals preference for hiring because the city never asks an applicant anything about sexual preference. . . . So what will change if we pass an anti-gay measure here? Nothing will change about how homosexuals are treated by the city. The library will have the same books it has now. Schools won't be affected. However, things will change. First, Timbertown will be thrown into an ugly and divisive battle. If this measure passes, as it well might, Timbertown will get a ton of bad publicity and two tons of grief. . . . The OCA doesn't give a rip about you and me. This is about money and power. . . . Our charter ain't broke. Let's not allow the OCA to "fix" it.[31]

Without embracing an explicitly pro-gay agenda, the *Gazette* tended to promote a liberal pluralist "we are all different" stance that was consonant with its commercial and institutional needs to appeal to a broad cross section of the community and be "everyone's newspaper." On the issue of homosexuality, the newspaper embraced the notion of sexual essences—gays just can't help it—echoing CAN's position. In July 1993, after geneticist Dean Hamer, studying homosexual brothers, reported finding a genetic link to homosexuality in an X chromosome inherited from the mother, an editorial suggested that the study "adds a big piece to the puzzle of how homosexuals become the way they are. It is one thing to demonstrate that homosexuality runs in families. It is something quite different to show that it is an abnormality of the X chromosome. (It now appears that it is the mother's fault after all, but not in the way we used to think.)"[32]

During the course of the campaign, from the day the OCA unveiled its plans to run the measure on January 20, 1993, to the day of the election, on May 18, 1994, seventy-one issues of the newspaper were published; of these, fifteen featured editorials opposing the OCA initiative. There were also a series of editorial cartoons that offered stinging criticisms of the OCA and its religious zealotry. One depicted a massive Lon Mabon figure poised on a soapbox, carrying copies of the ballot proposal, and declaring "I'm Baaa-ack!" Standing off to the side, dazed and confused, were three stunned Timbertown residents, wiping sweat from their brows. Another cartoon pictured the OCA as a helmeted crusader perched on a steed, carrying a sword with an antigay petition on one end. He rides into city hall and addresses an employee who fearfully is hiding behind her desk: "We're here to share the love of God with the Homosexual Community. . . . Where do they Live?" Yet another cartoon depicted Lon Mabon playing checkers with a beaver identified as "Joe Legislator." A stack of papers, "Actual State Business," languishes on the legislator's desk. Mabon moves a checker on the board and tells the beaver legislator, "King Me."

The letters to the editor column, perhaps the most widely read part of the paper, offered a broader range of opinions about the proposed charter amendment. During the campaign, the newspaper published eighty-three letters to the editor on the charter measure controversy. Of these, a majority—forty-eight in all—opposed the OCA-backed measure. A greater range of people wrote letters opposing the measure than supporting it, creating the impression that CAN had a larger pool of activists and active supporters than the OCA and its allies had. The small core of OCA activists, who frequently wrote letters to the editor, became familiar names in the paper. Barney Wooten's claim to fame was that he had over fifty letters to the editor published in area newspapers, a fact of which he was especially proud.

Of the other major issues facing the community, only two rivaled the ballot measure in terms of the attention it commanded in the pages of the newspaper: a controversy surrounding a proposed plan to build a cavernous Wal-Mart on an eighteen-acre parcel of land outside of town, and an effort to pass a bond issue to finance a new high school, to alleviate the consequences of a property tax limitation approved by voters in 1990, which slashed the education budget. Under the headline "New High School, Not OCA Is the Big Local Issue on May Ballot," Perez editorialized:

> The city charter amendment will probably pass here. After it passes nothing will change. The city will not root out homosexuals in our midst. No homosexual will get fired (if, indeed, any work for the city now). The City will be prevented from promoting homosexuality, something it

would never do anyway. . . . The educational park vote, on the other
hand, will make an enormous difference. . . . We get a new high school.
The old school is in sad shape.[33]

Despite his suggestion that the ballot measure was a waste of time and
money, and ineffectual at best, however, the issue dominated the
pages of the newspaper for months. Identity-politics trumped small-
town politics-as-usual. During the seventeen-month period that began when the OCA declared its intention to place the measure on the
ballot and ended on Election Day, twenty-nine news articles focused
on the ballot measure battle, and the vast majority were lead stories on
the front page with accompanying photographs. For the first six
months of the campaign, the story was given more prominence than
either land use or education, the other two issues that were hotly debated in town. Education and development issues were important but
often boring. The gay rights issue made good copy. It had a human
face, pit well-known personalities in town against one another, and
was high on drama.

Week after week, the front page of the *Gazette* featured stories
about some OCA leader in town—Jeri Cookson, Pamela Sneed, or
Sally Humphries most prominently—gathering signatures to place
the measure on the local ballot, condemning the permissive society,
criticizing the city council for wavering on whether to place the measure on the local ballot, railing against the Oregon state senate for trying to circumvent the measure, and rallying the troops when Lon Mabon came to town. "Battle Is Back," "OCA Renews Attack on Gay
Rights," "OCA Complaints Allege Violations," "OCA Cries Foul
Over New City Ordinance" were typical headlines. And each such
action was met by a response from those who opposed the OCA:
"Timbertown Council Opposes Anti-Gay Campaign," "Showdown
Looms on OCA Initiative," "Mayor, Councilors, Feel Stress." Such
stories conveyed the impression that OCA activists were engaged in
combat and reveling in confrontation, and that the town of Timbertown, forced to respond, tried valiantly but unsuccessfully to keep
the peace.

If the reporters and editors of the newspaper tended to find Christian conservative views objectionable, their views were tempered
by a small-town ethos that values coexistence amid adversity. Like
many others in town, *Gazette* staffers suggested that while the OCA
might be a reprehensible organization, rank-and-file OCA mem-

bers were often good, well-meaning folks, and the paper never editorialized against local OCA activists by name, preferring instead to target Lon Mabon and other leaders who lived outside of the community. Chuck Mendip, who worked as a reporter for the *Gazette* during the campaign, drew a familiar distinction between OCA leaders, whom he termed "political," meaning they did things to amass power, and supporters, and those who opposed abortion and homosexuality because they honestly thought it was wrong. "I think Pamela Sneed is political, and I think Mabon is political," he told me. Their followers, on the other hand, are "doing what their faith tells them to do."

But subtlety does not make for stinging campaign slogans—or for good newspaper copy. Despite the best intentions of individual reporters to "report the story as they saw it," media conventions and routines, which favored images of visual conflict, often won out. The mass media feasts on drama and conflict and loathes historical contextualization, and the harsher the words, the greater the chance that newspapers would publish a letter to the editor or a quote from an activist, or run a photo of someone holding a placard emblazoned with a swastika on the front page. At a city council meeting, when Martha Jensen compared the OCA's use of propaganda with that of the Nazis, the next day her comments appeared in the pages of the *Gazette*. Social movements in a mass-mediated society must use the media to get their message across; in order to use the media, they must conform to certain definitions of what is newsworthy.[34] OCA leaders certainly knew this and framed their press releases, public actions, and press conferences accordingly, emphasizing conflict, confrontation, and hyperbole. But the media is a double-edged sword. The more they used the media, the more beholden they were to it, and the less control they had over how the conflict was framed.

Jeri Cookson wrote a letter to the editor of the Timbertown *Gazette* complaining that her words had been "twisted and used on the front page . . . to create controversy, sell papers, and create division in our community."[35] Another woman complained about a photograph accompanying an article about the OCA: "You really must have taken a lot of pictures to find one as unflattering. . . . I mean, that lady looks as if she's ready to do some major gay bashing! Actually she was probably just squinting into the sun. But only your photographer knows for sure and your readers only see what you let them. I'm surprised you didn't have a picture next to it of someone from the [opposing side] with a big smile, handing out ice cream cones to small children."[36]

When she read the newspaper, Sally Humphries was often taken aback. "What could I possibly have to do with the Nazis?" she wondered, confused and hurt that anyone would possibly think or say such things in public. When a letter to the editor in the *Gazette* called Humphries an "articulate bigot" an alternative weekly in Eugene picked up the story, running her photo above the caption, "I'm Sally Humphries. Just call me an articulate bigot." As Sally said to me, "I don't feel like a bigot, and I don't feel that I'm very articulate either!" Friends made light of it, stopping her on the street and greeting her with "Hi, articulate bigot!" But she felt stung by the criticism. "Being called a Nazi made me realize how hateful people can be, how people can turn your words against you." "The media doesn't like Christians," said John James, who proceeded to tell me about a Gallup poll that found that 87 percent of newspaper reporters never go to church. "That's way under the national average. They are not very representative of the cross section of the American people." James believes that if Christians wanted accurate news, they must to listen to their own radio and television stations.

Charged with promoting "liberal bias," the publisher of the Timbertown *Gazette* responded with the following:

> I think there's no doubt about it: most of the news people I know are liberal on these issues. I doubt that Measure 9 got more than fifteen percent of the vote in the newsrooms I know. Why is that? Is there some liberal conspiracy in the media? I think there are three chief reasons why folks in the newsroom are more liberal than the average man or woman. The first reason has to do with education. Higher education trains people to value diversity, an open mind and a healthy skepticism. Educated people tend to be more "liberal" and news people are almost all college educated. Second is the matter of self selection. Newsroom people tend to be idealistic (beneath a thin cover of cynicism) and not very materialistic. Third, a reporter's job is likely to make him or her tolerant. . . . Reporters and editors run into a wide variety of people representing the spectrum of opinion and background. People who deal with a broad variety of people are more likely to see all kinds of people as individuals and not label them as part of a group.[37]

Because newspaper reporters and editors reflect—to a great extent—the dominant culture and embrace a liberal pluralist "we're all different" ethos, Christian conservative views do not play well in the media; newspaper coverage portrayed OCA activists as religious zealots who were dividing Timbertown.[38] This coverage had unintended consequences and carried hidden costs. It fueled the anger of OCA activists, and provided evidence that society really does hate Christians and that they must stick together and make common cause.

WE ARE NOT NAZIS—WE ARE VICTIMS

An OCA flyer asked: "When you speak out against the homosexual agenda in your County or town, have you been called a bigot, a Nazi, a hatemonger? Don't fall for it! And don't be intimidated by such tactics. These tactics have been used before! You have the right to defend the common good of society. YOU NEED TO RECOGNIZE THESE TACTICS. Who's doing the name calling? Who's acting hateful? Who's using fascist tactics? DO NOT ALLOW YOURSELF TO BE INTIMIDATED. YOU HAVE A RIGHT TO PROTECT YOUR COMMUNITY, FAMILY AND VALUES."[39]

Lon Mabon criticized Governor Roberts for comparing his group with the Nazis. The governor should be ashamed of such comments, he said. "There are many people in OCA who fought in WWII. To denigrate their sacrifice is unconscionable."[40] "I'm one of those Christian fundamentalists you warn my neighbors about," an OCA activist in Timbertown wrote to the editor of the *Gazette*. "I live in a personal relationship with the God who created me. . . . However, I didn't realize that I was such a threat. I haven't blown up any buildings yet, or gone on a suicide mission. I haven't even raised a rifle and shouted 'Jihad!' Would you like me to wear a yellow star, er . . . I mean cross, just to identify myself as a potential problem?"[41]

Conservative Christians' claims that they alone knew the truth, the word of God, discredited them as religious loonies and hateful people. They needed a different way of representing themselves to the broader public, in a fashion that would appeal to the general values shared by most Americans. As sociologist Frank Lechner suggests, Christian fundamentalism is inherently an ambivalent stance; much the same could be said of politicized Christian conservatives in general. On the one hand, they reject secularism, with its separation of church and state; its efforts to include individuals of different cultures, races, religions, and values; and its support of a pluralistic society in which only the most general values are common to all. Their belief in the absolute authority of the Bible and their quest to impose a particular set of moral standards on all of society are thus rejections of the tenets of modern secular liberal society. Yet their very existence and ability to make any claims at all are based on those very tenets. As a minority often viewed with derision, they must appeal to the inclusiveness and tolerance of American society to reserve a place for themselves in the cultural debate. So on the one hand, then, religious traditionalists attempt to dictate "correct" beliefs and behaviors to its adherents, as well as to export them to the larger society. On the other hand, they can hardly reject completely the right and responsibility of individuals to base commitments on their own consciences. It becomes necessary to appeal to the broad general values shared by all Americans, which are likely to allow for more tolerance and ambiguity than are consistent with core fundamentalist beliefs.[42]

Recognizing this, to elicit broader sympathy, the Christian right began to usurp the rhetoric of victimhood, redefining itself in the language of interest group liberalism and identity politics.[43] Deborah Lipstadt, who has written about Holocaust deniers and revisionists, provides a clue as to why this rhetoric is so powerful. "The general public tends to accord victims . . . a certain moral authority," she writes. "If you devictimize a people you strip them of their moral authority, and if you can in turn claim to be a victim . . . that moral authority is conferred on or restored to you."[44] Shifting from an earlier notion of Christians as guardians of the status quo who represent the "moral majority" to an understanding of Christians as an oppressed minority composed of social outcasts, the Christian right claimed that it was misunderstood and maligned by the "liberal media," heckled, mocked, and abused by communities who claim to celebrate diversity. OCA members began to shift the terms of the debate, arguing that they were in fact the victims, *they* were the persecuted minorities—not gays. In the "Holocaust frame," they began to cast themselves as the Jews.

OCA leader Janice Henry complained that someone painted a swastika on her family's "Yes on 9" sign, explaining that her husband chased the car and helped police apprehend two women, and when she told the story to four reporters, she said, the press wouldn't touch it. "Painting the OCA as Nazis is a common theme for these folks," she declared. "They got the strategy straight out of *Mein Kampf*—

accuse your opponents of what you are, and get the jump on them so they'll look so bad they won't accuse you." Like many OCA activists, she thought of herself as a good citizen who had the nation's best interests at heart. The real haters, the real Nazis and KKKers, were *over there,* in the South, or in Europe. *We* are good, caring people.

Of course, progressives were dedicated to making the opposite argument, and they mobilized Holocaust memories to do so. In 1992, after a neo-Nazi group leafleted a high school in the small town of Sweet Home, Oregon, local human rights groups sponsored a showing of an exhibit based on the life of Anne Frank, the girl whose story has become synonymous with the Holocaust for many Americans, thanks to the postwar publication and circulation of her diary, which was made into a movie and play. The traveling exhibit, which details the everyday lives of Frank and her family while hidden in an attic during the Nazi occupation of Amsterdam, and includes photographs and memorabilia documenting the persecution of Jews, gypsies, the disabled, and Communists during the war, ends with a series of panels that depict other instances of hatred and intolerance: neo-Nazi movements in postwar Europe, institutionalized racism in 1950s America, and Christian right homophobia.

The exhibit made its debut in the early 1980s at the Anne Frank House in Amsterdam, which attracts tens of thousands of visitors annually, and travels throughout the world to communities willing to sponsor it and undertake local educational efforts associated with it. During the course of the campaign against Ballot Measure 9, groups opposing the OCA sponsored the Anne Frank exhibit in cities and towns throughout Oregon, and an estimated thirty thousand people saw it from December 1992 through May 1994.[45] As a consequence, it became highly politicized. When the exhibit was shown in Eugene, an OCA member was incensed by its effort to draw links between anti-Semitism and homophobia, calling it "pro-homosexual propaganda," and wrote a letter to the editor of the *Eugene Register-Guard:*

> The displays showed how the popular social movement stirred ancient prejudices against the Jewish people, calling first for boycotts of their businesses, then for their removal from places of influence, and then stripping society of anything that alluded to their religion. Finally, the displays showed how the "politically correct" exterminated them. The chill hit me as recent hateful accusations made against fundamentalist

> Christians. . . . Like Germany of the 1930s, no views but the politically
> correct are tolerated today—especially in Eugene, where the slogan
> "honor diversity" is just another way of saying, "See it my way, you igno-
> rant narrow-minded bigot!" I realized if you change the name of the
> faith from Judaism to evangelical Christianity . . . you might just wonder
> if history is starting to repeat itself. I wonder if my children will be forced
> to wear yellow crosses instead of stars.[46]

Christian conservatives had turned liberal secularists who support gay
rights into "politically correct" storm troopers—echoing radio talk
show host Rush Limbaugh's rants against "feminazis." Speaking of
the traveling exhibit about the life of Anne Frank, a gay rights sympa-
thizer asked, "Did this letter's author go to the same exhibit my family did?"

> Christians make up the majority of the population; they are not a minor-
> ity by any means like the gays and Jews were during the 1930s and today.
> The right-wing Christians started the whole "gay agenda" mess with
> many of the same arguments the Nazis used. . . . I am sick of seeing real-
> ity twisted by Oregon Citizens Alliance types until the very same persons
> who are denying a group's basic rights are claiming that they are the ones
> who are the victims.[47]

The more they were called names—Nazis and bigots—the more
OCA members positioned themselves as victims and martyrs. And
then they began to deliberately provoke their opponents to call them
such names. In the midst of the Timbertown campaign, the OCA appeared in the annual Eugene Celebration parade whose theme was
"Honor Diversity." A gay/lesbian activist group warned its supporters
against taking action that would incite the OCA's wrath. "Remember, as bizarre as it sounds, OCA members see themselves as the victimized parties, and they will probably record any negative responses
for use as 'proof' in future campaign propaganda," it warned. "Let's
not rise to the bait." The group invited gay rights supporters to march
with its contingent in the parade. "If you feel you must make a statement," it advised, "turn your back as OCA passes by."[48] The OCA
contingent appeared in the parade with a float depicting three family
values scenes: a wedding; a family gathered around the dinner table;
and a grandfather reading to his grandchildren. Each tableau was
staffed by living, breathing OCA members and their family members.
As predicted, when the float passed by, thousands of onlookers turned

their backs, and a handful of people threw eggs at the float and attempted to block the route.

"They've been caught with their pants down, exposing the intolerance and violence that mark their movement. So much for hon-
oring diversity!" proclaimed OCA spokesperson Pamela Sneed the
day after, railing against those who "turn their back on people with
whom they disagree," and charging that a boy on the float was hit
with a piece of ham, and mooned by a male parade participant who
"dropped his jeans (skirt? whatever . . .) and bent over to reveal a message on the back of his black under-shorts: Gender neutral zone."[49]
"Traditional Christianity is now the Evil Empire for the politically
correct," said spokesperson Janice Henry. "We are labeled as intolerant and hateful people. Do gay and bisexual people shrivel up in horror at the sight of happy families, like vampires confronted with a
cross? Are OCA members the only ones who eat dinner, go to weddings, read aloud to children?"[50]

The rhetoric of victimhood resonated with many OCA members
who thought of themselves as members of a moral minority demonized by a secular society. "I'm one of those nasty right-wing nuts,"
said sixty-five-year-old Jeri Cookson facetiously when I interviewed
her in her home. She distrusted me, assumed that I—very much like
the media—was out to make her look bad, yet at the same time she
was pleased, flattered that I took the time to ask for her opinions. Despite her initial hesitation, Jeri held forth for several hours. "You
know I don't usually talk to people like you," she said. "I don't think
a whole lot of those people up at the university." For Jeri, "university
people" are liberal, morally lax secular humanists who can't be
trusted. Like many other OCA activists I interviewed, she seemed
guarded, leery of my intentions, and wondered whether I would portray her as a shrill, intolerant old biddy.

When asked her how she would describe her religious beliefs,
Erica Williams replied, "I'm a very conservative, Bible-believing
Christian, one of those 'mean-spirited' ones." Is that how she
thought of herself? "Well, that's what they describe people who are
very conservative Christians: mean-spirited," she replied. Which
people? "The people in the press, people around town," she said. Has
anyone in town ever called her these things? "Not to my face, no. But
I'm sure they say it in private." In describing the Oregon Citizens Alliance, Barney Wooten asserted, "We've been enormously demon-

ized in this state. They label us as 'hateful' or 'bigoted' or 'narrow-minded.'"

OCA activists' rhetoric of victimhood was consciously staged to win the public's sympathy. But it was powerful because it spoke to the widespread belief among conservative Christians that they truly were persecuted by a culture dominated by secular and commercial values. Because they are committed to an ethos of individual self-reliance, conservatives can't acknowledge the real roots of their victimhood. Because they see feelings of shame as a sign of weakness, they deny them. Political rhetoric that speaks to their sense of victimhood, locates a cause, and offers them the possibility of seeing themselves as strong, independent beings helps them to transform unacknowledged shame into anger—and displace it on to others.

In recent years, the notion that Christians are oppressed has become a centerpiece of national Christian conservative rhetoric. In September 1996, more than one hundred thousand American congregations observed an International Day of Prayer for the Persecuted Church, coordinated by the World Evangelical Fellowship, which joins national and regional associations of evangelical churches around the world. Convinced that Christians have become "special targets" around the world, particularly under Communist regimes such as those in China, North Korea, and Vietnam, and militant Muslim movements in the Sudan, Pakistan, and Iran, evangelical leaders urged such bodies as the U.S. Congress and the Immigration and Naturalization Service to give higher priority to the religious persecution of Christians.

When I attended a service at Caroll Neitz's Pentecostal church one Sunday, I heard a sermon about missionaries in Goma, Zaire, who were "burned out of their houses." Over "five hundred Christians died in Zaire last year!" Neitz told his congregation. "Let's pray for all of the persecuted Christians the world over." In a newsletter, photographs of tortured pastors and burned churches urged churchgoers to pray and collect funds for the victims. The emphasis upon Christians as persecuted people resonated with their belief in redemption through suffering and suggested that a discourse of victimhood had become pervasive in American political culture. When conservative critic Charles Sykes charged the left with transforming America into a "nation of victims," he could hardly have predicted that the right, too, would jump on the victim bandwagon.

In the 1990s, a movement for fetal rights spoke of the plight of the "smallest victims," providing evidence, in Lauren Berlant's words, that "the national victim has become a cultural dominant in America" and that "political authenticity depends on the individual's humiliating exile" from power and privilege.[51] On both the theological left and right, the *New York Times* reports, a consensus is emerging. "After decades of soul-searching over the indifference or even complicity of some Christians in the Holocaust and in genocidal wars in Rwanda and Bosnia, Christians are seeing themselves as the victims and martyrs of the moment."[52] This rhetoric had particular appeal for Timbertown's conservative Christian activists.

If confrontations with the secular public helped conservative Christians strengthen their commitment and solidarity, clashes with the media, which they viewed as part of the liberal elite establishment, had much the same effect. If the right initiated these conflicts, the left—equating Christian activists with Nazis—ate the bait. Adopting the language of liberal democracy, the right, in turn, reveled in the belief that *they* were aggrieved victims. Such rhetorical excesses, writes James Davison Hunter, are characteristic of the contemporary "culture wars" in which different groups utilize hyperbole to appeal to the emotional predispositions of the public.[53] If neither CAN nor the OCA could reasonably hope to recruit many outsiders to its cause, by using exaggerated claims each urged the broader public to dis-identify with the other. "Promoting dis-identification," writes Cindy Patton, "produce[s] at least temporary allies."[54]

The media amplified the conflict, drawing the sides in an even more polarized fashion than they had done themselves, but both sides were, to varying degrees, complicit in this process. The OCA very deliberately tried to polarize the battle and force people to choose sides. CAN, in contrast, tried to run an nonconfrontational campaign, but was backed into a corner and forced to participate in a knock-down-drag-out fight. Many people in town, even those who sympathized with CAN, were alarmed by how deeply the confrontation polarized Timbertown. "Beat them with a stick. That's what they do, both groups," said Chuck Mendip, a timber-worker-turned-journalist and Democratic Party activist. "They beat you with a stick. Whoever can draw blood wins. It's not a way to run a country. It's not a way to run a city. It doesn't work." But the damage was done.

CHAPTER 9

Whose Side Are You On?

The public fight over homosexuality was initially waged by a fairly small group of activists at the extremes. There were probably no more than forty or so activists in the OCA and CAN combined, people who became involved because the campaign spoke to their strong convictions: Christian conservatives who wished to make a stand for the universality of Christian values, and liberals who wanted to affirm pluralism and individual choice. The ambivalent middle, the vast majority of people in town, weren't particularly enamored of homosexuals but most didn't want to deprive them of their rights either. In the course of the campaign, each side tried to persuade this ambivalent majority to take a stand. It was, initially, a difficult task.

Linda Mabley expressed concern that her elementary school–age kids might suffer repercussions if she came out against the OCA. "I worried a little about whether people wouldn't want their kids to play with my kids anymore, and whether there would be any fallout for them." Her family urged her not to take a stand on the issue, worrying that it would alienate them from the community. OCA supporters, for their part, had similar experiences. In public, whenever activists stood at the freeway intersection holding up signs that read "Save Our Children" and "Stop Special Rights," a number of "secret disciples" approached them and told them that they subscribed to their family-values principles but were afraid of appearing with them in public. "Small towns can be kind of repressive," said Barney Wooten. "People would come up and almost whisper to us that they support us and hope we kept it up, and then say, 'I worked for the school system and can't really say anything,' or 'I'm glued to my job' and that kind of stuff." In small towns, as a newspaper reporter told me, "any time you voice your opinion, you become an activist." Taking a stand on a divisive issue can therefore be a scary prospect, threatening the pervasive belief in small-town solidarity.

Supporters of CAN made a point of wearing their buttons around town. "It was strange wearing that button," said Janice Trump, because it implied guilt by association: so inconceivable was the notion that heterosexuals might take a stand on behalf of gay rights that many people assumed that supporters of gay rights must be gay themselves. "People at the grocery store would stare at you from the corner of their eyes," said Janice, "and you just knew they were wondering, Is she gay?" When Sally Humphries attended city council meetings when the charter measure was discussed, she was often surprised by the presence of so many women she assumed were lesbians. Were they really lesbians? I asked her. "They must've been," she replied. "They looked like lesbians, and they spoke out for gay rights. They were kinda unkempt, messy. They didn't wear makeup, and they wore blue jeans."

But appearances could be deceiving. The vast majority of the unkempt activists clad in blue jeans and sensible shoes were in fact heterosexual women, and sometimes the straightest-looking Timbertowners were actually queer as a three-dollar bill. At one point during a heated city council discussion of the measure, Sally Humphries leaned over to Cindy Barber, standing with two of her children, and told her she was amazed by how many lesbians there were in town, evidenced by the turnout. Cindy's feminine self-presentation and her appearance with her children meant that her sexuality remained unmarked, so Sally assumed she was straight and was therefore on her side. If "real" lesbians, in Sally's view, were unkempt and masculinized, lesbian mothers barely existed. The OCA's homosexual bugbear—the aggressive, macho gay man—was all but nonexistent in Timbertown. Describing the scene at city council meetings during the campaign, Sally noted, "The men were never there. I would say to my husband, 'What about the men? Where are they?'"

To OCA activists, lesbians were a secondary threat—they might be aggressive and masculine, but they were women first and foremost which meant they were essentially nurturers and therefore less threatening than gay men. Right-wing rhetoric divided society into two groups: hypermasculine warrior men and ultrafeminine women, revalorizing biblical interpretations of absolute gender differences. Homosexual men who are aggressively masculine and lesbian women who are mothers and who exhibit other traditionally feminine traits threatened the Christian right belief in absolute gender differences, and revealed a fundamental incoherence in its discourse. When they did encounter a real lesbian, as Sally Humphries's meeting with Cindy Barber suggested, if she didn't conform to their preconceptions of what lesbians look like, OCA activists assumed she was straight. One could not be a masculinized aggressive predator and also a mother, as conservative Christians define mothers—nice and pure and normal; lesbian mothers were therefore a contradiction in terms, defined out of existence.[1] Much the same was true in relation to male homosexuals: if they did not parade around town as out, open, and aggressively masculine, they were for all intents and purposes invisible.

If OCA activists encountered queer people and imagined they were straight, the taint of homosexuality attached itself to unsuspecting heterosexuals, including a bank teller named Gay who, in the course of the campaign, became a source of great curiosity—and alarm. The OCA campaign proclaimed that since gays had higher incomes than most, attempts to extend them legal protections constituted "special rights." Some Timbertowners, convinced by these claims, imagined that the special privileges gays enjoyed included their own line at the bank, and avoided the line at all costs, imagining it was the "gay line." When the teller began to realize that many patrons of the bank refused to use her services, she insisted that the bank place her last name on her name card instead of her first, and normality resumed.

When conservative-leaning individuals looked around and began to imagine the homosexual threat lurking everywhere, liberals surveyed the scene and saw nice people who suddenly seemed mean inside. Cassie Smith, who worked as a secretary at the middle school, began to realize that some of her coworkers, whom she had liked very much, supported the OCA initiative. "I assumed that everybody had basically the same philosophy as I did if they were of the same age and background. But I was wrong." Some of those who supported the OCA surprised Cassie, including the principal of one of the schools. "This person works in public education! He and his family were churchgoers and circulated petitions for the OCA. When people would call him on it, he'd say, 'I love the sinner but hate the sin,' whatever that line is." At one point during the campaign, she had a loud discussion with a male teacher in the lounge, while Barbara Hammer, whom Cassie knew to be a lesbian, sat across from them. "I guess he didn't have a clue. And he was going on and on loudly: I don't want those people in a position of leadership, where they can influence. It was funny to me that after all those years he didn't know, and if he knew he didn't care if he was offending her or changing her perceptions of him."

Sometimes, conflicts destroyed friendships. Cindy Barber and her girlfriend, Sammie, occasionally substituted at a gas station in town to earn money to supplement their bookstore earnings. They befriended a woman named Jackie who watched their store while they moonlighted at the gas station. Eventually, the three women became very close, playing cards every month, and exchanging presents at Christmas. Cindy and Sammie never talked about being lesbians, but nor did they hide their relationship from her. But when Cindy became an outspoken opponent of the OCA-sponsored measure, Jackie's sister Marcy felt threatened, and drove by the store yelling, "Dyke!"

When the OCA staged a rally on the corner outside of the Cindy and Sammie's bookstore, Marcy was out there with the rest of them, carrying antigay signs and chanting slogans. But when Cindy and Sammie's across-the-street neighbor, whose kids had played with their kids every day for years, stood up at a city council meeting and argued in favor of the charter measure, that was the final straw. Cindy was floored. Did he not know the impact that would have on his lesbian neighbors? Or did he simply not care? she wondered. "It was ugly, ugly, ugly." It changed the way she viewed the town. "Before I could walk down the street and say this is my home, but suddenly everyone seemed to become my enemy. It was no longer just a political situation that was going on all over the state. Some of these people were my friends. These were my friends that were coming out and saying, 'I hate you for what you are.'"

As owners of local businesses, lesbian and gay men had a lot to lose. During the campaign, Harry Boyle, a small business owner who is straight, told me that he often asked people if they would patronize gay-owned businesses, and most replied that they would not. "Well, you do," he told them. "Two restaurants, a couple of businesses, and a bar are owned by lesbians. And a few businesses are run by gay men." The day Cindy Barber placed a sign in their bookstore window opposing the charter amendment, people began to talk. "Did you see that sign in their window?" they asked. "Those women must be, you know, lesbians." If previously they were fairly invisible as a lesbian couple, during the course of the campaign, people began to put two and two together: the fact that they were two women who had a store, who lived together, who raised kids together was no coincidence—though June and Janice Trump, sisters who owned the new bookstore down the block, were also assumed to be lesbians. But in Cindy and Sammie's case the claim was true, and that made all the difference. One day, a young man who had been a regular customer stopped into the store to chat, as he often did, about goings-on around town, and occasionally about books. He saw the anti-OCA poster in the window and told Sammie she was a sinner who would burn in hell, and that he would never return to the store again.

As small business owners took stands in favor of or against the measure, their clientele often shifted. When Sammie and Cindy began to openly oppose the OCA, their customer base dropped by nearly 50 percent but the loss was offset by liberals in town who went out of their way to patronize them because of their gay rights stand. One day, one woman bought fifty dollars' worth of books, most of them priced seventy-five cents or a dollar, and told Cindy: "I wouldn't be buying from you if it wasn't for your sign. I'm concerned that your business is not going to survive this OCA campaign." Cindy bought a bunch of gay rights buttons and began to sell them at the store, and she and Sammie began to meet other business owners who were also CAN supporters, like June and Janice Trump, who also experienced a strain in their relationships with some customers.

Janice Trump had a basket of CAN buttons for sale near the cash register in her store, which was also the only ticket outlet for the community theater. One day OCA activist Erica Williams sauntered in to purchase a ticket for a performance and spotted the buttons. "Is there any other place to get a ticket?" she inquired. Janice replied, "Nope, we're the only outlet." Soon, other OCA supporters also stopped shopping in the store. When a small business owner who was also a city councilor voted to keep the initiative off the ballot, the OCA and their supporters boycotted her business and harassed her, forcing her to consider resigning from the council.[2]

CAN supporters also engaged in informal boycotts of businesses owned by OCA supporters. Sonia Mellen, a forty-six-year-old lesbian health worker, told me she regularly bought gas from an independent gas station, paying higher prices because she believed in supporting small businesses in the community. During the charter campaign, she began to scrutinize the businesses she regularly patronized and asked the two older men who ran the gas station how they stood on the charter issue. "This is outrageous but I need to know whether or not you are going to vote to call me perverse and unnatural and all the rest of it," she said. One of the men looked at her and said, "I am going to vote that way." And so Sonia replied, "Well, I can't buy my gas here." The man retorted, "You know, it really doesn't cost that much more here," and Sonia said, "That's not the point," and drove away in tears.

Even pastors who supported the OCA expressed surprise at how polarized the town became. When he first became involved in the campaign, Lance White of the Timbertown Christian Center thought it was clear and simple—we don't want to give special rights to homosexuals. "A hound dog might battle a skunk, but it's worth a battle." At a rally where his congregation and other OCA supporters stood on one side of the street chanting and holding signs in favor of the charter measure and CAN members stood on the other side of the street shouting and holding signs against the charter measure, he began to rethink his involvement. White failed to anticipate the extent to which the campaign would split the town, and he became increasingly ambivalent about participating openly in the campaign. Other conservative church leaders had similar misgivings.

Caroll Neitz agreed with the OCA's claim that homosexuality was immoral, but he began to wonder whether morality should or could be legislated at the ballot box. "Sometimes we're going to win, sometimes we're going to lose as far as what the Lord would do. But where it's really worked out is in personal relationships. If I have a homosexual friend, is he going to see Christ's likeness in me? That's more important than which box I check at the polls." And Bob Harrison, of Mountaintop Church, who was initially an enthusiastic supporter of the OCA began to back off a bit, fearing that his antigay stance might alienate some members of his congregation. When several pastors in the ministerial association placed an ad in the *Gazette* endorsing the OCA-backed measure on behalf of their churches, Harrison began to wonder: "We do have a political agenda of righteousness but we don't want to ostracize people. I'm not hesitant to say things in the building about going to the ballot box, but if we're in the street we're identified with a political agenda. That can be dangerous."

Every year, the city of Timbertown, like many small towns throughout the nation, sponsors an annual Mayor's Prayer Breakfast, a communitywide public gathering in which an inspirational speaker addresses the mayor and other civic leaders, along with representatives from the religious community. Typically, these breakfasts are fairly ecumenical affairs featuring benign motivational speakers, but the arrival of the OCA encouraged the ministerial association to press for a more conservative speaker. A group of evangelical pastors including Irwin Callow, Ben Jaeger, and Lance White nominated conservative firebrand Marshall Foster, the founder and president of the Mayflower Institute, which seeks to "teach America's biblical inheritance of liberty," to be the featured speaker at the Mayor's Prayer Breakfast. Foster, a former director of the University of Southern California's Campus Crusade for Christ, is best known for his belief that natural disasters—floods, earthquakes, and pestilence—are God's punishment for sinful transgressions, and that San Francisco's 1989 earthquake was divine retribution for the city's reputation for tolerance. Foster's visit would include a prayer breakfast, a seminar for church leaders hosted by Bob Harrison at the Mountaintop Church of Christ, and a communitywide church service entitled "The Battle for the 21st Century."

Once liberals in town caught wind of the plan, the proverbial shit hit the fan. "Our founding fathers went out of their way to carefully separate church and state while guaranteeing religious freedom for all," longtime Democratic Party activist Marianne Woods argued. Foster, in contrast, "promotes the idea of Puritan leaders as national leaders" and excludes members of the faith community. A Christian leader in Timbertown retorted: "Nothing could be further from the truth. One need only look at the increasing crime, overflowing prisons, teenage pregnancy, racism, and distrust we feel with our religious institutions to see that our society is in need of healing. The May-flower Institute is a nondenominational educational foundation." He closed with a plea for liberal tolerance for conservative Christians: "Please respect every citizen's right to freedom of speech and assembly."[3] Still, many people in the community felt the breakfast would be divisive, that it was part of the OCA's strategy to reconstruct the community along religious lines and dismantle the barriers separating church and state. The mayor, fearing controversy, decided to withdraw her endorsement of the event.

''KIDS CAN BE PRETTY MEAN''

In small towns, the school is often the glue in the community. In Timbertown, it's the single institution that most people have a stake in: it is both glue and a principal source of division. After the timber industry scaled back its operations, the school district, employing 350 staff members, became the largest employer in town, along with the hospital. People turn up for high school football and basketball games en masse, and they also fight over what students are taught in school, and about how and how much to fund schools. It is perhaps unsurprising, then, that the high school also became the site of some of the most violent confrontations around gay rights.

During the 1992 Measure 9 campaign, the atmosphere of the school noticeably shifted. In a mock election held before the statewide measure, more than half of Timbertown high school students voted in favor of the measure, and 13 percent were undecided.[4] Many parents and teachers noted a rise in violent conflicts among kids during the feverish campaign. A group of boys constructed plywood figures hanging from nooses with "kill fags" written on them and wore them on chains around their necks. "Kids who were different were called names, and got beaten up," said Janice Trump. Many people believed that the OCA gave schoolchildren a license to hate. "Kids can be pretty mean," said Cindy Barber. The few out gay students at the high school became particular targets of harassment, as did the children of lesbians.

Sammie Melton's son Hal, a feisty sophomore, wore a campaign button on his hat in support of his lesbian mother. He was harassed, picked on, and one time, as she described it, "trapped and ketchuped"—squirted with ketchup from head to toe. Every day he wore his gay rights button, he was attacked and humiliated. Kids broke into his locker and stole his books. When his mothers complained to the school district they were told that Hal incited the attacks and should remove his button. "You make all the kids wearing OCA buttons remove theirs, and I'll remove mine," he told the teachers. They didn't take their buttons off, and the conflicts continued. Cindy Barber's twelve-year-old daughter Ginny walked arm in arm with her friend Laurie in front of the junior high school one day. Some kids knew that they identified as bisexual, and that Ginny had a lesbian mother. They kicked them, screaming, "Dyke," and threatened "to beat the living snot" out of them. Even Cindy's younger daughter Andrea, who was boy-crazy, was attacked: she was harassed and called a lesbian by another girl. But Andrea, a tough, strong-willed girl, retaliated and told the harasser to leave her sister alone, or "she would beat the crap out of her if she didn't shut her big fat mouth." Eventually, the harassment stopped.

These and other incidents tested the mettle of Barbara Hammer, who was vice principal and athletic director of the high school. As an administrator, Hammer thrived by being good at what she did, by being fairly nonchalant about her lesbianism, and by playing her cards wisely. She befriended potential enemies, lunching with conservative Christians, and was a gradualist, introducing reforms slowly and by being moderate in relation to controversial subjects like sex education. Barbara, a small-town Oregonian, knew how to speak her constituents' language. "We try to be responsive to what the parents want, and we also try to have pretty candid conversations with them: 'Okay, I understand what you want but have you thought about this, or have you thought about that?' We try to push them a little bit." And much of the time, she says, "they respond pretty well."

When I asked Barbara whether the school district's sex education curriculum includes discussions of homosexuality and other forms of sexual diversity, she explained that the teachers introduce the subject in the eighth grade, "although they're pretty cautious about it, pretty sensitive." In the tenth grade, in the sexuality unit, "it's presented as a choice." Parents rarely if ever complain—it's the topic of abortion that raises more hackles. But Barbara admits that in relation to its treatment of gay kids, and the kids of gay parents, the school district "probably doesn't do a very good job."

Nor did the school district do enough to deal with conflicts that broke out at the high school during the charter measure campaign, according to a number of parents and teachers. Since the school system was bound by law to remain neutral on electoral matters, it required its staff, who tended to oppose the OCA, to refrain from openly stating or displaying their opinions of the charter measure: they could discuss the content of the measure, and its possible ramifications, but could not express how they felt about it openly. There was, acknowledged Hammer, "a lot of anxiety on the part of members of the staff. They had strong opinions about the charter measure." Some teachers defied their union's orders to remain neutral and expressed their opposition to the charter measure, including a lesbian who wore a CAN pin. This teacher was attacked by a student, and later quit her job.

Hammer was called in to break up some of the scuffles, and as a school staff member she was forced to restrain herself from taking a stand against the OCA. By not intervening, Cindy Barber believed, she and other school administrators permitted hate to spread: "Neutrality was impossible in this circumstance. The schools should've protected the kids, at the very least, but they didn't." School board member Sylvia Watkins, who saw the dilemma through the eyes of an administrator as well as that of a parent, was more forgiving, "We were caught between a rock and hard place. We couldn't take a stand, because all hell would break loose." Eventually, sexuality was no longer the primary subject of the clashes: the conflict spilled over to race as well.

Two of the most visible cliques in the high school were called the "cowboys" and the "rappers." The cowboys were a small band of down-home country tough kids who dressed in Western gear and enjoyed hunting and risk taking, and were known to bully other kids. The rappers were a small group of Asians and Latinos and their white friends who wore baggy pants, listened to hip-hop music, and played soccer. The cowboys frequently taunted the rappers and called the white kids among them "wiggers," white niggers. Matt Cogan, the only black student at Timbertown High School, was popular among the "rappers," but cowboys were none too fond of him. "Matt seemed like a nice guy at first," one of the cowboys said, "but then he started wearing headbands and acting like he owned the world." Matt had recently arrived in town from Dallas and lived in a small house in the center of town with his two black siblings, a white stepmother and her three white children, and his father, who worked as a cook at a pancake restaurant.

One evening, on the night of a basketball game, twenty cowboys, current and former students at the high school, surrounded Matt as he left the gym, incensed that one of the cowboy's girlfriends was interested in the new hip black kid in school. They threatened to beat him up if he went out with the girl. In the past, kids of color tended to turn the other cheek when threatened by the cowboys. But Matt, who had come from a racially mixed urban school, lashed back, hitting Bill Munsey, one of the cowboys. The following day, three minority students, friends of Matt's, retaliated against the cowboys, and a series of brawls erupted. The three attackers were suspended for two to four days. The next day, the *Gazette* pictured five cowboys sporting shit-eating grins, baseball caps, and cowboy hats in front of a pickup truck. The cowboys claimed to be harassed by those "baggy pants people." Bill's mother supported his claim: "That Negro kid sidewinded Bill. I tell my son, you can't hit a Negro, they'll call you racist." Besides, she said, he couldn't fight back—he was already on probation. An editorial declared: "Prejudice and discrimination have finally reached their boiling point at Timbertown High School."

A few days later, things took a turn for the worse. Matt Cogan returned to school after receiving apologies from several of the cowboys who assaulted him. But one night, his father smelled gasoline at their house. Cogan looked outside and spotted someone running from the house, and noticed that gasoline had been poured along the back of the house. The community was shocked. Nearly one hundred people attended a meeting at the Presbyterian church, where students, parents, teachers, administrators, and school board members vented their concerns and frustrations. A popular cheerleader of mixed race ancestry recounted tearfully that she was the frequent victim of verbal and physical harassment at school.[5] Others spoke of the town's history of racism.

"Timbertown is known for racism and for fighting," said a student whose ancestors settled in the area 130 years ago. A woman suggested: "Older Timbertowners can remember the twenties and thirties, when blacks were publicly chased out of town by leading citizens. In recent years the persuasion has been more subtle. Still, most blacks don't stay long."[6] Laurie Sokol, a reporter for the *Gazette,* recalled: "I have seen a lot of emotional issues, but that community meeting at the church was the most amazing thing I've ever seen. Many were driven to tears by frustration and anger, but they wanted to confront it and make something positive from it." When these incidents occurred, said Sylvia Watkins, "it really made people go, 'Oh my God, all of these things are happening to our town.'"

Others came forward, testifying that racism was indeed rampant in Timbertown. "You wouldn't think that in rural Oregon I'd have to worry about becoming a target for racial harassment," said a letter to the editor. "After all, I'm white, male, armed, and in a bad mood most of the time." He then proceeded to tell readers that he owned a business that produced Japanese specialty mushrooms—called shiitake—and shipped them to Southern California. "I was silly enough to list the business, address included, in the Yellow Pages as Oregon Shiitake, Inc. In hindsight I guess I should have called it Willamette Mushrooms, or, better yet, the John Wayne Mushroom Ranch." One day, he received a message on his answering machine that threatened to kill him. The caller was under the mistaken impression that he was a mushroom buyer of Asian, possibly Vietnamese, heritage.

> I guess this experience places me in the rather small category of white males who have been subject to racial harassment by white males—of some sort. Life can be goofy. . . . What would it be like to really have a skin color different from pale and pink? . . . I know that I can walk down the street, go into stores, talk to people, and my skin color will not be an issue at all. The above mentioned phone call was more of a freak accident. However, in my mind the question inevitably arises: What is it like to know that such a phone call can come at any time? That you could be harassed when you shop for groceries? That your children may get into a shoving match at school and, therefore, someone wants to burn down your home?[7]

Many liberals noted that the OCA campaign exacerbated existing racial tensions in the town. The white mother of an adopted South Asian boy described "the bitterness seeping into the town" in the course of the campaign. "My son used to be a happy-go-lucky kid." He was conscious of being different from most kids in town, but "when the OCA came we began to see people on street corners shouting at one another."[8] Cassie Smith said, "Lines were drawn during the Measure 9 campaign in 1992. It's just kind of snowballed from that." And another woman suggested that

> the OCA gave many students in Oregon the message that prejudice, discrimination and intolerance were not only condoned but embraced. . . . You cannot blame the children for their behavior; they are simply emulating their role models. As long as respected members of our community support OCA policies . . . discrimination will continue to surface in the way our children treat each other.[9]

Others saw the problem largely in terms of economics. "The cowboy ethic is a dead-end vestige of the good old days in Timbertown when teenagers could just raise hell and not be serious about school because they were assured of decent jobs in the woods and the mills."[10] In other words, the cowboys were part of a declining working class, whose families were employed by the timber industry, and whose future was now uncertain. And then there were psychological explanations. Herman Fields, pastor of the Living Brook Church, blamed the cowboy phenomenon on a culture of violence, abuse, and drunkenness. "I guarantee you that most of those kids were abused. They see life in terms of dominance and submission." Given what I'd learned of Timbertown's macho culture, this explanation certainly seemed plausible. But singular explanations failed to grasp the wide scope of changes in motion. Global economic shifts simultaneously threatened the logging economy (and the traditional gender patterns it fostered) and also brought an influx of new immigrants, changing the composition of the town.

A counselor in the school district suggested, "Small towns everywhere are changing, becoming increasingly mixed. It's really healthy."[11] Simon Perez, in an editorial in the *Gazette,* proclaimed: "The days of cowboy culture are over. We have to deal with it, Timbertown. This isn't Honky Haven anymore. . . . We are going to see an increasing number of Hispanics, Asians, African-Americans, Jews, Muslims, homosexuals and who knows what else living among us. I say welcome."[12] A group called Students Together Ending Prejudice met daily during lunch to organize a high school assembly on racism. They invited two college football players, who challenged the students to disagree with their parents if they heard racist remarks at home. Students also organized a forum at the high school called Building Bridges that featured poems, skits, and songs addressing diversity issues. School district staff members attended a prejudice reduction leadership training. In an exercise in the elementary school, students answered questions such as Who has an *abuela?* Who knows what Rosa Parks did? Why did the Irish emigrate to the United States in the 1880s?

Editorials in the newspaper denounced racism. The mayor read a proclamation encouraging the appreciation of differences. A local group therapist invited city and school officials and representatives from the South Lane Ministerial Association to a community meeting on race. More than fifty Timbertown government workers attended a play by a multiethnic ensemble that challenged the audience's racial stereotypes. It was designed, in the words of a city official, to make people think about a lot of "subtle things they do with day to day interaction with others, when they might be stepping on people's toes and not even realizing it."[13] Within a couple of months, virtually every student and public employee in town had been exposed to a program or forum addressing the importance of tolerance of difference.

But professions of liberal tolerance that welcomed diversity, unaccompanied by an appreciation for the plight of timber workers, often fell upon deaf ears. Many long-time Timbertowners felt that relatively affluent liberals in town were willing to bend over backward to make minority groups feel welcome, yet when it came to the worsening position of the town's timber workers, hardly a tear was shed. This position, never publicly articulated, was expressed in private conversations and grumblings, and it gave the OCA "special rights" message more credibility among Timbertown's angry white men and women, as for this OCA activist:

> The great majority of people in this town know that skin color has nothing to do with your level of humanity, morality, spirituality, etc. But how did you include sexual orientation in this argument? When did this become a race issue? I think the race issue and the sexual orientation issue must remain separate, for they are both difficult issues that should not be mixed together under racism. It is possible, after all, to feel one way about racism and another way about homosexuality. Lumping them together just puts more people on one side of the fence or the other, and I'm not

sure that the side you support would gain in that circumstance. . . . Any-time we begin to classify these young citizens as "cowboys," "blacks," "Hispanics," etc. we further the racism in our community. . . . They don't need minority "sensitivity training." You'll probably teach them some new cuss words they don't even know yet. Let's teach them to get along. Period.[14]

As working-class Timbertowners projected their anxieties about the economic and cultural changes taking place around them upon homosexuality, CAN activists responded with the claim that homosexuals were a legitimate minority group that deserved protection under the law and tolerance in the community. And they turned up the volume by invoking the memory of fascism and its horrific consequences fifty years ago.

ANNE FRANK IN OREGON

As racial conflict rocked the town and Election Day loomed, CAN activists, in keeping with their "we all live in this community" theme, looked for ways to draw connections between racial and sexual discrimination. Several members of the group had seen the exhibit on the life of Anne Frank when it had traveled to Eugene during the previous year, sponsored by human rights groups. They were moved by the ways it subtly tied together racial, sexual, and other forms of prejudice, drawing lessons for today, and decided to bring the exhibit to Timbertown. "Anne Frank is a response to discrimination in our community. We want people to come and view it and think about their own lives, how discrimination affects their own lives," said Cassie Smith. "Without beating people over the head, members of CAN hope that the public sees a connection between the issues explored in the exhibit, the upcoming charter amendment vote, and the racial incidents at the high school," said Robin Bergman. "Let's remember discrimination as it existed in the past and try to eradicate it."

A CAN press release read: "In recent months, our town has experienced incidents of racial tension and the divisive categorization of 'us vs. them.' A central purpose of having this nationally acclaimed exhibit . . . is to help all of us understand that we are part of the same human family." In addition to Anne Frank panels, CAN gathered materials and resources to include a "Timbertown Experience" display that, a flyer announced, would "parallel the way discrimination begins with groups of targeted people and snowballs to the horrors of Nazi Germany and the Holocaust. We will be interviewing and depicting personal experiences of local people and tying those experiences with the exhibit. . . . If you are a WWII buff or if your own life experiences go back to that era in Europe or you have connections with someone who had those experiences, Cassie wants to talk to you!"[15] Cassie also sent a letter to school district staff soliciting artwork by preschool- to high school–age students dealing with themes of discrimination, hatred, and the Holocaust. "Themes that could be used include: 'isolation,' 'friendship,' 'sadness,' 'helping others,' etc. For older students, themes that relate more closely to the Holocaust, Anne Frank, WWII, discrimination issues, etc. are appropriate." The organizers also invited volunteers to be docents, leading groups and individuals through the exhibit.

Robin Bergman informed the local press that the exhibit "is not a political action; it's not a political statement." Cassie Smith agreed. The Anne Frank exhibit "refrains from forcing a particular position down people's throats. It asks people to make connections themselves," she declared.[16] But they dramatically underestimated the extent to which the exhibit, by virtue of the fact that it was sponsored by a human rights group, and mounted just days before the charter measure appeared on the town ballot, would be interpreted in political terms. Even if CAN never compared the OCA to the Nazis in so many words, the "OCA as Nazis" frame had already been constructed in the course of the campaign, in numerous letters to the editor across the state, and had been planted in the minds of many rural Oregonians. At the time, Steven Spielberg's film *Schindler's List* and the U.S. Holocaust Memorial Museum were making the Holocaust a growing presence in American culture. As CAN readied the Anne Frank exhibit, a Timbertown woman wrote to the *Gazette* describing her response to the movie:

> I cried during the three hours and found myself wishing that all of my wonderful community would watch this film. My heart was heavy on the drive home as I thought of my history lessons from school. The Holocaust started with a small group of fearful, prideful people who thought they knew what was best, thought that the eradication of one particular flavor of people would make this a better place. . . . It starts with something that some people are afraid of and ends in death. . . . I am sad for the state of affairs in which we find the little town of Timbertown.[17]

Anticipating that the exhibit would be used against them, as it had earlier been used by groups opposing the OCA during the statewide ballot campaign, OCA activists contacted the school district office to protest the fact that the school seemed to be sanctioning an exhibit that drew a moral equivalence between homosexuals and Jews, and overstated gay claims to Holocaust victimhood. Pamela Sneed: "The OCA would be the first to oppose violence against homosexuals. Homosexuals as a group were not targeted for extermination in Nazi Germany."[18] And she mentioned an additional point that would later become a prominent theme in OCA literature: many Nazi Party members were themselves homosexuals.

"Everyone should take the time to go and see [the Anne Frank exhibit], for we must not forget the horror of the holocaust," wrote Erica Williams in a letter to the editor. "However, neither should what happened in the holocaust be used as an excuse to extend special rights to homosexuals. This is propaganda when one group seeking legitimacy attaches itself to another group that already has legitimacy. . . . In the early years of the Third Reich homosexuals were not singled out for persecution. Hitler was friendly to homosexuals and in his youth hung around with homosexual groups. When Hitler ruled Germany, many of his inner circle, including his personal bodyguard, were known homosexuals."[19] Certainly there were homosexuals among the Nazis, as there are among all social movements, on the left and the right. This does not prove that there were a disproportionate number of homosexuals within the fascist movement, however.[20] Through such claims, conservatives sought to strip gays of the moral authority that comes with victimhood and paint them instead as the "oppressor," the enemies not only of the religious right, but also of Jews, who are along with blacks a legitimate minority group. The "true" victims emerge as the guardians of "common sense morality," conservative Christians.[21]

It wasn't the first time the Anne Frank exhibit had been criticized for drawing links between anti-Semitism and homophobia. Jewish groups had in the past decried that the Anne Frank exhibit falsely universalized Jewish suffering during the Nazi period, and drew false a equivalence between anti-Semitism and homophobia, and other human rights abuses around the world. Timbertown's school administration replied that the exhibit was purely "educational" and that it was "designed to help the community address issues of discrimination and intolerance—not to make a political point." When interviewed by the *Gazette,* the county superintendent of schools said that he did not see the Anne Frank exhibit as a "political statement." Nonetheless, the local school district agreed to be "mindful of any political overtones that might occur." OCA activists also contacted the Anne Frank Center in New York, sponsor of the exhibit, prompting them to send the following letter to Cassie Smith:

> The Anne Frank Community Exhibit has enjoyed a very successful and encouraging response in Oregon. . . . Unfortunately, there is an element in Oregon which does not understand that the exhibit is a universal appeal for respect and compassion. . . . The Anne Frank Center USA stands firmly behind civil rights for gay men, lesbians, and bisexuals. The fact that some individuals and groups have defined civil rights for a minority as "special rights" is disturbing and undemocratic. The death of tens of thousands of homosexuals during the Holocaust is a historical truth acknowledged by historians and institutions, including the US Holocaust Memorial Museum in Washington, DC. German homosexuals were among the first groups stripped of their civil rights during Hitler's reign of terror. The current nationwide movement to vilify the gay and lesbian community and deny them their rights is certainly reminiscent of these tactics. Organizations hosting the exhibit champion equal rights and civil rights for every American citizen. . . . The exhibit should be used as a catalyst for change, not as a political football. Critics of the exhibit and the organization sponsoring the exhibit have not been able to set aside their own prejudices and have taken it upon themselves to promote their own brand of what is right. Conversely, organizations sponsoring the exhibition which exclude certain members of the community are also in the wrong and could lose their right to sponsor the exhibition. The Anne Frank Center USA will not tolerate discrimination in any form.[22]

Surprised by extent to which the exhibit had become politicized, Cassie Smith lamented: "I thought this would be a great way to bring the community together. Now I can see where people will use it as an issue to divide us and that makes me really sad."[23] Nonetheless, she and other CAN activists read the letter from the exhibit's sponsors as affirmation of their attempt to link racial and sexual discrimination. In response, they decided to open participation up to all members of the community, including those whose political views they found reprehensible. Three OCA activists, including Erica Williams, signed up to be docents, and led people through the exhibit.

On May 1, 1994, the exhibit opened at Timbertown Middle School. On the opening day, a "service of remembrance and commitment" welcomed visitors. It began with solemn music and a meditation:

> The universe whispers that all things are intertwined. Yet at times we hear the loud cry of discord. To which voice shall we listen? Although we long for harmony, we cannot close our ears to the noise of war the rasp of hate. How dare we speak of concord, when the fact and symbol of our age is Auschwitz? The intelligent heart does not deny reality. We must not forget the grief of yesterday, nor ignore the pain of today. But yesterday is past. It cannot tell us what tomorrow will bring. If there is goodness at the heart of life, then its power, like the power of evil, is real. Which shall prevail? Moment by moment we choose between them. If we choose rightly, and often enough, the broken fragments of our world will be restored to wholeness.

This invocation was followed by two readings from Anne Frank's diary, and Hebrew prayers for the dead, recited by Presbyterian pastor Henry Chomsky, a rabbi from nearby Eugene, and two Jewish children from Timbertown, who lit a *yahrzeit* candle, a Jewish memorial ritual. Representatives of the Catholic and Buddhist communities in town were also given roles, as was the conservative faith community, represented by Pastor Lance White of Timbertown Christian Center, who introduced the hymn "Amazing Grace." A Presbyterian of Dutch descent who was interned with her husband in prison camps in Java under the Japanese spoke, as did an OCA activist who described the plight of her parents, Japanese Americans who lost their family land in Southern California during World War II and were placed in an internment camp during the war.

Students were engaged in exercises to draw links between the Holocaust and contemporary instances of intolerance in their community:

> Ask the students to name and discuss people who help others in emergency situations nowadays. What do the students think they themselves would or could do to help other people in a risky situation? Have some students take photographs of racist graffiti in their neighborhood or city.

> Let the students talk about their own experiences with racism. What was their own role in the incident? Were they victims, bystanders, spectators, or offenders? What did they do? What did other people do? Be sure to be open-minded in allowing the students to say what they think and feel. Tolerance is important. Ask the question: Could today's racism lead to something like the Holocaust?

There were also local events, including a talk by a resident who was one of the first liberators of the Dachau concentration camp, and a local man who as a fifteen-year-old fled Nazi Germany for Denmark, which saved the vast majority of its Jewish population.

Amid the paeans against intolerance, if there was any mistaking the organizers' intended message, the last line of a program circulated at the opening event made it perfectly clear: "Vote No on Discrimination. It's just plain mean." And as CAN anticipated, OCA members used the exhibit as an opportunity to speak out against gay rights. Erica Williams informed students passing through the exhibit that many of Hitler's closest advisers were homosexuals. She was reprimanded by the exhibit organizers, as were a group of high school students who chanted, "White Power," in front of a Nazi flag. "All of a sudden," a CAN activist lamented, "it seemed more like a battleground than a memorial."[24] CAN supporters responded by criticizing the OCA's efforts to link homosexuality with Nazism. "The upholders of the macho-centered culture of Nazism felt threatened by the very existence of homosexuality," said a local rabbi.[25]

Others proceeded to reinforce the "OCA as Nazis" theme. "Even though the OCA "are no brown-shirted storm troopers goose-stepping in our streets," they "swaddle themselves in the sheep's clothing of conservative Christians" while they "walk the walk and talk the talk of the Fuhrer's Schutzstaffel."[26] But not all of the OCA's critics supported CAN's efforts to equate gay rights with the plight of Jews during the Holocaust. Such claims were overstated, said a concentration camp liberator who lived in town, arguing that the OCA's efforts are misguided, but that comparisons between Nazism and the OCA were "hysterical, paranoiac, and exaggerated," and asserting, "Most Americans would not tolerate a persecution of the type that occurred in Germany."[27] Katie Wolf, a forty-three-year-old child of survivors from New York who was one of Timbertown's baby boom back-to-the-landers, felt ambivalent about the Anne Frank exhibit as

well. On the one hand, she said, "It's important to make those connections, to show the similarities between the Holocaust and Bosnia,
and prejudice in general." But as she toured the exhibit and looked at
the photos of the destruction of a young girl's world, she thought of
her parents, who had fled Vienna, losing their families in the carnage.
When she looked at the people of Timbertown, and their lack of
connection to that history, all she could hear were children's laughing
faces and the sheer normality of the scene.

In an effort to position the event above the political fray, an ecumenical closing ceremony, entitled "Of Things Spiritual," began
with a reading from the Torah and included selections from the diary
of Anne Frank and a "Communal Litany of Creation's Diversity":
"God believes in diversity; God the creator commanded that the
earth produce all kinds of plants, those that bear grain and those that
bear fruit; God commanded that the earth produce all kinds of ani-
mal life—tame and wild, large and small. Then God created human
beings—male and female. God the Son called as his disciples, fish-
erman, tax collectors, and political extremists. The spirit works
through different people in different ways." It ended with a pastoral
reflection from a local minister and the song "We Shall Overcome."

During its five-day stand, seventy-two volunteers guided three
thousand people through the exhibit, including nearly every fourth
and fifth grader in Timbertown. On white butcher paper hung near
the exit, individuals inscribed their responses to the exhibit: graffiti
tags like "Alex" and "Craig" and "Joe Was Here" juxtaposed with
Stars of David, peace signs, the Hebrew word "shalom," and "We will
remember." In a blank book sitting on a table, they wrote one-line in-
scriptions:

> To Ann [sic], I'm sorry for all that happened.

> Persecution is not okay

> We must remember.

> See this so history doesn't repeat itself.

> This is cool.

This exibit [*sic*] is the best Anne Frank exhibit! I really enjoyed coming here! And I hope I can come again!

It was sad

It is sad to see what we are really like

How could they?

Watching all this really makes me feel bad. I think it is very bad for all these people from long ago get hurt like they did and all this stuff is really neat.

It was sad to see how many people died and bulldosed [*sic*] away

I should have cousins and aunts and uncles throughout Europe. This exhibit explains why I have none

I hope this will help our town learn tolerance

After seeing the exhibit I plant to encourage people to vote no on 20–15

There is only one hope in this world—Jesus Christ

I like how she rote [*sic*]

This was disgusting seeing all the dead bodies but otherward [*sic*] it was GREAT

I love Anne Frank

Did the exhibit accomplish its goal of uniting the community around a shared commitment to human rights? The varied responses to the exhibit made that question difficult to answer. But a few days after it closed, Cassie Smith reported to the Anne Frank Center that the Timbertown event was "a great success."

Though the intent of the Anne Frank exhibit was to educate and help to build tolerance between the different factions of our community . . . we too believe that the exhibit should not be used as a political football and it was our intention not to let it be. . . . I believe though that it is impossible to not let it become an issue when towns like ours have the exhibit at the same time that they are also faced with political initiatives designed to limit rights to citizens. To me, and to many people, the limiting of rights and targeting of certain groups of our society smacks of early Nazism. The OCA loudly cries this isn't so but for many of us it is a scary thing to watch happen and we will do what we can to resist it. Timbertown CAN, like many of the similar groups that have formed, is made up mainly of women, most of whom are long-termed married mothers, and in some cases, also very religious. We have been accused of being self-serving lesbians but the truth of the matter is, we are common women and men who have become forced to become political activists and most of us thought that would never happen. We were forced when we realized what was happening. . . . I appreciated your letter and your firm stand against the targeting of gays and lesbians, but you have to realize that in this time, in this town and state, that in itself is indeed a very political statement.[28]

Three days later, the antigay ballot measure won 57 percent of the vote despite the fact that its sponsors were outspent by their liberal opponents. Only one third of eligible voters turned out to the polls. In nineteen towns and seven counties across Oregon, the measure also passed. Editor Simon Perez concluded in the *Gazette:*

> As the debate over the OCA-sponsored city charter amendment finally falls silent, we need to recall that we are all still here. And we have to live together. Bosnia and Northern Ireland can serve as reminders of what happens when cultural differences escalate. Elections, by their nature, force us to think about matters that divide us. Now that the election is over, we need to think about the things that make us a community.[29]

CHAPTER 10

Living with Strangers

Centuries ago, the Puritans' Massachusetts Bay Colony, formed as a beacon of religious faith, a "city on a hill," suffered a series of reversals that threatened its sense of identity. How would the colony assert itself and reconstruct the flagging bonds of faith? Members of the community proceeded to identify a number of local girls, marginal characters of various sorts, as witches, and once they were identified, proceeded to root these "others" out. Accounting for the witch trials in the aftermath of the McCarthy "red scare," sociologist Kai Erikson suggested they served a social function: by defining certain people as deviant, he argued, we "guard the cultural integrity of the community." By declaring who is strange, we come to know who is familiar.

The longing for familiarity, for a community that is home, is a central theme in American history, and indeed in modern life. It is the community, writes Erikson, "that cushions pain, the community that provides a context for intimacy, that represents morality and serves as the repository for old traditions."[1] Talk of community surfaces most when communities are under threat—and frequently leads people on quests to repair them. The campaign against homosexuality in Timbertown was, too, a quest for belonging and security—and reparation. True to Erikson's predictions, the campaign emerged at a time when long-standing bonds of trust and reciprocity were eroding. Small-town Oregonians live with a sense of gnawing insecurity, a world of dissolving marriages, "flexible" employment, and shifting selves. By the early 1990s, they were more likely than ever to undergo life transformations that shifted the balance of power in marriages, reconfigured friendship and family networks, and encouraged geographic mobility.

Timbertowners seemed more reticent than ever to join with their neighbors to address their problems, and participation in community organizations declined, and with it civic engagement in general. People complained obsessively about the sorry physical state of the high school, and yet refused repeatedly to pass a levy to replace the old, dilapidated building.[2] At the same time, Timbertowners talked endlessly about their desire for connection, for solidarity, for a sense of something larger than themselves. If the state was suspect, faith seemed to stand above the fray; I was often surprised by how central God's authority, or at least God language, was to many Timbertowners' sense of self. Faith shaped friendship networks, work environments, political opinions, and even home improvement projects. It transformed ambient fears into hope and gave people the sense they were engaged in constructing a community of individuals united by their passionate commitment to God.

With many citizens looking to churches for a sense of connection and belonging, conservative Protestant leaders took up the challenge of reconstructing the community. Evangelical churches provided a vocabulary and infrastructure through which these communal aspirations and ambient fears could be articulated, and a Christian right organization gave these fears a face and a name: homosexuality. To traditionalists, lesbians and gay men epitomized the unencumbered self, and all the flexibility and refashioning that such a self implied. Ironically, many of the most devout Christian conservatives spoke of their own lives in similar terms: as having gone through a period of transformation and rebirth which shed their old, false selves. Homosexuals were problematic because they signified a retreat into self-indulgence and individualism and flouted the moral authority of centuries of tradition, the right argued.

For those who feel that their only solace lies in making familial bonds more rather than less compulsory, the option of choosing an identity, and refashioning intimate relationships at will was anathema. Emancipated from the procreative imperative, gay sexual unions were provisional, fleeting, unmoored to the larger project of family and community well-being, they declared. But in speaking with anti-gay activists, I found something deeper, more troubling, at stake. When they come out publicly, lesbians and gay seek to disavow feelings of shame; many Christian conservatives, in contrast, deny their shameful feelings. Because they can not admit to having these feelings, they seek to alleviate them by displacing them on to others, the strangers in their midst.

A century ago, sociologist Georg Simmel defined "the stranger" as the one who arrived today and stays tomorrow, who embodies a strange mixture of nearness and distance. In Simmel's world, Europe at the turn of the century, Jews were the principal "others." In small-town Oregon at the end of the millennium, where there is little racial or ethnic diversity, lesbians and gay men play a similar role: they—we—are both familiar and alien, the same and different from the majority population. Haunted by the new-found knowledge of the stranger who lived next door, Timbertowners looked around, wondered whether homosexuality was far more pervasive than they had ever imagined, and began to question their friends, neighbors, their own families, and even themselves.

It wasn't difficult: the lesbians and gay men in town were strangers who were not all that strange: they tended to have families, respectable work; they shared many, if not most of their values, and even looked and acted very much like them—perhaps their very ordinariness made them even more threatening.[3] People of color inspired a different type of anxiety and endured a different kind of wrath. Rather than representing a small minority group set off from society, queer people signaled a nightmare version of the direction American society seemed to be heading—that's what made them seem so threatening. The only solution conservatives could imagine was to draw tight boundaries that would exclude gays from the community through legislative means.

LIBERALISM'S LIMITS

Why did Timbertown's proposed charter amendment gain as much support as it did? If it was a culture war, it was a war that was waged on shaky ground, by individuals whose opinions were more shifting than solid; it was a war that created social divisions more than it reflected them. Even the most pious conservative activists, when engaged in one-on-one discussions, seemed far less certain of themselves and their beliefs than I had anticipated, and the churches in which they placed their trust much more fractious. Rather than announce a sense of certainty and moral fortitude, the campaign seemed to do quite the opposite: it revealed a pervasive underlying sense of insecurity, place-lessness, and existential mistrust.

If the truth be told, most Timbertowners seemed far less con-cerned with the moral threat posed by homosexuality than with a host of other problems: the changing roles of men and women and the quickening pace of marital dissolution and family change, the de-cline of their small community and the fear that global, faceless cor-porations have more and more power to make decisions about what people will eat, how they will work, and where they will live. One out of every three American workers have been in their jobs for less than one year. Two out of every three have been in their present jobs for less than five years. Uncertainty, increasingly, is a fact of life. As liberals spoke about the importance of inclusion, tolerance, and equality, many longtime Timbertowners wondered, Who was pro-tecting *their* rights, *their* livelihoods? Who was championing *their* needs when they lost their jobs, when their homes were repossessed, when they struggled to maintain their community? Who was making *them* feel included?

Talk of victimhood on the right appealed emotionally to popular fears of dispossession. If boundaries of all sorts were eroding—those between men and women, those separating small towns from urban engulfment, and those shielding lily-white America from a growing multiculturalism—the OCA told Timbertowners they could erect a moral boundary that would say to the world: "not in our town"—and many were convinced by their claims. But despite all their good in-tentions, the left underestimated the extent to which antigay senti-ment was fueled by feelings of insecurity and the quest for belonging.

For one thing, liberals' claim that "they can't help it—they were born that way—" designed to allay fears that gay people were out to seduce and convert their children to their perverted ways, and to au-thenticate lesbians and gay men as a "legitimate" minority group, failed to address the widespread perception that the boundaries be-tween us and them, heterosexual and homosexual, *were* in reality quite malleable. Deep down, many heterosexuals know, queer people aren't *essentially* different from them—though they've made a series of different choices about how to live their lives, to create families outside of the realm of legal marriage, to claim an identity that sets them apart from their families of origin, and the teachings of many churches.

To those who had constructed lives around a taut regime of rules, obligations, and traditions, the notion of *choice* embedded in the idea of homosexuality spelled trouble. But you don't have to be a queer theorist to know that the "ethnic" model of homosexuality is fundamentally flawed: sexual boundaries *are* flexible and permeable; desire is a complex, unwieldy thing; and homosexuality is not always confined to homosexuals—even small-town Oregonians know this. Conservative Christians, for all their misguided righteousness, at least opened up a public discussion of sexuality, acknowledging that the personal is political, that intimacy is, for better or worse, a realm of power, and that sexuality is a primal human concern that deserves public discussion.

Witness the public's fascination with sex scandals—and the lives of Monica Lewinsky, O. J. Simpson, Lorena Bobbitt, and their ilk— which has dominated U.S. media in recent years because, as Ellen Willis suggests, "they dramatize the central conflicts and obsessions of contemporary culture, especially issues of sexual morality and male-female relations."[4] In a culture that is already heavily sexualized by an endless stream of media images, the liberal response—that sexual matters should be private—is untenable. Had liberals in Timbertown recognized this, they could have taken a bolder, proactive— and pro-sex—stance. Instead, they tried to cleanse homosexuality of its sexual connotations.

The issue of sexuality nonetheless became freighted with a host of symbolic meanings, manipulated by the right.[5] If the campaign was a fight against sexual "others" it was also a fight against risk and insecurity at a time when communities and family ties, once based upon face-to-face relationships, are increasingly ruled by the market and by experts, when tradition is rapidly loosing its hold, and individuals are "forced to negotiate lifestyle choices among a diversity of options."[6] There is a progressive element to this story to be sure: individuals are more and more capable of standing apart from their families and communities of origin, and construct "reflexive projects of the self," as Anthony Giddens terms them. Lesbians and gay men, among others, have benefited from these new possibilities, and have, in turn, expanded their reach.

But individuals seem to require a certain degree of constancy and certainty in order to operate in society, to feel like full human beings. They need to construct lives peopled by significant others who can give them love and support, and develop economic and political institutions that can offer shelter and sustenance. In the late 1980s and early 1990s, many Timbertowners rapidly lost the capacity to fulfill these needs. In this vacuum emerged a campaign to re-embed a community identity and assert the primacy of the heterosexual family, which symbolized continuity and tradition. The liberal response—exhortations for pluralism and tolerance—failed to provide an expansive enough counter-vision. Suggesting that the OCA were Nazis bent on destroying gays (read Jews) only fanned the flames of resentment, and made it easier for the OCA to claim that it was the wronged party. In retrospect, Marianne Woods, a CAN activist, provided a sobering assessment: "We were all pretty green and did not really know how to go about it," she lamented. "The kinds of things we did made sense to us but may have only exacerbated the situation here. The process of raising consciousness not only did not have positive results, it was resented by otherwise very good people."

After the election, CAN disbanded, exhausted by the protracted nature of the fight against gay rights, though many activists went on to participate in a number of other seemingly more pressing issues. Some became involved in a campaign to improve bus service for Timbertown residents who commute to jobs in the surrounding area, a proposal that was opposed by many local businesses and longtime residents who feared that easier access to the town would encourage people to shop elsewhere, and would weaken local autonomy even further. When Timbertown lost its only hospital because the corporation that owned it deemed it unprofitable, placing residents with acute health needs in jeopardy, many local citizens, including members of CAN, organized to lobby for federal subsidies to replace it. Others became involved in local school politics. Robin Bergman was elected to the school board and was instrumental in establishing an alternative charter school where kids would follow their interests and not be subjected, in her words, to the "mind-numbing" routines of traditional classrooms.

Today, several years after the ballot measure campaign, the issue of lesbian/gay rights no longer dominates the pages of the local newspaper, but people seem more aware of existence of sexual diversity than ever before. Some of the few out lesbians and gay men left town, uncomfortable with their newfound visibility, while others say they feel much more connected to the community than ever, vowing to stay and fight. An organization called the Rural Organizing Project became active in scores of small communities, including Timbertown, fusing a concern for the protection of the human rights of sexual, racial, and ethnic minorities with proactive campaigns for economic justice and democratic political reform. So while many liberals in Timbertown ended up feeling demoralized by the charter measure's passage, in practical terms the campaign's results were mixed, and the right's tangible gains, aside from filling the OCA's campaign coffers, were few.

NOT DEAD YET

The campaign against lesbian/gay rights in Timbertown, for all its talk about changing charters and laws, was largely a symbolic protest that was, in practical terms, destined to fail. Shortly after the election, within the space of about a year, the American Civil Liberties Union filed a lawsuit on behalf of three local residents seeking a permanent court injunction barring enforcement of the amendment on the grounds that it violated state and federal constitutional rights to free expression; the OCA failed to pass another statewide antigay ballot measure; and the U.S. Supreme Court found Colorado's Amendment 2 (upon which the local Oregon charter measures were modeled) unconstitutional on the grounds that it was too broadly drafted to meet a legitimate state interest, and that "a state cannot so deem a class of persons a stranger to its laws."[7]

Although Republicans controlled the House of Representatives for the first time in forty years, religious conservatives still couldn't accomplish what they set out to do: make abortion illegal, rescind the ban on school prayer, and turn public opinion against homosexuality. In 1998, the Oregon Court of Appeals issued a precedent-setting ruling that "sexual orientation is a protected category" and therefore the state must extend health insurance and other benefits to state employees' same-sex partners.[8] Even corporate America seemed to be recognizing the legitimacy of same-sex relationships. In 1990, only 6 national companies provided some type of spousal benefits to unmarried partners and their dependents; eight years later, more than 350 such companies did.[9] Legislative efforts to limit gay rights, it seemed, were severely stalled.

Today, more and more Americans refuse to discriminate against lesbians and gays when it comes to rights to fair housing, equal treatment on the job, and access to health care—but they refuse to fully accept homosexuality as the moral equivalent of heterosexuality, entitled to all the same rights and privileges. Testifying to the extreme variability and flux of public opinion even within the same region on this issue, in 1998 voters in the state of Maine repealed a statewide ordinance prohibiting discrimination against lesbians and gay men; two years later, the state of Vermont voted to give lesbian and gay couples the same rights and benefits afforded married couples under state law. Alan Wolfe, surveying thousands of suburbanites on this and other issues declared that "many of us swear eternal fidelity to religious rules and then bend those rules to fit secular reality," predicting that right-wing efforts against gay rights "will fall apart from the weight of its own contradictions."[10]

In 1999, Paul Weyrich, a prominent longtime religious right activist, publicly admitted that conservatives had lost the culture war. "It is very clear," he told *60 Minutes,* "there is no longer—if there ever was—a moral majority."[11] Across the nation, conservative churches turned against the Christian Coalition and other attempts to bring politics into the pulpit, refusing to distribute the voters pamphlets that they had so readily embraced a few years earlier. (In Timbertown, after witnessing the division it had sown, many church leaders who had gladly joined the OCA bandwagon wanted no part of the organization a few years later.) Throughout the country, Republican Party stalwarts tried to distance themselves from conservative Christians, fearing guilt by association; splits in the national organizations of the Christian right led many to doubt its continuing influence; and insiders declared that the religious right's strategic alliance with the Republican Party was a failure.[12]

Still, announcements of the religious right's death seem premature—particularly if we see it as a movement for the hearts and minds of Americans, for cultural power and emotional succor, rather than as a movement narrowly concerned with advancing a legislative agenda. For even when they lose, legislative campaigns often help to mint new leaders—sometimes among the most unlikely people, as the example of Sally Humphries, Timbertown's "Martha Stewart for the Christian set," suggests. Sally parlayed her newfound visibility in town into a seat on the city council, where she continued to stand up, she told me, for "good values and morals," and in favor of business interests. Most of the time, Sally laments, in her typical self-deprecating manner, "I don't know how much I can contribute, being a housewife, a lot of these issues are so technical." Nonetheless, her activism has given her a sense of purpose, and a feeling that she is standing up for what she believes in. And that is important—for it keeps activists going over the long haul.

In the mid-1990s, as the national organizations of the religious right began to cast a wider net, moving beyond "family values" to issues of taxes and term limits and making antigay politics less central to its national agenda, local efforts to fight the normalization of homosexuality continued. Campaigns against gay families and queer presence in the schools supplanted "no special rights" campaigns, and Defense of Marriage Acts, prohibiting gay marriage, were passed in twenty eight states. The OCA, though a shadow of its former self, continues fighting. In 1998 it joined with the Christian Coalition to try to end late-term abortion, which was unsuccessful, as were its efforts to redefine "family" as one man and one woman, and to rescind insurance coverage for same-sex partners of state employees. In November 2000, voters narrowly rejected another statewide ballot initiative, the "Student Protection Act," which would have prohibited discussions of homosexuality or bisexuality in the schools "in a manner which encourages, promotes, or sanctions such behaviors."

Wolfe's predictions that the issue will die out aside, Americans seem to be divided on the issue of whether lesbians and gay men are the moral equivalent of heterosexuals. Typically, the same percentage of Americans who support equal treatment for lesbians and gays in employment, housing, and credit institutions oppose our right to children and our claim to family.[13] This division in public opinion has made sexuality a continuing "wedge" issue for the right. Knowing this, many of Timbertown's right-wing activists continue to be sanguine about the future of their movement. When I asked Jeri Cookson what she thinks she and her fellow activists accomplished, she replied: "I think we got a lot of information out. We educated a lot of people on different issues, and that's very important." Barney Wooten was similarly optimistic: "No war is won without setbacks or stalled progress in some corner of the battlefield. Missionaries work years or decades before their ministries bear fruit. What we don't accomplish will be our legacy to our children and grandchildren."[14]

Those who have pronounced the death of the Christian right fail to understand that it thrives on the margins, that it speaks to the aspirations and fears of millions of Americans—often more effectively than the left—and that it feeds on conflict and controversy, utilizing local campaigns as opportunities to create public spectacles that help define its friends and enemies. Social movements, it seems, are more often a source of vision and voice than the vanguard of a new world. Since their goals are often overdrawn, their importance "lies more in their moral visions than their practical accomplishments."[15] The right articulated a moral vision, however impoverished and mean-spirited, which gave activists the sense that they were engaged in a struggle of historic significance. While some battles will inevitably be lost and others won, right-wing activists reassured themselves, fighting for what one believes in is itself a virtue—and that's what keeps them going despite the fact that they have accomplished so little in concrete terms.

Because liberalism begins with the assumption that morality is complicated and shifting, and that tradition alone can never be a basis for community, it has been much more difficult for liberalism to make moral claims with the same vigor and vision—particularly as it tends to assume that individuals exist to maximize their own self-interest.[16] During a television debate during the statewide ballot measure campaign, a lesbian activist told OCA head Lon Mabon, "You're trying to impose your moral position on me," to which he replied, "All laws are moral positions." Mabon was, it turned out, correct. Liberalism lacks a moral vocabulary that is adequate to sensibly discuss the link between family, morality, and politics. Its language of rights lacks an understanding of what is right and good. It understates the extent to which selves are embedded in a web of relationships that provide meaning, without which social life is unimaginable. Supporters of lesbian/gay rights in particular, and multiculturalism in general, have yet to generate a language that speaks to the anxieties and aspirations of Americans, that makes a convincing argument for the importance of sexual diversity. How, then, can we develop such a vocabulary, and upon what models can we draw?

INTIMATE CITIZENSHIP AND THE ETHICS OF OTHERS
Thirty years ago, sexual politics was dominated by the language of "liberation." Lesbian/gay activists argued that sexual freedom would

require the abolition of compulsory heterosexuality, and the creation of a society where sexual labels would be meaningless. Today, theorists and activists seem far more interested in gaining citizenship rights than in calling for liberation. The state enforces heteronormativity, defining those who remain outside of heterosexual marriage as "others." We need to extend the privileges of citizenship to those who have historically been classified by the state as subjects without legal rights, they argue. We must make lesbians and gay men, and transgendered people, full citizens and grant them the right to marry, to have equal employment benefits, and to participate openly as queer citizens. The expansion of citizenship rights on the basis of sexuality represents a movement toward "emotional equality," and the democratic "transformation of intimacy," they suggest.[17]

These claims, and the activism they inspire, are progressive in many respects, but they also raise a number of questions. How will lesbians and gay men define themselves as they position themselves as full citizens: Will they emphasize their differences or similarity from the heterosexual norm? If lesbians and gay men are increasingly integrated into society as full citizens, what will happen to other more marginalized groups, such as poor women on welfare? Does equality for some necessarily lead to equality for all?

Today, our sense of social obligation has diminished. A resurgent anti-immigrant sentiment seeks to seal off America's borders from immigration; politicians who are "tough on crime" seek solutions to urban problems by speeding the flow of incarceration. These are, clearly, simplistic solutions to complex social problems. They seek to hold off the enormous cultural and economic shifts that are creating a multicultural America, and an increasingly global culture. In an earlier capitalist age, mass movements of workers successfully redressed some of the problems of the market. Threats to security, certainty, and safety appeared as temporary nuisances that could be cured; a scientific rationality would lead to the forward march of "progress." These progressive ideals were flawed—by their antipathy to the enduring power of differences of race, ethnicity, nationality, and gender, for one. But at least the left once possessed a unifying vision. Today hardships seem disconnected from one another. Faith in social institutions to solve social maladies has diminished; cutting back social entitlements is increasingly seen as a solution to inequality.

In this age, which Barbara Ehrenreich has dubbed "the end of caring," blaming the victim is all the rage. Consider the official title of the welfare reform bill: the Personal Responsibility and Work Opportunity Reconciliation Act. The federal government's retreat from its sixty-five-year commitment to its neediest citizens is cloaked in the language of morality and individual responsibility. As part of welfare reform, states receive tens of millions of dollars for "abstinence only" sex education programs in the schools. That efforts to stave off the normalization of homosexuality come at the same time when "promiscuous" welfare mothers are being routinely demonized is no coincidence. But as lesbians and gay men and teen mothers come to be seen as threats to "the family," we must ask, Whose family is being defended? An image of childhood innocence threatened by outsiders (incompetent mothers, government bureaucrats, lascivious men, and loose women) that is in need of protection and control continues to stir the passions and imaginations of many. Perhaps we haven't moved very far from the Puritan days: the contours of American citizenship are still defined partly through the exclusion of sexualized "others."

Thus far the most visible political spokespersons for an expanded notion of sexual citizenship have argued that lesbians and gays are "virtually normal"—"good" homosexual citizens who dutifully occupy the private sphere, exhibit appropriate respect for marriage and family values, and who deserve full citizenship rights on that basis— echoes of the stand that liberal gay rights supporters took in Timbertown. Illustrating this, a consortium of gay rights groups, including the Human Rights Campaign Fund, the largest gay lobby in the nation, placed a full-page ad in the *New York Times* that featured a smiling American family, Dave and Ruth Waterbury and their twenty-something lesbian daughter Margie, and the statement:

> We're living proof that families with lesbians and gay kids can be whole, happy and worthy of all that this great country promises. . . . Our lesbian daughter is the apple of our eye. . . . We now understand with all our heart and soul that Margie is as complete and dynamic a human being as our other wonderful daughter who happens to be heterosexual. . . . We are a typical American family, with old roots in the heart of America. We love our church, our community, and the beautiful Minnesota countryside. We bike. We cross-country ski. We're Republican. . . . Gay people and their families are people of faith. . . . All leading medical experts agree . . . gay people are just as likely to be healthy and happy as the rest of us.[18]

As this ad suggests, liberals have tried to develop a moral vocabulary to counter the right's claims, embracing a mixture of liberal rights talk and communitarian appeals. Rights talk seeks to integrate lesbians and gay men as full citizens, stressing that they are hardworking individuals rather than members of a community or collectivity who share common goals and aspirations. The communitarian approach suggests that lesbians and gay men are bound by the same mutual concerns and obligations—for family, community, and faith—of other Americans. As organizers of the Millennium March for Equality in Washington, D.C., in April 2000 explained, "We want to show middle America that we're mature people who work, just like them. This is our country and we pay our taxes."[19] Recent campaigns for gay marriage also tend to invoke "we're just like you and we want the same rights" arguments, reinforcing both the necessity and desirability of sexual coupledom. Thanks to the greater financial clout of mainstream gay organizations, these rather conservative arguments are ascendant.

But there are limits to a citizenship movement that seeks to expand its rights and entitlements without regard to other "others." Encouraging same-sex integration into married, monogamous family structures will not necessarily benefit nonmonogamous or single lesbians and gay men, or unapologetic sexual minorities-within-minorities such as transgendered people and out bisexuals, and indeed may further marginalize them.[20] Neither will it benefit poor women and men, or even the white/heterosexual but nonetheless anxious men and women that I have described in this book who, in the current period of rapid flux and change, have an investment in the creation of a more expansive rather than a narrowed vision of the Good Life. For increasingly, we are all in some sense strangers.

The question remains: How do we live in a contested moral order? And how do we live with the strangers in our midst? In the Puritans' world, declaring certain members of the community to be witches may have contributed to the stability of society by reinforcing commonly held norms and values, but in the contested moral order of late-twentieth-century America, conformity to the will of the majority is no longer a solution. As the case of Timbertown suggests, campaigns designed to root the "others" out, though they may succeed in the short run, end ultimately in division and despair. Much the same could be said for efforts to, in the words of the philosopher

Emanuel Levinas, "reduce the other to the Same"—forcing lesbians and gay men and other gender and sexual non-conformists to conform to white/heterosexual/middle-class norms in exchange for full citizenship rights.[21] Rather than try to codify goodness, writes Levinas, we should try to live an ethical life that values the "other." Only if we can truly see the "other" and listen to him or her can dialogue take the place of divisive conflict.

Shortly after the Timbertown campaign, a group of people not very far away attempted to put this philosophy into practice. A conflict resolution center organized a structured dialogue between Christian right and gay activists. After meeting together for several months, the group issued a statement decrying "the unconscious assumption in cultural warfare," that "if one side wins, the other side will simply disappear." Each side came to the conclusion that neither would fundamentally change, but that they must "all live in the community together."[22] Structured dialogues such as this may never be successful in bringing the most extreme adversaries to the table; nor will they necessarily reform the deep-seated but amorphous fears that give rise to hate. But perhaps they represent a much-needed effort to at least sit down face-to-face and begin to come to terms with strangers. By their very definition these strangers are not like us and in some respects will never be like us. Regardless, Levinas suggests, we have an obligation to love, respect, and honor them (and, I would add, to help sustain them materially as well). The success of these relationships, from which we may gain little or nothing tangible in return, is the very test of our humanity.

APPENDIX A

Methodological Notes:
What's a Nice (Queer) Jewish Girl Doing in a Place Like This?

Initially, I entered "the field" with trepidation. Would I be able to gain the trust of those who stood on the opposite side of this issue? How would I present myself to them? How could I represent their views in a way that would do them justice, that appreciates how they emerge from a very different set of circumstances and social contexts from my own? During the course of nearly two years, I talked with holy-roller preachers, had heart-to-hearts with people who wept with joy when they told me how they found the Lord, and listened as individuals spun elaborate tales of apocalyptic end times.

Because I wanted to paint a portrait of many different sectors of a small town as they became embroiled in this conflict, I made the decision to go beyond the relatively small number of people who took public roles in the campaign. I began with these public activists, whom I located fairly easily, through newspaper accounts and earlier contacts, and I asked each one to refer me to two other people in the community: one who shared that person's opinions on the issue of gay rights and who may or may not have been active in the campaign, and one who probably did not share his or her opinions. Several of these individuals no longer resided in Timbertown. A few lived in neighboring towns but nonetheless participated in the campaign. From this list, I selected a larger sample of interview subjects. I also interviewed a number of "opinion leaders," elected officials, businesspeople, and longtime residents who were well known in the town.

The interviews were loosely structured, to permit my subjects to focus upon those aspects of the campaign, their involvement in it, and their feelings about the issue of homosexuality that seemed salient to them. At the same time, I gathered biographical material about each person, trying to understand who they were as individuals, as political actors, and as residents of Timbertown. What were their relationships to the town? How did they feel about how the town was changing? What were their hopes and dreams for the future? I also gathered materials about the history of Timbertown. Most of the interviews, which lasted anywhere from an hour to three hours, were tape-recorded, and the tapes were later transcribed.

Quickly, I found that it is often easier to talk to a stranger than a friend about issues close to one's heart, and that, despite my fears, being an outsider worked to my advantage. My Jewishness, in particular, marked me as an outsider, and deemed me a relatively respectable, and sometimes even exotic outsider, and gave my Christian interviewees the freedom to express opinions about the world—that were both honest and forthright, yet whose operating assumptions were often diametrically opposed to those I took for granted. Throughout these conversations, I strove for what I call "critical empathy," trying to understand the interaction between personal biography and social context that formed my interviewees' opinions, without necessarily agreeing with them or liking them as people.

Lacking a nuanced conception of Jewishness, Christian conservatives often assumed that I was religious. In their world, the term "Christian" signifies "born-again Christian." The religious right activist Barney Wooten lamented that there were "only thirty-five million Christians" in this country, and that perhaps only half of those regularly vote. Thirty-five million? That figure seemed awfully low, I told him, until I realized that his definition of "true Christians" was an exceedingly narrow one that included only those who claim to have a "personal relationship with God." If born-again Christians were only a small minority in the Christian universe, the same, he reasoned, was true of Jews: self-identified Jews would tend to be orthodox. When he learned that I was a member of a synagogue, he was calmed, imagining that I shared his disdain for the secularizing influences of modern culture.

Being "out" as a Jew allowed me to downplay aspects of myself that would prove to be less palatable to my Christian right subjects.

Perhaps my Jewishness was more than enough for them to handle at one time, for they rarely if ever questioned me about my personal life, or my sexuality. Sally Humphries asked me if I was married, to which I replied yes. (It was true that I had been living with my partner for ten years. So what if she's a woman?) When she asked me if I had a child, I gleefully nodded. "Lewis is nine months old." A few months later, when I bumped into her in a supermarket in a strip mall near my home, she recognized me immediately and gave me a big, warm hello. I felt awkward, quickly introduced her to my son, and was relieved that my partner, Nancy, had decided to stay home that day.

Keeping my opinions to myself was the most difficult challenge of all. Because I wanted to get into their heads and understand how they saw the world, I never challenged people—even when I found their opinions misguided, reprehensible, or downright evil. When Erica Williams went on at great length about the fact that most of Hitler's SS henchmen were homosexuals, I gritted my teeth and nodded. When a preacher railed against cities and "the gays, Asians, New Agers, and other undesirables" that populate them, I bit my lip.

I used my role as a "neutral sociologist" to my advantage because I truly wanted to understand my subjects, and didn't want them to know anything about me that might get in the way. Knowledge of my lesbianism, I imagined, would cut off the discussion. But I was having a bad day when Beverly Allen told me that homosexuals could "cure" themselves through prayer, and I lost my cool. "If God's in it with you, miracles can happen, homosexuals could change, alcoholics can change," she told me, to which I politely replied that many gay people can't, or won't change, and that maybe we need to respect their wishes. She shot me a skeptical glance. That comment pierced the "heterosexual assumption" operating during the interview. "I don't even know about you," she said, wondering for the first time during our ninety-minute interview whether I really was the person she thought me to be.

What, in the end, did I learn from my adventures in American Christendom? I learned that though few small-town evangelicals have close relationships with living, breathing Jews, the most important figures in their symbolic universe—the Bible—are Jews, so they feel that they have a "special relationship" with us. I also learned that they are exceedingly willing to share their deepest, darkest secrets and their wildest dreams with a virtual stranger—a fact that made me uncomfortable at first. While they poured their lives out to me, I carefully tiptoed around some central facts of my own life, obscuring them from view. But I soon came to think of the interviews as an implicit bargain. Once I recognized that my subjects were also practicing the art of deception—agreeing to meet me so that they could affirm their specialness as Christians, and perhaps even entice me to join their flock—I began to see the interaction as an equal exchange. I learned all about the world of evangelical Protestantism, and they got to talk to a real live Jew.

INTERVIEW SUBJECTS
These are the people I interviewed, listed by pseudonyms. Activists in the campaign are identified by their affiliation with either the Oregon Citizens Alliance (OCA) or Community Action Network (CAN). Individuals who were not directly active in the campaign are identified by some other characteristic.
Beverly Allen, homeschooling mother
Ann Ashihara, secretary
Cindy Barber, CAN activist
Ginny Barber, high school student
Martha Bayles, CAN activist
Robin Bergman, CAN activist
Bob Bowen, religious sect leader
Harry Boyle, businessman and city council member
Annie Caponi, CAN activist
Henry Chomsky, pastor
Tony Congers, union leader
Jeri Cookson, OCA activist
Judy Dunlap, CAN activist
Bill Freeman, engineering consultant
Barbara Hammer, school administrator
Betty Harris, administrator
Bob Harrison, pastor
Vicki Harstrup, supermarket checker
Janice Henry, OCA activist
Sarah Henson, longtime resident and historical archivist
Sally Humphries, OCA activist

John James, OCA activist
Martha Jensen, former city councilor
Andrew Kenneth, church leader
Katherine Kinko, auto mechanic shop co-owner
Linda Mabley, liberal activist
Chuck Mendip, newspaper reporter
Sam Miller, wood products worker
Shari Mitchell, teacher
Carroll Neitz, pastor
Cynthia Newman, social worker
Sam O'Connor, former mayor
Toby Ramsey, CAN activist and X-ray technician
Chester and Martha Rideout, liberal activists
Susan Rogers, architect
Harvey Silko, retired teacher and church leader
Mary and Mel Skill, small businesspeople
Cassie Smith, CAN activist
Nancy Sunday, school aide
June and Janice Trump, CAN activists
Sylvia Watkins, CAN activist
Erica Williams, OCA activist
Marianne Woods, CAN activist
Barney Wooten, OCA activist

Text of Ballot Measures

COLORADO AMENDMENT 2

No Protected Status Based on Homosexual, Lesbian or Bisexual Orientation

Neither the state of Colorado, through any of its branches, or departments, nor any of its agencies, political subdivisions, municipalities, or school districts, shall enact, adopt or enforce any statute, regulation, ordinance, or policy whereby homosexual, lesbian or bisexual orientation, conduct, practices or relationships shall constitute or otherwise be the basis of or entitle any person or class of persons to have or claim any minority status, quota preferences, protected status or claim of discrimination. This Section of the Constitution shall be in all respects self-executing.

OREGON MEASURE 9

(1) This state shall not recognize any categorical provision such as "sexual orientation," "sexual preference," and similar phrases that include homosexuality. Quotas, minority status, affirmative action, or any similar concepts shall not apply to these forms of conduct, nor shall government promote these behaviors.

(2) State, regional and local governments and their properties and monies shall not be used to promote, encourage, or facilitate homosexuality, pedophilia, sadism or masochism.

(3) State, regional and local governments and their departments, agencies and other entities, including specifically the State Department of Higher Education and the public schools, shall assist in setting a standard for Oregon's youth that recognizes homosexuality, pedophilia, sadism and masochism as abnormal, wrong, unnatural, and perverse and that these behaviors are to be discouraged and avoided.

TIMBERTOWN MEASURE 20–15

The City of Timbertown . . . shall not make, pass, adopt, or enforce any ordinance, rule, regulation, policy or resolution that extends minority status, affirmative action, quotas, special class status, or any similar concepts, based on homosexuality or which establishes any categorical provision such as "sexual orientation," "sexual preference," or any similar provision which includes homosexuality.

OREGON HOUSE BILL 3500

"Be It Enacted by the People of the State of Oregon:

Section 1.

(1) A political subdivision of the state may not enact or enforce any charter provision, ordinance, resolution or policy granting special rights, privileges or treatment to any citizen or group of citizens on account of sexual orientation, or enact or enforce any charter provision, ordinance, resolution or policy that singles out citizens or groups of citizens on account of sexual orientation.

(2) Any person who believes that a political subdivision has enacted or is enforcing a charter provision, ordinance, resolution or policy in violation of this section may bring an action in circuit court to have the charter provision, ordinance, resolution or policy declared invalid, for injunctive relief and for such other relief as the court may consider appropriate. The court shall award reasonable attorney fees and costs to a plaintiff who prevails in an action under this subsection.

Section 2.

This Act being necessary for the immediate preservation of the public peace, health and safety, an emergency is declared to exist, and this Act takes effect upon its passage.

NOTES

1. Introduction

1. Paul Neville, "Tuesday's Vote Will Test OCA Comeback Strategy," *Eugene Register-Guard,* June 28, 1993, 1A, 4A.

2. Tad Shannon, "Reforms Wrong, Lawyer Tells Court," *Eugene Register-Guard,* May 5, 1998, 1A.

3. On various moral panics and moral crusades, see Stanley Cohen, *Folk Devils and Moral Panics: The Creation of Mods and Rockers* (Cambridge: Blackwell, 1972); Donna Gaines, *Teenage Wasteland* (New York: HarperCollins, 1990); Nicola Beisel, *Imperiled Innocents: Anthony Comstock and Family Reproduction in Victorian America* (Princeton: Princeton University Press, 1997); Gayle Rubin "Thinking Sex: Notes for a Radical Theory of the Politics of Sexuality," in *Pleasure and Danger,* ed. Carole Vance (Boston: Routledge, 1984); Estelle Freedman, " 'Uncontrolled Desires': The Response to the Sexual Psychopath, 1920–1960" (in *Passion and Power: Sexuality in History,* ed. Kathy Peiss and Christina Simmons (Philadelphia: Temple University Press, 1989, 199–225); Steven Seidman, "Transfiguring Sexual Identity: AIDS and the Contemporary Construction of Homosexuality," *Social Text* 19/20 (1988):187–205; Debbie Nathan and Michael Snedeker, *Satan's Silence: Ritual Abuse and the Making of a Modern American Witch Hunt* (New York: Basic Books, 1995). John Gerassi, *The Boys of Boise: Furor, Vice, and Folly in an American City* (New York: Macmillan, 1966), is an early examination of a moral panic over homosexuality. On moral panics more generally, see Erich Goode and Nachman Ben-Yehuda, *Moral Panics: The Social Construction of Deviance* (Cambridge and Oxford: Blackwell, 1994). For a critique of the "moral panics" literature on the grounds that it understates the rational, material underpinnings of moral movements, see Nicola Beisel and Brian Donovan, "The Problem with Moral Panics," *Culture* (newsletter of the American Sociological Association) 12, no. 2 (Winter 1998):1–3.

4. James Davison Hunter, *Culture Wars: The Struggle to Define America.* (New York: Basic Books, 1991), 4.

5. There is a debate among sociologists over the usefulness of the "culture wars" concept, against the claims set forth in James Hunter's *Culture Wars* and *Before the Shooting Begins: Searching for Democracy in America's Culture War* (New York: Free Press, 1994). Some contend that the American population is not nearly as polarized as Hunter and others suggest. For example, Christian Smith et al., in *Cultural Wars in American Politics: Critical Reviews of a Popular Myth,* ed. Rhys Williams (New York: Aldine de Gruyter, 1997), argue that "the actual culture wars that we do see on television—shrill fights over abortion, homosexuality, prayer in schools, obscenity in art, and so on—are being waged by a fairly small group of noisy,

entrepreneurial activists at the extremes, whose interest are served by the impression that all of American has taken up arms to join their fight" (175–77).

6. James Jasper, *The Art of Moral Protest: Culture, Biography, and Creativity in Social Movements* (Chicago: University of Chicago Press, 1998), 94.

7. Horace M. Kallen, *Culture and Democracy in the United States: Studies in the Group Psychology of the American Peoples* (New York: Boni & Liveright, 1924), 13.

8. See Kristin Luker, *Abortion and the Politics of Motherhood* (Berkeley: University of California Press, 1984).

9. Harry Esteve, "Democrats Concentrated in Large Cities," *Eugene Register-Guard,* November 5, 1998, 1A.

10. On boundary marking and maintenance, also see Frederic Barth, *Ethnic Groups and Boundaries: The Social Organization of Culture Difference* (Oslo: Universistetsforlaget, 1969); Pierre Bourdieu, *Distinction: A Social Critique of the Judgment of Taste* (Cambridge: Harvard University Press, 1984); Norbert Elias, *The Established and the Outsiders* (London: Sage, 1984); Eviatar Zerubavel, *The Fine Line: Making Distinctions in Everyday Life* (New York: Free Press, 1991).

11. Michael Ignatieff, *Ethnic War and the Modern Conscience* (New York: Metropolitan Books, 1998).

12. Kai Erikson, *Wayward Puritans: A Study in the Sociology of Deviance* (New York: John Wiley and Sons, 1966), 8–19.

13. Robert Scott, and Jack Douglas, *Theoretical Perspectives on Deviance* (New York: Basic Books, 1972), 29.

14. Anna Marie Smith, "A Symptomology of an Authoritarian Discourse," in *Cultural Remix: Theories of Politics and the Popular* ed. Erica Carter et al. (London: Lawrence & Wishart,

1995), 224; Michael Paul Rogin, "The Countersubversive Tradition in American Politics," *Berkeley Journal of Sociology* 31 (1986):1–33. But the right does not have exclusive claims to boundary making. See my *Sex and Sensibility: Stories of a Lesbian Generation* (Berkeley: University of California Press, 1997); and Joshua Gamson, "Must Identity Movements Self-Destruct? A Queer Dilemma," in *Queer Theory/Sociology,* ed. Steven Seidman (Cambridge: Blackwell, 1996).

15. Quoted in Nancy Chodorow "The Enemy Outside: Thoughts on the Psychodynamics of Extreme Violence with Special Attention to Men and Masculinity," *Journal for the Psychoanalysis of Culture and Society* 3, no. 1 (1998):26.

16. See Zymunt Bauman's discussion of "Strangers" in his *Thinking Sociologically* (Cambridge: Blackwell, 1990).

17. Mary McIntosh, "The Homosexual Role," *Social Problems* 16 (1968):262–70.

18. John D'Emilio, *Sexual Politics, Sexual Communities: The Making of a Homosexual Minority in the United States* (Chicago: University of Chicago Press, 1983); Kath Weston, "Get Thee to a Big City: Sexual Imaginary and the Great Gay Migration," *GLQ* 2 (1995):253–77.

19. Anthony Giddens, *The Transformation of Intimacy* (Stanford: Stanford University Press, 1992); Alice Echols, *Daring to Be Bad: Radical Feminism in America* (Minneapolis: University of Minnesota Press, 1989).

20. Steven Epstein, "Gay Politics, Ethnic Identity: The Limits of Social Constructionism," *Socialist Review* 17, nos. 3–4 (1987):9–50; Lisa Keen and Suzanne Goldberg, *Strangers to the Law: Gay People on Trial* (Ann Arbor: University of Michigan Press, 1998).

21. Steven Epstein, "Gay and Les-

bian Movements in the US," in *Gay and Lesbian Movements Since the 1960s,* ed. Barry Adam, Jan Willem Duyvendak, and Andre Krouwel (Philadelphia: Temple University Press, 1999.)

22. Carey Goldberg, "Acceptance of Gay Men and Lesbians Is Growing, Study Says," *New York Times,* May 31, 1998, 15A; Alan Wolfe, *One Nation, After All* (New York: Viking, 1998).

23. Epstein, "Gay and Lesbian Movements in the US," 34.

24. Senator Bob Dole, quoted by Barry and Aimee Williams in letter to Don Anderson, Junction City School District, June 5, 1995.

25. Christian Smith, *American Evangelicalism: Embattled and Thriving* (Chicago: University of Chicago Press, 1998), found that twenty million Americans, or 7 percent of adults, identify themselves as evangelicals (1).

26. Sara Diamond, *Not by Politics Alone: The Enduring Influence of the Christian Right* (New York: Guilford Press, 1998), 8–9.

27. Mark Shibley, *Resurgent Evangelicalism in the US: Mapping Cultural Change Since 1970* (Columbia: University of South Carolina Press, 1996).

28. On evangelicals' gradual shift toward political involvement, see Diamond, *Not by Politics Alone;* Benton Johnson, "Theology and the Position of Pastors on Social Issues: Continuity and Change Since the 1960s," *Review of Religious Research* 39, no. 4 (June 1998):293–308.

29. Luker, *Abortion;* Faye Ginsburg, *Contested Lives: The Abortion Debate in an American Community* (Berkeley: University of California Press, 1989); Didi Herman, *The Antigay Agenda: Orthodox Vision and the Christian Right* (Chicago: University of Chicago Press, 1997).

30. Diamond, *Not by Politics Alone.*

31. Janice Irvine, "A Place in the Rainbow: Theorizing Lesbian and Gay Culture," in Seidman, *Queer Theory.*

32. This progressive reform movement also laid the basis for a new, more modern round of racial exclusion and segregation. See Peggy Pascoe, "Democracy, Citizenship, and Race: The U.S. West in the 20th Century," unpublished paper, Department of History, University of Oregon, 1999.

33. Technically, initiatives make new law while referenda repeal existing laws; however, some initiatives, such as Colorado's Amendment 2, can do both. In certain states, including Colorado, the initiative process can be used to amend the state constitution (Herman, *Antigay Agenda,* 141–42). See also Todd S. Purdham, "Ballot Initiatives Flourishing as a Way to Bypass Politicians," *New York Times,* April 1, 1998, 1A.

34. On the antigay ballot initiatives of the early 1990s, see Lisa Duggan, "Queering the State," *Socialtext* 39 (1994):1–14. Also see Herman, *Antigay Agenda;* Diamond, *Not by Politics Alone.*

2. The Personal Is Political

1. Janice Henry, "OCA Measure will Prevent Gays Getting Special Treatment," Timbertown *Gazette,* February 3, 1993, 5A.

2. Interview with author, March 4, 1998.

3. Letter to the editor, Timbertown *Gazette,* May 4, 1994, 5A.

4. Elaine Pagels argues that Christianity has historically defined the satanic not so much in terms of distant threats but in relation to intimate ones: "The most dangerous characteristic of the satanic enemy is that though he will look just like us, he will nevetheless have changed completely: How could one of *us* become one of *them?*" Quoted by Linda Kintz, *Between Jesus and the Market: The Emotions That Matter in Right-Wing America* (Durham, NC: Duke University Press, 1997), 73.

5. On the origins and significance of the "ethnic" model of homosexuality, see Steven Epstein, "Gay Politics, Ethnic Identity," *Socialist Review* 17, nos. 3–4 (1987):9–50. On gay civil rights strategies, see Lisa Keen and Suzanne Goldberg, *Strangers to the Law: Gay People on Trial* (Ann Arbor: University of Michican Press, 1998).

6. Gayle Rubin, "Thinking Sex: Notes for a Radical Theory of the Politics of Sexuality," in *Pleasure and Danger,* ed. Carole Vance (New York: Monthly Review Press, 1984).

7. Kai Erikson, *Wayward Puritans: A Study in the Sociology of Deviance* (New York: John Wiley and Sons, 1966); Robert Scott, "A Proposed Framework for Analyzing Deviance as a Property of Social Order," in *Theoretical Perspective on Deviance,* ed. Robert Scott and Jack Douglas (New York: Basic Books, 1972); Mary McIntosh, "The Homosexual Role," *Social Problems* 16 (1968):262–70.

8. Critiques of liberal individualism did not emerge from the right alone. See communitarian statements such as Amitai Etzioni, *The New Golden Rule: Community and Morality in a Democratic Society* (New York: Basic Books, 1996); Robert Bellah et al., *Habits of the Heart: Individualism and Commitment in American Culture* (Berkeley: University of California Press, 1985). On the relationship between the private and public spheres, see Lauren Berlant, *The Queen of America Goes to Washington City: Essays on Sex and Citizenship* (Durham, NC: Duke University Press, 1997).

9. Tad Shannon, "Reforms Wrong, Lawyer Tells Court," *Eugene Register-Guard,* May 5, 1998, 1A.

10. Stephen Braun, "Prayer Clubs Growing Phenomenon in Schools," *Eugene Register-Guard,* May 16, 1998, 17A.

11. James Jasper, *The Art of Moral Protest: Culture, Biography, and Creativity in Social Movements* (Chicago: University of Chicago Press, 1998), 215.

12. Marc Ramirez, "Lon Mabon Sets 'Em Straight," *Seattle Times,* October 3, 1993, 19.

13. Didi Herman, *The Antigay Agenda: Orthodox Vision and the Christian Right* (Chicago: University of Chicago Press, 1997), 5; Susan Johnston, "On the Fire Brigade: Why Liberalism Can't Stop the Anti-Gay Campaigns of the Right," *Critical Sociology* 20, no. 4 (1994):7; Lisa Duggan, "Queering the State," *Socialtext* 39 (1994):1.

14. Patty Wentz, "He's Back," *Willamette Week,* February, 11, 1998, 1. James Jasper draws a distinction between "fundis" and "realos," *Art of Moral Protest,* 375.

15. Right Watch, "Right Guide to the Other Side: Contributors to the OCA and its Companion PACs in the 1988–1994 Primary," Portland, Oregon, 1994.

16. Oregon Citizens Alliance, "Statement of Principles," Brooks, Oregon.

17. Ramirez, "Lon Mabon," 12–21.

18. "Targeted Rural Community Donation Analysis," Oregon Citizens Alliance, Brooks, Oregon, 1992.

19. Harry Esteve, "OCA Fund-Raising Dinner Draws Politicians Protests," *Eugene Register-Guard,* January 15, 1994, 1B.

20. Richard Slotkin, *Regeneration Through Violence* (Middletown: Wesleyan University Press, 1973).

21. Timbertown *Gazette,* April 3, 1969, 12A. See also James Davison Hunter, *Culture Wars: The Struggle to Define America* (New York: Basic Books, 1991).

22. Christian Smith, *American Evangelicalism: Embattled and Thriving* (Chicago: University of Chicago Press, 1998).

23. Edwin Scott Gaustad, *Historical Atlas of Religion in America* (New York: Harper & Row 1976), 123.

24. Letter to the editor, Timbertown *Gazette,* April 14, 1993, 5A.

25. Geoffrey Parrinder, *Sex in the World's Religions* (New York: Oxford University Press, 1980), 214.

26. Anthony Giddens, *Modernity and Self-Identity* (Cambridge: Polity Press, 1991).

27. On shifting gender ideologies in evangelical Christianity, see Judith Stacey, *Brave New Families* (New York: Basic Books, 1990); Judith Stacey and Susan Gerard, "We Are Not Doormats" in *Through the Prism of Difference: Readings on Sex and Gender,* ed. Maxine Baca Zinn, Pierette Hondagneu-Sotelo, and M. Messner (Boston: Allyn and Bacon, 1997); R. Marie Griffith, *God's Daughters: Evangelical Women and the Power of Submission* (Berkeley: University of California Press, 1997).

28. Letter to editor, Timbertown *Gazette,* July 28, 1993, 4A.

29. Letter to the editor, Timbertown *Gazette,* June 23, 1993, 5A.

30. See, for example, how these ideas play out in the ex-gay movement, as documented by Surina Khan, *Calculated Compassion: How the Ex-Gay Movement Serves the Right's Attack on Democracy,* October 1998, and *Challenging the Ex-Gay Movement,* reports from Political Research Associates, The Policy Institute of the National Gay and Lesbian Task Force, and Equal Partners in Faith, n.p. December 1998.

31. Interview with author, April 14, 1998.

32. Smith, *American Evangelicalism,* 188.

3. Resentment's Roots

1. Jim Leinfelder, "Letter from Portland: Logging, Fishing, Skating Falter as the Old West Fades," *Newsday,* February 20, 1994, 52.

2. Unidentified news article, Timbertown Historical Society.

3. Michael Thoele, *Bohemia: The Lives and Times of an Oregon Timber Venture* (Portland: Oregon Historical Society Press, 1998), 455.

4. Ibid., 269.

5. Ibid.

6. Works Progress Administration, *Oregon: End of the Trail* (Portland: Binfords and Mort, 1940), 60.

7. Michael Hibbard and James Elias, "The Failure of Sustained-Yield Forestry and the Decline of the Flannel Shirt Frontier," in *Forgotten Places: Uneven Development in Rural America,* ed. Thomas A. Lyson and William W. Falk (Lawrence: University Press of Kansas, 1993), 197.

8. "Timber Keeps Community Green," Timbertown *Gazette,* April 3, 1969, 6A.

9. Norbert Elias, *The Established and the Outsiders* (London: Sage Publications, 1994).

10. Beverly Brown, *In Timber Country: Working People's Stories of Environmental Conflict and Urban Flight* (Philadelphia: Temple University Press, 1995).

11. Tee Corinne, "Southern Oregon Lesbians and the Back-to-the-Land Movement of the 1970s–80s," paper; Tee Corinne, "Resources for Southern Oregon Women on the Land," paper, Sunny Valley, Oregon, August 1991.

12. Lynne Isaacson, "Delicate Balances: Rearticulating Gender Ideology and Rules for Sexuality in a Jesus People Communal Movement" (Ph.D. diss., University of Oregon, 1996).

13. David Hupp and Jeff Malachowsky, "Rural Divide: The Politics of Polarization," *Western States Center News,* Summer 1993, 1.

14. A brochure from the local Chamber of Commerce listed "Twelve Good Reasons to Live in Timbertown,"

including, "Your vote counts in local elections" and "A chance for fame (or notoriety) as a guest on the local radio call-in show." Chamber of Commerce, *Chamber of Commerce Membership Directory and Community Profile* (Timbertown, 1997), 1.

15. Elias, *The Established*, 153–54.

16. Ibid., ii.

17. Lance Robertson, "Cutting a Deal Comes Slowly," *Eugene Register-Guard*, April 15, 1993, 1F, 5F.

18. William R. Freudenberg, Lisa Wilson, and Daniel O'Leary, "Forty Years of Spotted Owls? A Longitudinal Analysis of Logging Industry Job Losses," *Sociological Perspectives* 41, no. 1 (1998):1–26.

19. Hibbard and Elias, "Failure of Sustained-Yield Forestry," 207.

20. Brown, *In Timber Country*, 24. Between 1980 and 1991, eighty-three sawmills and sixty-nine plywood and veneer plants in the state were closed. Housing starts were at a forty-five-year low, representing less than half its 1972 level (Thoele, *Bohemia*, 446).

21. Thoele, *Bohemia*, 473.

22. "Oregon Tops List for Mill Closures Throughout West," *Eugene Register-Guard*, August 18, 1992, 1B, 2B.

23. Mike Page-English, "Taking a Fall," Timbertown *Gazette*, March 10, 1993, 1A.

24. Hibbard and Elias, "Failure of Sustained-Yield Forestry," 209.

25. James Greenberg, "Hip City," *Harper's Bazaar*, May 1, 1994, 117.

26. Jim Leinfelder, "Letter from Portland," 52.

27. Mike Thoele, "Romantic View of Small Towns Ignores Troubles," *Eugene Register-Guard*, March 25, 1990, 51G.

28. Chamber of Commerce, *Community Profile and Business Directory* (Timbertown, 1992).

29. City of Timbertown brochure, 1992.

30. Many loggers also chose to remain working in the woods, though typically at lower salaries: "Resilient Loggers Find Ways to Stay in Woods," *Eugene Register-Guard*, November 22, 1998, 12D.

31. Rick Bella, "An Uncertain Future," *Eugene Register-Guard*, April 8, 1990, 1A.

32. Thoele, "Romantic View of Small Towns;" Ed Whitelaw, "Rich Oregonian, Poor Oregonian," *Oregon Quarterly*, Summer 1995. In the 1980s the distribution of income in the nation as a whole became more polarized. See Katherine Newman, *Declining Fortunes* (New York: Basic Books, 1993), 41.

33. Center for Population Research and Census, Portland State University, Portland, Oregon.

34. On the phenomenon of equity migrants, see Ibid., 13. It is noteworthy that America's seniors are far better off than any other age group in the country, a trend that is accelerating. In 1986, the elderly made up 21 percent of the population but had one third of the nation's wealth (Newman, *Declining Fortunes*, 36). The political impact of these trends could be seen in the West in the early 1990s, as rural counties in Montana, Nevada, and portions of Wyoming, Oregon, and Washington gained population due to migration. These migrants were more likely to be affluent and conservative according to "Rural Isn't What You Think," *Western States Center Newsletter* (Spring/Summer 1999):3.

35. Many immigrants from California took high-profile roles in local antitax campaigns, which resembled California's Proposition 13 tax revolt of the previous decade, and they fought to protect the environment and property

values of their own neighborhoods through exclusionary zoning. See Brown, *In Timber Country,* 14–15.

36. Georg Simmel, "The Metropolis and Mental Life," in *The Sociology of Georg Simmel,* ed. Kurt Wolff (New York: Free Press, 1950). In the late 1980s, when I interviewed lesbian women living in the San Francisco Bay Area, many spoke of the contrast between the rural life they once lived and the freedoms that were possible in the city. If they moved to cities, gay people could take their place alongside Italian Americans, Jewish Americans, and African Americans as members of a full-fledged minority group—or so many believed. See my *Sex and Sensibility* (Berkeley: University of California Press, 1997).

37. Frances Fitzgerald, *Cities on a Hill: A Journey Through Contemporary American Cultures* (New York: Simon & Schuster, 1986), 23.

38. Robert T. Michael et al., *Sex in America: A Definitive Survey* (Boston: Little, Brown, 1994); Edward O. Laumann et al., *The Social Organization of Sexuality* (Chicago: University of Chicago Press, 1994).

39. David Firestone, "Murder Reveals Double Life of Being Gay in Rural South," *New York Times,* March 6, 1999, 1A.

40. Mary McIntosh, "The Homosexual Role," *Social Problems* 16 (1968):262–70.

41. Zygmunt Bauman, *Postmodern Ethics* (Oxford: Blackwell, 1993), 156.

42. Brown, *In Timber Country,* 251. Bauman, *Postmodern Ethics,* suggests that modernization undermines morality; Anthony Giddens, in *Modernity and Self-Identity: Self and Society in the Late Modern Age* (Cambridge: Polity, 1991), writes of the "disembedding" of local relations as they become integrated into systems of standard transactions and

professional expertise. But the decline of localism has been exaggerated, according to William W. Donner, "Assimilation and Localism: Some Very Small Towns in Mass Society," *Sociological Inquiry* 68, no. 1 (1998):61–82. "There are continued efforts to maintain and re-embed local identities and spheres of intensified social relations . . . which serve expressive, local purposes and maintain some degree of face-to-face intimacy" (62). Indeed, the campaign I am describing may be seen as an effort to re-embed a local identity in Timbertown, against economic and other pressures to assimilate into the larger region and lose its small-town identity.

43. Brown, *In Timber Country,* 119.

44. Thoele, "Romantic View of Small Towns," 51G.

4. Community Reimagined

1. Pierre Bourdieu, *Distinction: A Social Critique of the Judgment of Taste* (Cambridge: Harvard University Press, 1984); James Jasper, *The Art of Moral Protest: Culture, Biography and Creativity in Social Movements* (Chicago: University of Chicago Press, 1998), 238.

2. Whether Pentecostals should be included in the spiritual universe of fundamentalism is a subject of debate among scholars. In Linda Kintz and Julia Lesage, eds., *Media, Culture, and the Religious Right* (Minneapolis: University of Minnesota Press, 1998), 55–113, Nancy T. Ammerman distinguishes the two and says that Pentecostals should not be included. Charles Strozier ("Christian Fundamentalism and the Apocalyptic in the 1990s," Chi Rho Lectures, Central Lutheran Church, Eugene, Oregon, November 6–8, 1998) acknowledges that Pentecostals are not as "aggressively literal"

as fundamentalists but nonetheless believes that they share enough core beliefs to consider them together. Didi Herman in *The Antigay Agenda: Orthodox Vision and the Christian Right* (Chicago: University of Chicago Press, 1997), says much the same. As she suggests, close to half of the population would describe themselves as "born again," a larger group than the one I am describing (12–13). And they believe in an apocalyptic theory of ultimate death that the world is coming to an end, and when that end comes, true Christians alone will be saved; Strozier considers this to be the "ideological core" of the movement. On the relationship between fundamentalism, evangelicals, Pentecostals, and charismatics, see John C. Green, "The Spirit Willing: Collective Identity and the Development of the Christian Right," in *Waves of Protest: Social Movements Since the Sixties,* ed. Jo Freeman and Victoria Johnson (Lanham, MD: Rowman & Littlefield, 1999), 153–67.

3. Christian Smith, *American Evangelicalism: Embattled and Thriving* (Chicago: University of Chicago Press, 1998), 33.

4. Terence O'Donnell, *That Balance So Rare: The Story of Oregon* (Portland: Oregon Historical Society Press, 1988), 30.

5. Patricia Nelson Limerick, "Believing in the American West," in *The West: An Illustrated History,* ed. Geoffrey C. Ward (Boston: Little, Brown, 1996), 208; Raymond Gastil, *Cultural Regions of the US* (Seattle: University of Washington Press, 1975), 48; Oregon Office of the Secretary of State, *Blue Book 1998* (Salem, OR: n.p., 1998), 402; Rodney Stark and William S. Bainbridge, *The Future of Religion* (Berkeley: University of California Press, 1985).

6. Joe V. Peterson, "Jesus People: Christ, Communes, and the Counterculture of the late Twentieth Century in the Pacific Northwest" (master's thesis, Northwest Christian College, 1990); Marion S. Goldman, *Passionate Journeys: Why Successful Women Joined a Cult* (Ann Arbor: University of Michigan Press, 1999).

7. A similar movement is true of the nation as a whole, as mainline Protestantism has lost ground to evangelicalism. While the Episcopal Church has decreased by 44 percent as a proportion of the U.S. population, the Church of God in Christ has increased by 863 percent. Most striking is how new many of the fastest-growing congregations are: of the approximately one thousand six hundred religions and denominations in the United States today, about eight hundred were founded since 1965. Russell Shorto, "Belief by the Numbers," *New York Times Magazine,* December 7, 1997, 60. See also Robert Wuthnow, *The Restructuring of American Religion* (Princeton: Princeton University Press, 1988); Dean Kelley, *Why Conservative Churches Are Growing* (New York: Harper & Row, 1986).

8. Bruce Bawer, *Stealing Jesus: How Fundamentalism Betrays Christianity* (New York: Crown, 1997), 5.

9. Smith, *American Evangelicalism,* 91.

10. Archie Robertson, *That Old-Time Religion* (Boston: Houghton Mifflin, 1950), 5.

11. Edwin Scott Gaustad, *Historical Atlas of Religion in America* (New York: Harper & Row, 1976), 123.

12. Mark Shibley, *Resurgent Evangelicalism in the United States: Mapping Cultural Change Since 1970* (Columbia: University of South Carolina Press, 1996).

13. Gustav Niebuhr, "New Groups Fuel Christians' Growth," *New York Times,* January 31, 1998, 23A; Donald E. Miller, *Reinventing American Protes-*

tantism (Berkeley: University of California Press, 1997).

14. Miller, *Reinventing American Protestantism;* Shibley, *Resurgent Evangelicalism.*

15. Peter L. Halvorsen and William M. Newman, *Atlas of Religious Change in America 1952–1990* (Atlanta: Glenmary Research Center, 1994), 104; Rev. Steven Overman, senior pastor of the Faith Center, Eugene, Oregon, "Signs of the Spirit: Reconciliation and Revival in America," International Church of the Foursquare Gospel website (www.foursquare.org).

16. On the Promise Keepers, see Sara Diamond, *Not by Politics Alone: The Enduring Influence of the Christian Right* (New York: Guilford Press, 1998); Susan Faludi, *Stiffed* (New York: William Morrow, 1999).

17. Smith, *American Evangelicalism,* 16.

18. Linda Kintz, *Between Jesus and the Market: The Emotions That Matter in Right-Wing America* (Durham, NC: Duke University Press, 1997), 6–7.

19. Emily Nussbaum, "For Evangelical Teenagers, Jewelry for Jesus," *New York Times Magazine,* November 15, 1998, 93–94. During the early 1990s, the sales of Christian products in bookstores exceeded $3 billion annually, according to Colleen McDannell, *Material Christianity: Religion and Popular Culture in America* (New Haven: Yale University Press, 1995), 222. See also Gustav Niebuhr, "Ministries Flourishing in a World of Tattooing," *New York Times,* March 21, 1999, 16.

20. In 1998, Southern Baptists amended their faith statement to declare that a "wife is to submit herself graciously" to her husband's leadership (Gustav Niebuhr, "Southern Baptists May Rule Against Women as Pastors," *New York Times,* May 19, 2000, 16A).

21. Diamond, *Not by Politics Alone,*

234. On the influence of feminism on evangelicalism, see Judith Stacey and Susan Gerard, "We are Not Doormats," in *Through the Prism of Difference: Readings on Sex and Gender,* ed. Maxine Baca Zinn, Pierette Hondagneu-Sotelo, and Michael Messner (Boston: Allyn and Bacon, 1997); R. Marie Griffith, *God's Daughters: Evangelical Women and the Power of Submission* (Berkeley: University of California Press, 1997).

22. Marion S. Goldman and Lynne M. Isaacson, "Enduring Affiliation and Gender Doctrine for Shiloh Sisters and Rajneesh Sannyasins," *Journal for the Scientific Study of Religion* 38 (1999):411–23. Lynne Isaacson, "Delicate Balances: Rearticulating Gender Ideology and Rules for Sexuality in a Jesus People Communal Movement" (Ph.D. diss., University of Oregon, 1996), found that 94 percent of former Shiloh members said that homosexuality was condemned by the Bible, though 35 percent thought gays and lesbians deserved equal protection under the law.

23. Tim and Beverly La Haye, quoted in Kintz, *Between Jesus and the Market,* 63.

24. "White As Snow," words by "L. N.," Desert Foothills United Methodist Church, Phoenix, Arizona, Website: http://hwmin.gbgm_umc.org/churches/DesertFoothillsAZ/PPBLISS/wtasn.html.

25. Limerick, "Believing in the American West," 207.

26. Bawer, *Stealing Jesus;* Daniel Wojcik, *The End of the World as We Know It* (New York: New York University Press, 1997).

27. Charles Strozier, *Apocalypse: On the Psychology of Fundamentalism in America* (Boston: Beacon Press, 1994).

28. Kintz, *Between Jesus and the Market,* 210.

29. "Affiliation is higher where there is a dominance of one denomination

rather than a thoroughgoing mixture of religious groups of more or less equal strength, as in Oregon" (Gastil, *Cultural Regions,* 48). Roger Finke and Rodney Stark, *The Churching of America 1776–1990* (New Brunswick, NJ: Rutgers University Press, 1992), disagree: the greater the competition from other religions and denominations, they argue, the more commitment there will be. One might say that commitment breeds intimate ties among members and church stability.

30. Robertson, *That Old-Time Religion,* 168.

31. Rudy Brueggmann, "Righteous Indignation," Timbertown *Gazette,* April 20, 1994, 1A.

32. Finke and Stark, *Churching of America.*

33. Jon Stone, *On the Boundaries of American Evangelicalism* (New York: St. Martins, 1997).

34. This is true of the denomination as a whole, according to Wuthnow's *The Restructuring of American Religion* (Princeton: Princeton University Press, 1988).

35. Historically, pressures to become more diverse have led to schism, as in the 1860s when the Presbyterian Church (U.S.A.) split from the Southern Presbyterians over the issue of slavery.

36. Jeffery L. Sheler, "An American Reformation," *U.S. News & World Report,* July 19, 1999.

37. Jody Shapiro Davie, *Women in the Presence: Constructing Community and Seeking Spirituality in Mainline Protestantism* (Philadelphia: University of Pennsylvania Press, 1995), 19.

38. In recent years, struggles over homosexuality have continued to divide Presbyterian and other mainline Protestant denominations. See Dawne Moon, "A Hetero Haven in a Heartless World: Homosexuality and the Prob-

lem of Politics in Church," paper presented at the American Sociological Association meetings, Chicago, August 1999; Jeff Wright, "Church Wrestles Morality," *Eugene Register-Guard,* March 7, 1998, 1A; David Briggs, "Lutherans Step Squarely into Sexuality Debate," *Eugene Register-Guard,* October 23, 1993, 6A; Keith Hartman, *Congregations in Conflict: The Battle Over Homosexuality* (New Brunswick, NJ: Rutgers University Press, 1996); Gustav Niebuhr, "Ban on Ordaining Homosexuals Is Upheld," *New York Times,* June 26, 1999, 14A; "Debate Over Same-Sex Marriage Splits a Methodist Church Near Atlanta," *New York Times,* June 24, 1999, 16A; Matt Smith, "The Holy War Over Gay Marriage," *SF Weekly,* November 4, 1998, 26; Gustav Niebuhr, "Laws Aside, Some in Clergy Quietly Bless Gay Marriage," *New York Times,* April 17, 1998, 1A; Gustav Niebuhr, "Methodist Faces Trial for Uniting Two Men," *New York Times,* March 25, 1999, 18A.

5. Decorating for Jesus

1. Judith Stacey and Susan Gerard, "We Are not Doormats" in *Through the Prism of Difference: Readings on Sex and Gender,* ed. Maxine Baca Zinn, Pierette Hondagneu-Sotelo, and Michael Messner (Boston: Allyn and Bacon, 1997).

2. Cited in Linda Kintz, *Between Jesus and the Market: The Emotions That Matter in Right-Wing America* (Durham, NC: Duke University Press, 1997), 173.

3. Ibid., 17; R. Marie Griffith, *God's Daughters: Evangelical Women and the Power of Submission* (Berkeley: University of California Press, 1997).

4. Colleen McDannell, *Material Christianity: Religion and Popular Culture in America* (New Haven: Yale University Press, 1995), 248.

5. Christian Smith, *American Evangelicalism: Embattled and Thriving* (Chicago: University of Chicago Press, 1998), 104.

6. Individuals are constantly involved in the quest to abide by "feeling rules" in order to "protect face" and minimize the public display of negative emotions (Erving Goffman, *Interaction Ritual* [New York: Doubleday Anchor, 1967]; Arlie Hochschild, *The Managed Heart* [Berkeley: University of California Press, 1983]). Emotions, both positive and negative, are inseparable from social interactions. Recent literature on the interaction of social movements and emotions has considered what Sandra Morgen, "Towards a Politics of Feelings: Beyond the Dialectic of Thought and Action," *Women's Studies* 10, no. 2 (1983):203–23, calls the "politics of feeling." (Also see Alberto Melucci, *Nomads of the Present: Social Movements and Individual Needs in Contemporary Society* [London: Century Hutchinson, 1995]; Verta Taylor and Nancy Whittier, "Collective Identity in Social Movement Communities: Lesbian Feminist Mobilization," in *Frontiers of Social Movement Theory,* ed. Aldon Morris and Carol Mueller [New Haven: Yale University Press, 1992]). Yet there has been little research on how the right taps into emotional needs. This is surprising in view of an earlier tradition of research that examined the psychological dimensions of right-wing activism, seeing such movements as an irrational playing out of paranoid fantasies (Richard Hofstadter, *The Paranoid Style in American Politics and Other Essays* [New York: Vintage, 1967]) or as disorganized, relatively spontaneous "panics" (Erich Goode and Nachman Ben-Yehuda, *Moral Panics: The Social Construction of Deviance* [Cambridge and Oxford: Blackwell, 1994]). Certainly, many movements embody irrational dimensions. But moral movements such

as the contemporary Christian right, much like their counterparts on the left, are much more complex, and more organized, than this. As Kintz, *Between Jesus and the Market,* suggests, we must move beyond the view of emotions and fantasy as "an unbridled irrationalism without any logic" (67). Emotions do possess a logic, and movements give shape and public voice to those emotions.

7. Thomas J. Scheff, "Socialization of Emotions: Pride and Shame as Causal Agents," in *Research Agendas in the Sociology of Emotions,* ed. Theodore D. Kemper (Albany: State University of New York Press 1990), 281.

8. Helen B. Lewis, *Shame and Guilt in Neurosis* (New York: International Universities Press, 1971), 41

9. Ibid, 197; Scheff, "Socialization of Emotions," 298.

10. Richard Sennett and J. Cobb, *The Hidden Injuries of Class* (New York: Knopf, 1992).

11. Alan Wolfe, *One Nation, After All* (New York: Viking, 1998).

12. Katherine Newman, *Declining Fortunes* (New York: Basic Books, 1993).

13. James Dobson, quoted in Michael Milburn and S. Conrad, *The Politics of Denial* (Cambridge: MIT Press, 1996), 20.

14. Sigmund Freud believed that punitive child rearing facilitates the process of moral development by forcing the child to identify with "the aggressor"—the parent. But post-Freudian observers have suggested that when children are socialized to deny their feelings, this may impact upon children and society in negative ways. In the wake of World War II, Theodor Adorno and his colleagues suggested that rigid, punitive parents create what he called the "authoritarian personality." Decades later, psychologist Alice Miller criticized the "poisonous peda-

gogy" embedded in "normal" child-rearing practices in the West. See ibid.

15. George Lakoff, *Moral Politics* (Chicago: University of Chicago Press, 1996).

16. Milburn and Conrad, *Politics of Denial,* 8.

17. Didi Herman, *The Antigay Agenda: Orthodox Vision and the Christian Right* (Chicago: University of Chicago Press, 1997), 81–82.

18. On the good gay-bad gay distinction in conservative rhetoric, see Anna Marie Smith, "A Symptomology of an Authoritarian Discourse," in *Cultural Remix: Theories of Politics and the Popular,* ed. Erica Carter et al. (London: Lawrence & Wishart, 1995), 299–330. Also see Johnston, "Paradoxes of Identity: Liberalism, Bio-Power and 'Homosexual' Politics in Oregon" (Ph.D diss., University of Oregon, 1996). On the distinction as it plays out in popular films, see Steven Seidman, "From Pollution to Normalization: Shifts in the Social Logic of Normative Heterosexuality" (paper given at Workshop on Sexuality and the State, International Institute for the Sociology of Law, Spain, June 2000). One could argue that by making a stand in favor of normative heterosexuality, OCA appeals were also directed much more broadly toward heterosexuals who harbored homosexual desires, whether or not they acted upon them.

19. Paul Neevel, "Wake Up Call," *Eugene Weekly,* March 17, 1994, 7.

20. Zygmunt Bauman, *Postmodern Ethics* (Oxford: Blackwell, 1993), 155.

21. Ibid., 156.

6. **Angry White Men and Women**

1. Alan Wolfe, *One Nation, After All* (New York: Viking 1998), 55.

2. Ibid., 322.

3. Paul Neville, "Money, Power and the OCA," *Eugene Register-Guard,* October 24, 1993, 1A.

4. In 1963, 60 percent of men aged twenty to twenty-four earned enough to keep a family of three out of poverty, whereas by 1984, only 42 percent could do so (Stephanie Coontz, *The Way We Never Were: American Families and the Nostalgia Trap* [New York: Basic Books, 1992], 263). Nationally, these shifts are producing a proliferation of different family forms: families headed by single mothers, divorced women cohabiting with one another, new families forming when fragments of extended families come together. Judith Stacey, *Brave New Families* (New York: Basic Books, 1990), found that "recombinant" working-class families were remaking American family life, and were a creative adaptation to a changing political economy. But for many Timbertowners the traditional family was an object of longing, often tied to a nostalgic appreciation for small-town life.

5. Kathleen Gerson, *No Man's Land: Men's Changing Commitment to Family and Work* (New York: Basic Books, 1993), 260.

6. George Lakoff, *Moral Politics* (Chicago: University of Chicago, 1966), 33–35.

7. Barry Adam, "Theorizing Homophobia," *Sexualities* 1, no. 4 (1998):387–404.

8. Thomas E. Wood, quoted in Lydia Chavez, *The Color Bind: The Campaign to End Affirmative Action* (Berkeley: University of California Press, 1998), 22.

9. Didi Herman, *The Antigay Agenda: Orthodox Vision and the Christian Right* (Chicago: University of Chicago Press, 1997), traces the history of right-wing anti-homosexual discourses differentiating between the "old moralist" discourse and a "new pragmatism." See also Anna Marie Smith, "A Symptomology of Authoritarian Discourse,"

in *Cultural Remix: Theories of Politics and the Popular,* ed. Erica Carter et al. (London: Lawrence & Wishart, 1995), 299–330; Susan Johnston, "On the Fire Brigade: Why Liberalism Can't Stop the Anti-Gay Campaigns of the Right," *Critical Sociology* 20, no. 4 (1994):3–19.

10. Thomas A. Lyson and William W. Falk, eds., *Forgotten Places: Uneven Development in Rural America* (Lawrence: University Press of Kansas, 1993).

11. Katherine Newman, *Declining Fortunes* (New York: Basic Books, 1993), 41; Tamira Miller, "The Two Oregons: Comparing Economic Conditions Between Rural and Urban Oregon" (report to Oregon's Joint Legislative Commission on Trade and Economic Development, Salem, Oregon, 1990).

12. Northwest Job Gap Study, a project of the Northwest Policy Center, University of Washington, and the Northwest Federation of Community Organizations, Seattle, Washington, January 1999. *ROP Report,* January 1999, summarizing the "Searching for Work That Pays." The report suggested that a living wage in 1999 was $10.07 for a single person in Oregon and $16.36 for a parent with two children.

13. Charles Sykes, *A Nation of Victims: The Decay of the American Character* (New York: St. Martins, 1992).

14. The Personal Responsibility and Work Opportunity Reconciliation Act of 1996 seeks to restrict welfare recipients' reproductive behavior. It denies money for children born to recipients already on welfare, and gives substantial bonuses to states that demonstrate the greatest reduction of births out of wedlock without increases in the abortion rate.

15. Interview with author, May 27, 1998.

16. Anthony Giddens, *Modernity and Self-Identity: Self and Society in the Late Modern Age* (Cambridge: Polity, 1991), 3–4.

17. Mike Page-English, "Council Opposes Anti-Homosexual Rights Measure," Timbertown *Gazette,* February 10, 1993, 1A; *Lion's Roar* (Timbertown High School), February 26, 1993.

18. Letter to the editor, Timbertown *Gazette,* July 26, 1993, 5A.

19. Letter to the editor, Timbertown *Gazette,* March 17, 1993, 5A.

20. Letter to the Editor, Timbertown *Gazette,* June 16, 1993, 4A.

21. In November 1995, conservatives sponsored Measure 8, a statewide ballot initiative requiring public employees to contribute 6 percent of their pay to finance their retirement pensions. Though it passed, the measure was eventually ruled unconstitutional.

22. In a 1993 *US News & World Report* poll, 73 percent of those who said they knew someone who is lesbian or gay (53 percent of the total sample) supported equal rights for lesbians and gays. Only 55 percent supported gay rights among the 46 percent of the total sample who said they did not know someone who is lesbian or gay. Cited by Judith Howard, "Prejudice," in *Lesbian Histories and Cultures: An Encyclopedia,* ed. Bonnie Zimmerman (New York and London: Garland, 2000), 605.

23. Ellen Goodman, "Gays in the Military Compromise Simply Incompatible with Reality," *Eugene Register-Guard,* July 11, 1993.

24. OCA flyer.

25. OCA flyer citing the *Wall Street Journal,* July 18, 1991, 1B. For a refutation of these figures, see Lee Badgett, "The Wage Effects of Sexual Orientation Discrimination," *Industrial and Labor Relations Review* 48, no. 4 (July 1995):726–39. Herman, *Antigay Agenda,* points out that in this discourse gays are "Jewed": they emerge as a symbolic "fat cat," getting rich off the backs of the average American (125).

26. June Brainard, commentary, "We Shouldn't Give Homosexuals Minority Status," *Eugene Register-Guard,* September 8, 1993.

27. Stuart Hall, "Cultural Identity and Cinematic Representation," *Framework,* no. 36 (1989):15; Michael Omi and Howard Winant, *Racial Formation in the United States* (New York: Routledge, 1986).

28. Arlene Stein, *Sex and Sensibility: Stories of a Lesbian Generation* (Berkeley: University of California Press, 1997).

29. Jody Rolnick, "Parents Oppose Books for Library," Timbertown *Gazette,* March 9, 1994, 1A.

30. Louise Denman-Sparks and the ABC Task Force, *Anti-Bias Curriculum: Tools for Empowering Young Children,* National Association of the Education of Young Children, Washington, D.C., 1989.

31. Rosamund Elwin and Michele Paulse, *Asha's Mums* (Toronto: Women's Press, 1990).

32. Interview with author, May 10, 1998.

33. Paul Neville, "OCA Rips Head Start Curriculum," *Eugene Register-Guard,* March 5, 1994, 1C, 2C. Letter to the editor, Timbertown *Gazette,* March 16, 1994, 4A.

34. Letter to the editor, Timbertown *Gazette,* March 16, 1994.

35. Letter to the editor, Timbertown *Gazette,* March 16, 1994.

7. **We Are All Queer—Or Are We?**

1. Letter to the editor, Timbertown *Gazette,* January 27, 1993, 5A.

2. Editorial, Timbertown *Gazette,* January 20, 1993, 4A.

3. Jodi Dean, *Solidarity of Strangers: Feminism After Identity Politics* (Berkeley: University of California Press, 1996), 6.

4. Robert Jay Lifton, *The Protean Self* (New York: Basic Books, 1993), distin-guishes among empathy, sympathy, and identification as sources of collective action. Identification requires you to *become* the other to participate in activity on behalf of that group. Sympathy requires you to *admire* the other. Empathy is different from both of these.

5. Cheryl Raffe, "How Do You Talk with a Fundamentalist?" *The Response,* Religious Response Network (Oregon), December 1993, 2.

6. Steering Committee, Rural Organizing Project. See also Blue Mountain Working Group, "A Call to Defend Democracy and Pluralism," in *Eyes Right: Challenging the Right Wing Backlash,* ed. Chip Berlet (Boston: South End Press, 1995).

7. Religious Response Network workshop, Timbertown, March 6, 1993.

8. Flyer, Timbertown CAN.

9. George Lakoff, *Moral Politics* (Chicago: University of Chicago Press, 1996), 34.

10. Ibid., 110.

11. Letter to the editor, Timbertown *Gazette,* July 14, 1993, 4A.

12. Letter to the editor, Timbertown *Gazette,* May 11, 1994, 5A

13. Flyer, Timbertown CAN, May 1994.

14. Ibid.

15. Jody Rolnick, "Out of the Closet: Parents of a Gay Son Tell their Story," Timbertown *Gazette,* February 17, 1993, 1A, 2A.

16. Joe Kidd, "Council Opposes Antigay Campaign," *Eugene Register-Guard,* February 9, 1993, 1D, 2D.

17. Timbertown City Council Minutes, February 8, 1993.

18. Resolution No. 1194, Timbertown City Council, February 8, 1993.

19. Editorial, Timbertown *Gazette,* July 13, 1993, 4A.

20. CAN Letter to mayor, August 2, 1993.

21. "The OCA's Loser," editorial, *Eugene Register-Guard*, August 13, 1993, 14A.

22. Pamela Sneed, Op-Ed, *Eugene Register-Guard*, July 30, 1993, 14A.

23. Letter to the editor, *Eugene Register-Guard*, August 6, 1993, 14A.

24. "The OCA Victories Show Our Deep Cultural Divisions," editorial, Timbertown *Gazette*, September 29, 1993, 4A.

25. Lynn Rea, "OCA Complaints Allege Violations," Timbertown *Gazette*, July 21, 1993, 1A.

26. Jody Rolnick, "Community Braces for Brewing Battle," Timbertown *Gazette*, August 11, 1993, 1A.

27. Letter to editor, *Eugene Register-Guard*, July 10, 1993, 15A.

28. Letter to the editor, *Eugene Register-Guard*, May 11, 1993, 14A.

29. Eve Sedgwick, "How to Bring Your Kids Up Gay," in *Fear of a Queer Planet*, ed. Michael Warner (Minneapolis: University of Minnesota Press, 1993).

30. Constance Penley, "Feminism, Psychoanalysis, and the Study of Popular Culture," in *Cultural Studies*, ed. Lawrence Grossberg, Cary Nelson, and Paula Treichler (New York and London: Routledge, 1992), 479–94.

31. Zygmunt Bauman, *Postmodern Ethics* (Oxford: Blackwell, 1993); Judith Butler, *The Psychic Life of Power* (Stanford: Stanford University Press, 1997). In the campaign against Measure 9 the previous year, gay rights supporters encouraged all concerned persons to wear and display pink triangles. Similarly, in a much-publicized public action, citizens protesting KKK violence against Jews in Billings, Montana, displayed pictures of Hanukkah menorahs proclaiming "not in our town." These political responses subverted the notion of sexual or racial "essences" writes Abby Ferber, *White Man Falling: Race, Gender, and White Supremacy* (Lanham, MD: Rowman and Littlefield, 1998), 156.

8. I Shout, Therefore I Am

1. A 1991 study of seventy-five teenage girls arrested for prostitution in a northwestern city found that a majority of the girls' parents identified as Christian fundamentalists, suggesting that having a fundamentalist religious background may increase the likelihood of one's becoming a prostitute. Michael Milburn and Sheree Conrad, *The Politics of Denial* (Cambridge: MIT Press, 1996), 93.

2. Cindy Patton, "Tremble, Hetero Swine!" in *Fear of a Queer Planet*, ed. Michael Warner (Minneapolis: University of Minnesota Press, 1993), 143–77, argues that the Christian right and lesbian/gay movements operate in dialectical relationship to each other.

3. Letter to the editor, *Eugene Register-Guard*, March 8, 1994, 14A.

4. Cheryl Raffe, "How Do You Talk with a Fundamentalist?" *The Response*, Religious Response Network (Oregon), December 1993, 2.

5. Dan Savage, "Savage Love," *Village Voice*, February 3, 1998, 167.

6. Alisa Solomon, "Notes on Klez/Camp," *Davka* (Winter):71–11; Anti-OCA flyer, unattributed.

7. For an analysis of "The Gay Agenda," see Julia Lesage, "Christian Coalition Leadership Training," in *Media, Culture, and the Religious Right*, ed. Linda Kintz and Julia Lesage (Minneapolis: University of Minnesota Press, 1998).

8. Gayle Rubin, "Thinking Sex," in *The Lesbian Gay Studies Reader*, ed. Henry Abelove, Michele Barale, and David Halperin (New York: Routledge, 1993), 43.

9. "Governor Compares Nazis with Anti-Gay Rights Group," *Eugene Register-Guard,* August 25, 1993, 1A.

10. Barry Dank, "Bryant's Brigade Uses Hitler's Tactics," *Los Angeles Times,* October 23, 1977, 61.

11. AIDS activist and playwright Larry Kramer was largely responsible for popularizing the AIDS-as-Holocaust, or "genocide" frame. See his *Reports from the Holocaust: The Making of an AIDS Activist* (New York: St. Martin's Press, 1989).

12. Scott A. Hunt and Robert D. Benford, "Identity Talk in the Peace and Justice Movement," *Journal of Contemporary Ethnography* 22, no. 4 (1994):488–517; Michael Berenbaum, "The Nativization of the Holocaust," *Judaism* 35, no. 4 (1986):447–57; James A. Holstein and Gayle Miller, "Rethinking Victimization: An Interactional Approach to Victimology," *Symbolic Interactionism* 1 (1990):103–22.

13. D. J. Pipher, "Resist OCA Doctrines," *Eugene Register-Guard,* July 11, 1993, 9A.

14. Letter to the editor, *Timbertown Gazette,* August 11, 1997, 4A.

15. Irena Klepfisz, *Dreams of an Insomniac: Jewish Feminist Essays, Speeches and Diatribes* (Portland: The Eighth Mountain Press, 1990), 64.

16. Christopher Shea, "Debating the Uniqueness of the Holocaust," *Chronicle of Higher Education,* May 31, 1996, A7; Alan S. Rosenbaum, *Is the Holocaust Unique? Perspectives in Comparative Genocide* (Boulder, CO: Westview Press, 1996).

17. Chris Simpson, American University, personal communication, 1995; James Ridgeway, *Blood in the Face* (New York: Thunder's Mouth Press, 1995); Didi Herman, *The Antigay Agenda: Orthodox Vision and the Christian Right* (Chicago: University of Chicago Press, 1997).

18. Elizabeth McLagan, "A Peculiar Paradise: A History of Blacks in Oregon, 1788–1940," quoted in *ROP Report,* January 1990, 2–3.

19. Kathleen Blee, *Women of the Klan: Racism and Gender in the 1920s* (Berkeley: University of California Press, 1991), 25.

20. Ibid., 70.

21. Letter to the editor, *Eugene Register-Guard,* April 2, 1994, 8A.

22. Michelle Lefkowith, personal communication, 1995. Elsewhere in Oregon, in Prineville, a leader of the local militia also served as the chief OCA petitioner in town (May 1995 memo from Marcy Westerling, Rural Organizing Project, Scappoose, OR).

23. On the continuities between the Christian right and the far right, see Raphael Ezekiel, *The Racist Mind: Portraits of American Neo-Nazis and Klansmen* (New York: Viking 1995); Evelyn Schlatter, "Bibles and Buggery: The Historical Continuity of Right Wing Ideology" (paper presented at the 6th North American Gay, Lesbian, and Bisexual Conference, Iowa City, Iowa, 1994). Herman, in The *Antigay Agenda,* is more reticent to compare the far right with the religious right.

24. Elizabeth Young-Bruehl, *The Anatomy of Prejudices* (Cambridge: Harvard University Press, 1996), argues that Christian activists want to keep gays around and make them available for actual or fantasy sexual service. "They can love people of the same sex, and we can punish them for it," she explains. "They can do what is forbidden, and we can be the good ones by signing over our forbidden wishes to them. But meanwhile we can enjoy their loving vicariously" (158).

25. Robert Jay Lifton and Greg Mitchell, *Hiroshima in America: Fifty Years of Denial* (New York: Grossett/Putnam, 1995), suggest that after the

Holocaust and Hiroshima, many people are preoccupied with the image of a nuclear end, haunted by images of mass killing and dying, and by death in general (352).

26. Ruth Frankenberg, *White Women, Race Matters* (Minneapolis: University of Minnesota Press, 1993).

27. Abby Ferber, *White Man Falling: Race, Gender, and White Supremacy* (Lanham, MD: Rowman & Littlefield, 1998); see also Howard Winant, *Racial Conditions* (Minneapolis: University of Minnesota Press, 1994).

28. Editorial, Timbertown *Gazette,* March 30, 1994, 4A.

29. Marc Ramirez, "Lon Mabon Sets 'Em Straight," *Seattle Times,* October 3, 1993, 18.

30. Editorial, "Vote for Fairness," *The Sunday Oregonian,* June 13, 1993, 2J.

31. Editorial, Timbertown *Gazette,* January 20, 1993, 4A.

32. "Hysteria Continues to Dominate Gay Rights Debate," editorial, Timbertown *Gazette,* July 21, 1993, 1A.

33. Editorial, Timbertown *Gazette,* March 30, 1994, 4A.

34. Documenting the relationship between the antiwar movement of the 1960s and media coverage of that movement, Todd Gitlin, *The Whole World Is Watching: The Mass Media in the Making and Unmaking of the New Left* (Berkeley: University of California Press, 1980), has shown how the media concentrated on images of extremes, playing up the most dramatic, most radical elements of the student movement, thereby elevating marginalized leaders to positions of power. On the relationship between media and social movements, see also Joseph Gusfield, *Symbolic Crusade* (Westport, CT: Greenwood Press, 1980); James Davison Hunter, *Culture Wars: The Struggle to Define America* (New York: Basic Books, 1991).

35. Editorial, Timbertown *Gazette,* April 6, 1994, 4A.

36. Letter to the editor, *Eugene Register-Guard,* June 24, 1993, 14A.

37. Editorial, Timbertown *Gazette,* July 28, 1993, 4A.

38. Joshua Gamson, *Freaks Talk Back: Tabloid Television and Sexual Nonconformity* (Chicago: University of Chicago Press, 1997), shows in a study of tabloid television that when religious conservatives appear on tabloid talk shows, the "bigot becomes the freak": the audience and hosts turn antigay guests such as Paul Cameron, head of the right-wing Family Research Institute, and those who impose antigay morality into "sick, ungodly, bigoted, un-American freaks" (109).

39. OCA flyer, No Special Rights Committee, Wilsonville, OR.

40. "Governor Compares Nazis with Anti-Gay Rights Group," *Eugene Register-Guard* August 25, 1993, 1A.

41. Letter to the editor, Timbertown *Gazette,* June 23, 1993, 4A.

42. Quoted in Milburn and Conrad, *Politics of Denial,* 102.

43. Peter Steinfels, "Evangelicals Lobby for Oppressed Christians," *New York Times,* September 15, 1996, 26A; Jeffrey Goldberg, "Washington Discovers Christian Persecution," *New York Times Magazine,* December 21, 1997, 46–65; Laurie Goodstein, "A Move to Fight the 'Persecution' Facing Christians," *New York Times,* November 9, 1998, 1A.

44. Deborah Lipstadt, *Denying the Holocaust: The Growing Assault on Truth and Memory* (New York: Free Press, 1993), 7.

45. Anne Frank Foundation, USA.

46. Letter to the editor, *Eugene Register-Guard,* February 5, 1993, 14A.

47. Letter to the editor, *Eugene Register-Guard,* February 9, 1993, 15A.

48. Letter to the editor, *Eugene*

Register-Guard, September 16, 1993, 12A.

49. Letter to the editor, *Eugene Register-Guard,* September 23, 1993, 14A.

50. Letter to editor, *Eugene Register-Guard,* September 23, 1993, 14A.

51. Lauren Berlant, *The Queen of America Goes to Washington City: Essays on Sex and Citizenship* (Durham, NC: Duke University Press, 1997), 100; Peter Steinfels, "Evangelicals Lobby for Oppressed Christians," *New York Times,* September 15, 1996, 26A.

52. Goodstein, "A Move to Fight," 16A.

53. James Davison Hunter, *Before the Shooting Begins: Searching for Democracy in America's Culture War* (New York: Free Press, 1994), 46.

54. Patton, "Tremble, Hetero Swine!," 145.

9. **Whose Side Are You On?**

1. Didi Herman, *The Antigay Agenda: Orthodox Vision and the Christian Right* (Chicago: University of Chicago Press, 1997), 107; see also Kintz, *Between Jesus and the Market: The Emotions That Matter in Right-Wing America* (Durham, NC: Duke University Press, 1997).

2. Lynn Rea, "Mayor, Councilors Feel Stress," Timbertown *Gazette,* June 23, 1993, 1A.

3. Letter to the editor, Timbertown *Gazette,* February 15, 1994, 4A.

4. Jody Rolnick, "Measure Divides Students," Timbertown *Gazette,* October 28, 1992, 1A.

5. Ibid., 6A.

6. Letter to the editor, Timbertown *Gazette,* February 23, 1994, 4A.

7. Letter to the editor, Timbertown *Gazette,* February 23, 1994, 5A.

8. Paul Neevel, "Timbertown Accepts the Challenge," *Eugene Weekly,* April 28, 1994, 1.

9. Letter to the editor, *Eugene Register-Guard,* February 5, 1994, 11A.

10. Ibid.

11. Paul Neevel, "Timbertown Accepts the Challenge," *Eugene Weekly,* April 28, 1994, 1.

12. Editorial, Timbertown *Gazette,* February 2, 1994, 4A.

13. Rudy Brueggemann, "Government Workers Get a Taste of Diversity at Performance," Timbertown *Gazette,* March 30, 1994, 3A.

14. Letter to the editor, Timbertown *Gazette,* February 16, 1994, 4A.

15. *CAN News Notes,* Timbertown, March 1, 1994, 1.

16. Eric Mortenson, "Anne Frank, Timbertown Cross Paths," Timbertown *Gazette,* March 14, 1994, 1A.

17. Letter to the editor, Timbertown *Gazette,* April 6, 1994, 4A.

18. Letter to the editor, Timbertown *Gazette,* April 6, 1994, 4A.

19. Letter to the editor, Timbertown *Gazette,* April 6, 1994, 4A.

20. Erwin J. Haeberle, "Swastika, Pink Triangle, and Yellow Star: The Destruction of Sexology and the Persecution of Homosexuals in Nazi Germany," in *Hidden from History: Reclaiming the Gay & Lesbian Past,* ed. Martin Duberman, Martha Vicinus, and George Chauncey (New York: Plume, 1989), 374. The link between Nazism and homosexuality rests upon the belief that homosexuality is an essential component of aggressiveness among male soldiers. Despite the claim of a direct link between Nazi ideology and homosexuality, historical evidence points to the opposite conclusion: that while the Nazis may have idealized homoerotism to a point, they identified homosexuality with the emasculation of men, which they saw as a threat to the traditional patriarchal, procreative family which they idealized. See also Klaus Theweleit, *Male Fantasies* (Min-

neapolis: University of Minnesota Press, 1987).

21. This encapsulates the argument of Scott Lively and Kenneth Abrams *The Pink Swastika* (Keizer, OR: Founders Publishing, 1995), a carefully constructed piece of political rhetoric, mixing serious scholarship with lies and outright distortions. See my "Whose Memories? Whose Victimhood? Contests for the Holocaust Frame in Recent Social Movement Discourse," *Sociological Perspectives* 41, no. 3 (1998):519–40.

22. April 14, 1994 letter from Anne Frank Center, New York.

23. Rudy Brueggemann, "Focus Shifts Locally After JC Vote," Timbertown *Gazette,* March 30, 1994, 2A.

24. Jody Rolnick, "Volunteer's Comments Upset Anne Frank Spectator," Timbertown *Gazette,* May 16, 1994, 3A.

25. Letter to the editor, Timbertown *Gazette,* April 15, 1994, 4A.

26. Letter to the editor, *Eugene Register-Guard,* March 4, 1994, 12A.

27. Letter to editor, *Eugene Register-Guard,* March 8, 1994, 12A.

28. May 15, 1994, letter from Cassie Smith to Anne Frank Center, New York.

29. Editorial, Timbertown *Gazette,* May 18, 1994, 4A.

10. Living with Strangers

1. Kai Erikson, *Wayward Puritans: A Study in the Sociology of Deviance* (New York: John Wiley and Sons, 1966).

2. Robert Putnam, *Bowling Alone: The Collapse and Revival of American Community* (New York: Simon & Schuster, 2000). Nina Eliasoph's *Avoiding Politics* (Cambridge: Cambridge University Press, 1998) finds a plethora of community organizations but little actual political debate and discussion. After many failed attempts, Tim-

bertowners finally approved a bond measure to finance a new local high school in May 2000.

3. Kurt Wolff, ed. *The Sociology of Georg Simmel* (New York: Free Press, 1950).

4. Ellen Willis, "Monica and Barbara and Primal Concerns," *New York Times,* March 14, 1999, 31E.

5. See, for example, Gayle Rubin, *Thinking Sex,* in *The Lesbian Gay Studies Reader,* ed. Henry Abelove, Michele Barale, and David Halperin (New York: Routledge, 1993); George Mosse, *Nationalism and Sexuality: Respectability and Abnormal Sexuality in Modern Europe* (New York: Howard Fertig, 1985).

6. Anthony Giddens, *Modernity and Self Identity: Self and Society in the Late Modern Age* (Cambridge, Polity Press, 1991), 5.

7. Lisa Keen and Suzanne Goldberg, *Strangers to the Law: Gay People On Trial* (Ann Arbor: University of Michigan Press, 1998).

8. The Oregon Court of Appeals, in *Tanner* v. *Oregon Health Sciences University,* became the first court in the nation to decide that government—at any level—is constitutionally required to recognize domestic partnerships and offer the same benefits.

9. Ellen Forman, "Domestic-Partner Benefits Quickly Becoming the Norm," *The Oregonian,* December 11, 1998, 1D.

10. Alan Wolfe, "Religion, With a Grain of Salt," *New York Times,* June 14, 1998, 15.

11. "Religious Right Failing," *Freedom Writer,* Institute for First Amendment Studies, Great Barrington, Massachusetts, May/June 1999, 1.

12. Laurie Goodstein, "Religious Right, Frustrated, Trying New Tactic on GOP," *New York Times,* March 23, 1998, 1A. Frederick Clarkson, "Splits in the Religious Right Will Make It Hard to Recapture the Christian Coalition's

Glory Days," *Salon,* February 24, 1999 (www.salon.com/news/1999/02/24news.html).

13. In 1994, according to a CNN/Time survey, 52 percent of Americans thought "gay lifestyles" are acceptable, but 64 percent opposed gay marriage and the adoption of children. See Margaret Cerullo, "Family Values? Broadening the Debate," *Gay Community News,* Summer 1997, 26.

14. Barney Wooten, "OCA's Mission Is Still Alive and Well," *Eugene Register-Guard,* August 10, 1998, 11A.

15. James Jasper, *The Art of Moral Protest: Culture, Biography, and Creativity in Social Movements* (Chicago: University of Chicago Press, 1998), 379, 84.

16. George Lakoff, *Moral Politics* (Chicago: University of Chicago Press, 1996), 384. See also Michael Sandel, *Democracy's Discontent* (Cambridge: Belknap, 1996).

17. Anthony Giddens, *The Transformation of Intimacy* (Stanford: Stanford University Press, 1992). For other efforts to rethink the relationship of sexuality and citizenship, see Jeffrey Weeks, "The Sexual Citizen," *Theory, Culture & Society* 15, nos. 3–4 (1998):35–52; and Kenneth Plummer, *Telling Sexual Stories* (New York and London: Routledge, 1995); Lisa Duggan, "Queering the State," *Socialtext* 39 (1994):1–14; David Evans, *Sexual Citizenship* (London: Routledge, 1993); Diane Richardson, "Sexuality and Citizenship," *Sociology* 32, no. 1 (1998):83–100; Urvashi Vaid, *Virtual Equality* (New York: Doubleday Anchor, 1995).

18. *New York Times,* July 19, 1998, 19A.

19. Alisa Solomon, *Village Voice,* June 29, 1998, 63.

20. Gayle Rubin, "Thinking Sex"; Anna Marie Smith, "The Good Homosexual and the Dangerous Queer: Resisting the 'New Homophobia,'" in *New Sexual Agendas,* ed. Lynne Segal (Basingstoke: Macmillan, 1997). Queer theorists generally agree that all sexual "dissidents," including bisexuals, transsexuals, and even some heterosexuals have an investment in calling into question binary, bounded notions of sexuality. See, for example, Diana Fuss, ed., *Inside/Out: Lesbian Theories, Gay Theories* (New York, Routledge, 1991); Eve Kosofsky Sedgwick, *Epistemology of the Closet* (Berkeley: University of California Press, 1990); Judith Butler, *Gender Trouble* (New York: Routledge, 1990); Sabine Hark, "Disputed Territory: Feminist Studies in Germany and Its Queer Discontents" (paper presented at the University of North Carolina, Chapel Hill, September 1999).

21. My reading of Emmanuel Levinas is based primarily on the collection *Entre Nous: Thinking of the Other,* trans. Michael B. Smith and Barbara Harshav (New York: Columbia University Press, 1998). I am also indebted to Zygmunt Bauman's discussion of Levinas in *Postmodern Ethics* (Oxford: Blackwell, 1993). On the New Community Meeting, see Gretchen Miller and John Koekkoek, "We All Live in This Community Together," *Eugene Register-Guard,* November 27, 1994, 1B.

22. Ibid.

ACKNOWLEDGMENTS

Many people, in large and small ways, made this book possible. At the University of Oregon, I was fortunate to be associated with the wonderful Center for the Study of Women in Society, directed by Sandi Morgen. CSWS gave me a small grant to initiate this project, helped fund its completion, and provided, at a pivotal stage in my research, a forum for activists and academics in the Eugene area who were trying to make sense of right-wing politics. Linda Kintz, Mimi Goldman, Julia Lesage, Michelle Lefkowith, Sal Johnston, Kelley Weigel, Nancy Solomon, Val Burris, and John Lunsford were among those who participated in that group, and inspired a set of questions that eventually led to this study.

It was my great good fortune to be a recipient of a postdoctoral fellowship sponsored by the Social Science Research Council, with funds provided by the Ford Foundation. John Gagnon and Diane di Mauro managed the herculean task of initiating and administering the Sexuality Research Fellowship Program, which permitted me to devote myself to this project for two years, and for which I am enormously grateful. Conversations with fellow fellows Rosemary Powers, Dawne Moon, and Jessica Fields were helpful and always fun.

The Department of Sociology at the University of Oregon released me from my teaching responsibilities and provided administrative support for this project. Many thanks to Marnie McElhiney, Barbara Luton, and Mary Redetzke for practical assistance, and to my colleagues who picked up the slack while I was gone. The College of Arts and Sciences at the University of Oregon also provided some money to support the research.

When I began poking around in preparation for my fieldwork, Ellen Rifkin, Marcy Westerling, and Kelley Weigel provided me with a number of contacts, as did Mike Hibbard. Chip Berlet, Nadia Telsey, and Linda Kintz shared with me some materials that proved invaluable. Ann Strahm accompanied me on research expeditions to the hinterlands and did some library research for me, and Phil Zuckerman, Linda Fuller, and Ben Johnson joined me in my forays to church, offering spiritual and intellectual guidance, and just plain support. Marilyn Carter and Benny Monroe slogged through the interviews and transcribed them brilliantly.

A number of people offered useful feedback when I presented early versions of this book at the University of Oregon, the American Sociological Association meetings in San Francisco, the Coalition Against Malicious Harassment, Rutgers University, New York University, the University of Amsterdam, and the "Queering Democracy" conference in Berlin, organized by my friend Sabine Hark. Much appreciation to friends who talked with me about the book and gave me advice and encouragement: Joan Acker, Gerry Berk, Deborah Gerson, Lisa Kramer, Jeff Land, Greg McLauchlan, Judith Musick, Steven Seidman, Julee Raiskin, Mary Wood, Monica Szurmuk, Marcello Bergman, Jocelyn Hollander, and Ramon Torrecilha.

Many thanks, especially, to Lizzie Reis, Nancy Chodorow, Steve Epstein, Jim Jasper, Jeff Goodwin, Francesca Polletta, Jerry Himmelstein, Ben Johnson, Tom Scheff, Phil Zuckerman, Linda Kintz, Nancy Solomon, and Ann Weinstone for reading parts of the manuscript and giving me valuable comments on it. Big hugs to Miriam Johnson, Ken Plummer, Judith Stacey, and Joshua Gamson for reviewing much of the book in advance; its failings are my own.

Amy Caldwell, my editor, showed unwavering enthusiasm for the book, gave me insightful feedback, and ably shepherded it through the process of publication. Kathy Antrim expertly copyedited the manuscript. Nancy, Lewis, and Fred the dog gave me love and support over the long haul.

Finally, my abundant thanks to dozens of Timbertowners, who will remain anonymous along with the name of their town. I hope they will recognize themselves in the portrait I have painted and understand their world better for it.